Bergson and Russian Modernism, 1900–1930

Bergson and Russian Modernism, 1900–1930

Hilary L. Fink

NORTHWESTERN UNIVERSITY PRESS / EVANSTON, ILLINOIS

Northwestern University Press
www.nupress.northwestern.edu

Printed in the United States of America

ISBN 978-0-8101-2855-2

The Library of Congress has cataloged the original, hardcover edition as follows:

Fink, Hilary L.
Bergson and Russian modernism, 1900–1930 / Hilary L. Fink.
p. cm.—(Studies in Russian literature and theory)
Includes bibliographical references.
ISBN 0-8101-1610-3 (cloth : alk. paper)
1. Russian literature—20th century—History and criticism.
2. Modernism (Literature)—Russia (Federation) 3. Bergson, Henri, 1859–1941—Influence. I. Title. II. Series.
PG3020.5.M6F55 1998
891.709'112—dc21 98-27706
CIP

∞The paper used in this publication meets the minimum requirements of the American National Standard for Information Sciences—Permanence of Paper for Printed Library Materials, ANSI Z39.48-1992.

For my parents

Contents

Acknowledgments

I first conceived of this project in 1989 after reading a footnote by Jane Gary Harris in which she suggested that a book on Bergson and Russian modernism was "sorely wanting." I thank her for pointing me in the direction of such an exciting and fruitful topic.

I am indebted to a number of people who have generously given me their attention and assistance over the years. I am grateful to Alexander Woronzoff-Dashkoff and Maria Banerjee, who first showed me the richness of Russia's language and literature. My heartfelt thanks go to Robert Maguire for encouraging me to enter this field and for being a wonderful teacher, mentor, and friend. His comments on drafts of this manuscript were indispensable. Richard Gustafson introduced me to Russian religious thought, which informs the first chapter of the present work, and Irina Reyfman supervised my earlier project on Mandel'shtam and Bergson, helping me build a solid foundation on which to base my study of Bergson in Russia; I am indebted to them both for their many insightful suggestions. I owe much to Frank Miller for his good counsel and encouragement throughout all my years at Columbia University. Cathy Popkin and Cathy Nepomnyashchy provided guidance when needed most. Other colleagues whose scholarly advice has enriched my work include Ellen Chances, Vladimir Alexandrov, and Boris Gasparov. Judith Deutsch Kornblatt's scrupulous reading of the manuscript was particularly helpful. For their faith in this project, I thank Caryl Emerson and Susan Harris. My constant sources of friendship and support have been Milla Trigos and Jamie Bennett, and from a somewhat greater distance, Olga Briker and Judson Flanagan. Grants from the International Research and Exchanges Board, the Harriman Institute, and the Mrs. Giles Whiting Foundation provided much needed opportunities for research and writing in Moscow and at Columbia. Reference librarian Bob Scott of Columbia's Butler Library and the archivists of IMLI (Institut mirovoi literatury im. A. M. Gor'kogo [Gorkii Institute of World Literature]) and RGALI (Rossiiskii gosudarstvennyi arkhiv literatury i iskusstva [Russian State Archive of Literature and Art]) in Moscow greatly facilitated my research.

Finally, this book would not have been possible without the love and support of my family, to whom I am inexpressibly grateful.

An earlier version of Chapter 2 appeared as "Andrei Bely and the Music of Bergsonian Duration," in *Slavic and East European Journal* 41, no. 2 (Summer 1997): 287–302. An earlier version of Chapter 4 appeared as "The Kharmsian Absurd and the Bergsonian Comic: Against Kant and Causality," in *The Russian Review* 57, no. 4 (October 1998): 526–38. I thank the journals and publishers for permission to make use of this material.

A Note on References

Unless otherwise noted, all translations of Russian and French quotations are my own. References to the following works of Bergson correspond to the English translations listed below:

CE *Creative Evolution.* Trans. A. Mitchell. Introduction by P. A. Y. Gunter. Lanham, Md.: University Press of America, 1983. Originally published as *L'Evolution créatrice.* Paris: Félix Alcan, 1907.

CM *The Creative Mind.* Trans. M. L. Andison. New York: Citadel Press, 1992. Originally published as *La Pensée et le mouvant: Essais et conférences.* Paris: Félix Alcan, 1934.

IM *Introduction to Metaphysics.* Trans. T. E. Hulme. London: Macmillan, 1910. Originally published as "Introduction à la métaphysique" in the *Revue de métaphysique et de morale* 9 (1903): 1–36. Reprinted later as chapter 6 of *The Creative Mind.* Page references will be made to *CM.*

MM *Matter and Memory.* Trans. N. M. Paul and W. S. Palmer. New York: Zone Books, 1991. Originally published as *Matière et mémoire: Essai sur la relation du corps à l'esprit.* Paris: Félix Alcan, 1896.

TFW *Time and Free Will. An Essay on the Immediate Data of Consciousness.* Trans. F. L. Pogson. New York: Macmillan, 1910. Originally published as *Essai sur les donnés immédiates de la conscience.* Paris: Félix Alcan, 1889.

I have used the modified Library of Congress system to transliterate Russian texts; however, well-known proper names are given in their most commonly used forms (for example, Tolstoy, Bely, Kandinsky).

Preface

While the influence of Schelling, Hegel, and Nietzsche in Russia has been widely explored (Setschkareff 1939; Chizhevskii 1939; Rosenthal 1986, 1994; Clowes 1988; Kujundžič 1997) the topic of Bergson in Russia has received much less scholarly attention. Aside from Francis Nethercott's (1995) recent book-length study in French of Bergson's reception by pre-Revolutionary Russian philosophers, only a handful of articles (Harris 1982; Rusinko 1982; Curtis 1976; Nethercott 1991)—and some longer works focusing on other topics—deal with the Russian reception of Bergson. Scholars who touch on the Bergsonian influence on a particular Russian writer or thinker include Bethea and Rudova (Pasternak), Morson and Emerson (Bakhtin), and Toker and Foster (Nabokov).[1]

In this first book-length study of Bergson and Russian literature, I concentrate on several of the leading writers and thinkers of Russian modernism who have made explicit reference to Bergson in their writings and/or in whose work I have found particularly Bergsonian themes. I selected figures who would fit into the major genres of religious thought, Symbolism, Acmeism, Futurism, Suprematism, and the absurd in order to present a somewhat cohesive outline of the Russian literary scene in the first third of the twentieth century. Because they do not clearly belong to any of the groupings mentioned above, I have not included detailed discussion of such figures as Olesha, Pasternak, Shklovskii, or Nabokov, although these authors (and many others) played central roles in the shaping of Russian modernism and very likely embraced some of Bergson's ideas in their work.

To keep the focus on the Russian reception of Bergson's thought over the course of the modernist period, chapters are organized more chronologically than thematically; that is, a discussion of post-Symbolism follows an examination of Symbolism, rather than a chapter on "intuition," for example, following one on "time." While Russian modernism was a highly organic phenomenon with certain artistic concerns (such as intuition, time, language, and form) taken up by most groups, it was also a fairly well defined historical phenomenon, lasting roughly from the 1890s through the 1920s. A chronological approach, I believe, best reflects the changing modernist ethos as the landscape of Russian modernism was continually being reconfigured. Such an approach may at first seem reliant on the very notion of "progress" against which both Bergson and Russian modernists railed; however, it is not *progress* that this chronology examines, but *evolution,* a "creative evolution" (to borrow Bergson's most famous title) that precludes the very notion of determinism or causality. What is perhaps most fascinating is that artists with such different views of the artistic process could still exhibit very similar Bergsonian traits in their work.

Losskii, Frank, Hippius, Mandel'shtam, and Kharms read Bergson in the original French; it is more difficult, however, to determine whether this was the case with certain other Russian thinkers, like Bely. Bergsonian ideas were so much in the air during the second and third decades of the twentieth century that most Russian intellectuals were likely to be familiar with the basic themes of Bergson's *Introduction to Metaphysics* and *Creative Evolution.* Richard Lehan comments on the undeniable role of Bergsonian ideas even for those artists who were not directly influenced by him:

> Bergson's influence, direct or indirect, on modern literature cannot be denied or de-emphasized. I have here stressed the concurrent developments between Bergson and various literary minds working independently of his direct influence in order to show that the Bergsonian construct generated a realm of discourse from which modernism, as a literary movement, was inseparable.[2]

The question of influence is always problematic, but particularly so in the modernist period when artistic cross-fertilization between Europe and Russia was especially intense. I am less interested in influence as agency or causality (that is, in the task of proving that Bergson caused a particular writer to create in a "Bergsonian" way) as I am in considering the intertextuality of Russian modernism, or how Russian modernist works may be viewed through a Bergsonian prism, thus broadening our understanding of the period while suggesting new pathways for interpretation and further research. I use the term "intertextuality" not as a poststructuralist rejection of the notion of influence (as Kristeva and Barthes envisioned it),[3] but rather as a term that has recently been defined as "working out from the broad definition of influence to encompass unconscious, socially prompted types of text formation (for example, by archetypes or popular culture); modes of conception (such as ideas 'in the air'); styles (such as genres)."[4] Thus, it is not the causal "*A* derives from *B*" school of influence studies that is most pertinent to the present study; rather, attention is focused on the parallels (plus occasional differences) between works of Russian modernism and the philosophy of Bergson. In expounding his theory of literary history, critic R. W. Stallman (1955) proposes the following:

> In studying relationships between literary works *by the juxtaposition of parallelisms* I am concerned to show not that the one work necessarily derives from the other, but rather that the related works belong together by virtue of kindred techniques, symbolic devices and patterns—not superficially by surface echoes but at the core of their conception and theme. (26)

While Stallman focuses on poetic influence in his article, the essence of his comment on parallelisms between two poems also applies when considering a poem and a philosophy. It is my contention that "at the core of their conception and theme," many works of Russian modernism parallel Bergsonian thought, their root conception being an aversion to nineteenth-century scientific rationality, determinism, and causality, and their shared themes being intuition, duration, and a type of artistic theurgy. The notion of creativity and its relationship to life was perhaps the defining preoccupation of Russian modernists, who embraced, with greater intensity than their European counterparts, the theurgic impulse to transform reality through art (a central teaching of Vladimir Solov'ev, as read in the Russian tradition). As Paperno points out, the fusing of art and life (*zhiznetvorchestvo*) was central to Russian culture of the modernist period, while the resulting modernist conception of an "aesthetic utopia" relied on the rejection of nineteenth-century positivism in favor of the creative principle, such as that inherent in Bergsonian creative evolution (Paperno and Grossman 1994, 3–4). Perhaps the single most important reason for Bergson's popularity in Russia in the early twentieth century was that Bergson's pronouncements on the active role of artistic intuition in the process of life-creation and participation in existence satisfied the Russian modernist desire to unite word and world.

The question thus arises as to whether Bergson was a cause or merely a symptom of Russian modernism (*vliianie* or *veianie*). In one sense, Bergson could be seen as more of a symptom, a thinker who simply satisfied the "spirit of the age" by offering a philosophy of life that seemed to replace mechanistic science with the creative individual as the agent truly capable of uncovering the deepest layers of reality. Citing parallels to Aristotle, Dante, Petrarch, and Boccaccio, Paul Douglass (1983) points out that Bergson's notion of artist as creator is far from original: "Bergson has not changed fundamentally the Renaissance arguments that the poet's power derives from contact with the universe's creative center and that his function is to suggest a truth beyond everyday powers of seeing. For Bergson, too, the height of God's creation is the creative man" (240). The attraction of Russian artists and thinkers to Bergsonian thought may have reflected nothing more than a general modernist passion for various elements of neo-Romantic organic thought, which perhaps would have carried Russian modernists in the same direction with or without the publication of Bergson's *Creative Evolution.*

On the other hand, in addition to following along in the Renaissance tradition, Bergson has also indirectly been called "the father of modernism" for his unique role in the formation of the modernist age. Richard Lehan (1992), who implies that Bergson should occupy this lofty position, outlines the way in which Bergson was, in a sense, largely responsible for the genesis and survival of the modernist movement:

> Bergson challenged at the outset the priority of a mechanistic, Darwinian evolution that robbed the universe of a creative unfolding and man of the corresponding creative power of a deep subjectivity within which the mythic, the primitive, and the intuitive could thrive. Both Joyce and Ezra Pound once claimed Flaubert to be the father of modernism, and perhaps in an artistic as well as chronological sense they are right. But it was Bergson who created a systematic, rigorous philosophy that gave foundation to basic modernist trends, and it was Bergson who cleared the modernist landscape of a materialistic underbrush that would have choked modernism off at the outset. . . . If the moderns did not have Bergson, they would have had to invent him. (307–8, 311)

According to Lehan, Bergson was more a cause of modernism than a symptom in that he lay the philosophical groundwork for a modernist discourse that he himself was integral in generating through the popularization of such antimaterialist concepts as intuition, duration, and the élan vital (vital impulse). Bringing the tradition of Renaissance humanism to bear at the very outset of the modernist period, Bergson is seen by Lehan as instrumental in rejecting the scientific determinism of the nineteenth century that championed the power of external forces of nature over the active, creative role of the individual in the universe. Bergson is thus considered to have been the élan vital behind modernism itself. Although I share Lehan's view and believe that Bergson did, to some degree, "influence" the Russian modernist scene (I have pointed out instances of possible influence wherever it seems likely), the study of Bergson in Russia, once again, is less a study of causality than of conceptions and themes shared by certain Russian modernist artists and the French thinker whose philosophy dealt with the same ideas about language, time, space, and motion that lay at the heart of so many modernist works.

There is little consensus on how to distinguish between the terms "modernist" and "avant-garde," although Victor Erlich (1994) offers a helpful definition of the latter: "Though 'modernism' and 'avant-garde' are not considered synonymous, they are usually assumed to be intimately related. I am inclined to say that the most legitimate use of the latter term . . . is to underline the emphatically future-oriented, iconoclastic, antibourgeois strain in modernism" (3). I agree with Erlich in that, while the whole of the avant-garde is included in modernism, not all of modernism is included in the avant-garde, a term that might be applied to those individuals or groups who bring a sort of militancy to modernism in the determined effort to be the "front-runner" in the race toward the future. In this sense, the only figures in the present study who might be considered "avant-garde" are Khlebnikov and Malevich.[5]

As for the time frame of this study, I have chosen the starting date of 1900 because in that year the first of Bergson's works (*Le rire*) was published in Russia (Laughter, Smekh v zhizni i na stsene). It was not, however, until the Moscow publication of *L'Evolution créatrice* (Creative Evolution; Tvorcheskaia evoliutsiia) in 1909 that Bergson gained widespread popularity among Russian writers and thinkers, and that discussion of him in Russian periodicals began to appear. P. Mokievskii (1909) remarks that "Bergson's philosophy has recently acquired a certain popularity in Russia. Bergson has already been philosophizing for decades, yet until very recently his name has been completely unknown to the general public" (152). Even in 1911, Bergson's impact on Russian philosophy was only in its incipient stage, as noted by one observer of the Fourth International Congress on Philosophy held in Bologna: "Bergson's ideas are generally beginning to exert a decisive influence on the philosophical quests of our time" (Ruge 1911, 409–10). Nonetheless, Bergsonian thought was introduced into Russia in the first few years of the twentieth century (and, as will be shown, may even have played a role in Andrei Bely's conception of time as expressed in his *Second Symphony*, written in 1902). The study ends in 1930, the year the Oberiuty, the last true representatives of Russian modernism, dissolved their group under Party assault as "class enemies," although several of Kharms's posthumously published absurdist works of the 1930s are discussed in Chapter 4.

Studies of Russian modernism tend to focus on the differences between scattered avant-garde groups because, according to George Gibian, many people claim Russian modernism was not a cohesive movement but at best a "series of diverse tendencies and trends."[6] I hope to dispute this claim through the examination of a range of modernist responses to one common referent—Henri Bergson—whereby a rich portrait emerges of variations on the same Russian theme; namely, the *intellectual* attraction to a Neoplatonic "absolute" (the "logical essence" of the "thing-in-itself") as well as to the intuitive means of grasping it. Perhaps most significant, Bergson provided Russian modernists with an optimistic and fertile philosophical grounding from which could grow their innate theurgic impulse to transform the world through art; by intuitively grasping duration (reality), one becomes an active participant in the dynamic process of life, a process that itself can be molded through artistic creativity.

Bergson's terminology can often be problematic in that much of what he discusses fits into rather vague categories, such as "intuition" and "duration." As the historian of philosophy, Frederick Copleston (1946–53) points out, Bergson's use of imagery and metaphor, along with his lack of philosophical precision, "have contributed to his being depreciated as a philosopher by those who equate philosophy with logical or conceptual analysis and who attach great value to precision of thought and language" (9:179). As a result, observes Copleston, Bergson is often considered by analytical thinkers to be more of a poet than a serious philosopher—perhaps one of the reasons Russian modernists were especially drawn to him in their effort to mold the artist into the creator of meaning in the world. In any case, the most one can hope for in reading Bergson is to grasp the poetic essence of his terminology. In a sense, this is only right, as Bergsonian philosophy itself is based on a similar approach to reality; rather than reduce the world to its constituent parts (which is the function of the intellect, or analysis), we must rely on intuition, the immediate, "artistic" contemplation of reality in its ceaseless flow, or duration.

Bergson's lack of terminological exactitude, at times problematic for the Western reader accustomed to philosophical precision of expression, was much more easily accepted in the tradition of Russian thought, itself marked by a fundamental mistrust of language as reductive of the inherent "wholeness" of life. The Bergsonian terms "intuition" and "duration," for example, are construed by all Russian modernists in fundamentally the same way, "intuition" suggesting the immediate contemplation of the essence of things, and "duration" indicating the constant flow of divine reality that can be apprehended only through an effort of intuition. The Eastern Orthodox underpinning to the reception of Bergson in Russia is undeniable and can be traced throughout the present study, beginning with a detailed discussion in the introduction and Chapter 1 of the compatibility of Bergson's philosophy with the intuitivism of Russian religious thought.

Bergson and Russian Modernism, 1900–1930

Introduction

Bergson and Russian Modernism

> But open Bergson and new horizons loom on every page you read. It is like the breath of the morning and the song of birds. It tells of reality itself . . .
> —William James

> [Bergsonian intuition] is nothing other than the act by which the mind has an idea.
> —Julien Benda

> In those times [1910–20] Bergson's name resounded throughout the world. How could I not study Bergson in those times? . . . His book *Creative Evolution* made an impression on me that lasted my entire life.
> —A. F. Losev

BETWEEN THE YEARS 1907 and 1914, Henri Bergson was internationally renowned. In Paris the lecture halls of the Collège de France were overflowing with listeners,[1] Moscow University students were avidly discussing Bergsonian thought,[2] and Bergson's most important pre–World War I works—*Essai sur les donées immédiates de la conscience* (*Time and Free Will* in the English translation, 1889), *Matière et mémoire* (*Matter and Memory*, 1896), *Introduction à la métaphysique* (*Introduction to Metaphysics*, 1903), and *L'Evolution créatrice* (*Creative Evolution*, 1907)—were being translated in Europe, Britain, America, and Russia.[3] Bergson's popularity, which had soared following the publication of *Creative Evolution*, started to wane in Europe and America once the war began; in Russia, however, his ideas remained of interest through the 1920s for Russian modernists like Osip Mandel'shtam and Daniil Kharms. World War I extinguished Western European optimism in such antimechanistic forces as intuition, irrationality, and the occult, which Bergson had helped to popularize. Why then Bergson's continued presence in Russian intellectual and artistic circles in the 1920s? First, Russian society was thought by many still to be "creatively evolving" following the Bolshevik Revolution of 1917; second, Bergsonian thought found great resonance with certain specifically Russian trends that did not disappear after 1917, perhaps most important the deep-rooted intuitivism of Russian Orthodoxy. Many Russian modernists turned to Bergsonian intuition and *l'imprévisibilité* (see Hippius "Dnevnik" 1921, 93) as weapons against the determinism and materialism of Marxism-Leninism. At the same time, they spiritualized Bergson's secular ideas in accord with their inherently religious/theurgic impulse to uncover divine reality and to transform it through art (deification, like intuitivism, also playing a central role in Russian Orthodoxy and contributing to the sense of artist as creator of the wor[l]d).

What constituted the Bergsonian "revolution,"[4] leading one of Bergson's main critics, George Santayana, to admit in 1913 that the Frenchman was "the most representative and remarkable of living philosophers"? (1957, 58). As one of the most prominent opponents of neo-Kantian critical rationality (put forth in Russia primarily by A. I. Vvedenskii and I. I. Lapshin), Bergson stressed the limitations of pure, rational thought in apprehending the true nature of reality. Rather, the intellect must be combined with intuition that allows for direct contact with *durée réelle* (pure duration), the continual flow of forever-changing reality. A discussion of Bergson's philosophy in the context of the neo-Romantic reaction to nineteenth-century rationalism will be helpful before examining the Russian intuitivist tradition, which served as the backdrop for Bergson's reception by Russian modernists.

Bergson's philosophical "revolution" in the early twentieth century mirrored, in large part, the revolution in physics begun in the last years of the nineteenth century, which called into question the ability of science to explain all of reality.[5] Beginning in 1895–96 with the discovery of X-rays and radioactivity, and continuing with the development of the quantum theory, the new physics "chipped away at the classical picture of a static universe composed of fixed and permanent atoms and molecules. . . . A nondeterminist physics was gradually taking shape which created significant doubts about mechanical causation and which therefore struck at the very heart of mechanistic science" (Grogin 1988, 9). Late nineteenth-century thinkers no longer considered reality to be a closed system of phenomena, wholly discoverable by the laws of reason and mathematics; instead, reality was seen as dynamic, in many ways mysterious, accessible not through intellect or analysis but rather through religion, metaphysics, and intuition. As Jung, Freud, Einstein, and others sought to explore the mysteries of spirit, consciousness, and creativity, Bergson proposed a philosophy that would try to do the same. Grogin (1988) notes:

> Revisionists [in the philosophy of science] . . . now acknowledged the creative role of the individual and his intuition in amassing scientific knowledge. This could only lend substance to the growing philosophical revolt which was ultimately led by Henri Bergson against mechanistic determinism. Philosophers

could now more easily contend that free will was not an illusion and that the time for a fresh orientation towards the modern world had come. (11)

In opposition to the nineteenth-century conception of time as a measurable, quantitative entity, progressing linearly, Bergson conceived of a second kind of time that science could not measure, what he called "real time" or duration. This is the time of one's inner life, always in flux, changing, and therefore impossible to analyze mathematically or scientifically. Bergson defines pure duration as "the form which the succession of our conscious states assumes when our ego lets itself *live,* when it refrains from separating its present state from its former states. . . . Both the past and the present states [form] an organic whole, as happens when we recall the notes of a tune, melting, so to speak, into one another" (*TFW* 100). Bergsonian duration is thus similar to James's "stream of consciousness," the continual flow of psychic states that creates one's inner life. In *Time and Free Will,* Bergson argues that reality is not to be discovered according to the nineteenth-century empiricist approach based on the observation of external phenomena; instead, attention must be turned inward, the essence of reality being embodied in the "immediate data of consciousness." To be truly free means to grasp one's own duration, the "fundamental self": "We reach [the fundamental self] by deep introspection, which leads us to grasp our inner states as living things, constantly *becoming,* as states not amenable to measurement, which permeate one another. . . . But the moments at which we thus grasp ourselves are rare, and that is just why we are rarely free" (*TFW* 231).

As opposed to intellect (or what Bergson calls "the faculty of manipulating matter" [*CM* 85]), only intuition (or, as in the above quotation, "deep introspection") is capable of grasping the flow of inner duration and allowing for freedom of action.[6] While only touching on the role of intuition in *Time and Free Will,* Bergson goes on to develop his central theme in the short work *Introduction to Metaphysics,* wherein he addresses the possible charge of solipsism against his philosophy of intuition: "But if metaphysics is to proceed by intuition, if intuition has as its object the mobility of duration, and if duration is psychological in essence, are we not going to shut the philosopher up in exclusive self-contemplation" (162)? Not surprisingly, Bergson answers his own rhetorical question in the negative, explaining that "the intuition of our duration, far from leaving us suspended in the void as pure analysis would do, puts us in contact with a whole continuity of durations." The object of intuition, then, may be both one's inner life and external objects as well (and in this sense Bergsonian duration encompasses much more than does James's stream of consciousness):

> We call intuition here the *sympathy* by which one is transported into the interior of an object in order to coincide with what there is unique and consequently inexpressible in it. Analysis, on the contrary, is the operation which reduces

> the object to elements already known, that is, common to that object and to others. Analyzing then consists in expressing a thing in terms of what it is not. All analysis is thus a translation, a development into symbol. (*CM* 161)

Bergson shows that both human beings and the external world are constantly in a state of becoming or flux, and that through intuition, a "spiritual harmony with [a thing's] innermost quality" (200), one can grasp the vital principle within, and unique to, the object of perception. In this sense, intuition is the realm of the artist: "The intention of life, the simple movement that runs through the lines, that binds them together and gives them significance, escapes [our eye]. This intention is just what the artist tries to regain, in placing himself back within the object by a kind of sympathy, in breaking down, by an effort of intuition, the barrier that space puts up between him and his model" (*CE* 177).

At the beginning of the twentieth century, as part of the revisionist movement in the philosophy of science, the physicist Henri Poincaré put forth the notion that most scientific principles are based not on immutable truths but rather on what we, as creative human beings, surmise these truths to be. In summarizing Poincaré's position, Grogin (1988) observes: "Scientific theories are then not merely summaries of data, nor ideas deduced from axioms, but are largely artificial constructions. And those constructions often depend on the intuitive nature of the scientific imagination. This is what Poincaré meant by his famous dictum: 'Scientific formulae are not true; they are convenient'" (10). Bergson also stresses the intuitive side of science, thereby unifying science and metaphysics in the same way that he argues for the interdependence of intellect and intuition: "Science and metaphysics then meet in intuition. A truly intuitive philosophy would realize the union so greatly desired, of metaphysics and science" (*CM* 192). By emphasizing the necessity of such a union, Bergson is attacking what he purports to be the Kantian belief that any form of knowledge residing outside the boundaries of the intellect (for example, intuition) is impossible. Writing in 1901, Bergson states: "The doctrine that I defend . . . proposes to reestablish the bridge (broken by Kant) between metaphysics and science. This divorce between science and metaphysics is the great misfortune from which our philosophy suffers."[7]

Bergson was certainly not an impartial reader of Kant, whose philosophy is clearly more complex than that simply of "intellect over intuition." In fact, intuition plays a significant role in Kant's epistemology; for Kant, however, intuition is a passive means of perception (much, as will be seen, it is for Schelling), whereas for Bergson it is an active form of sympathy with an object's inner essence. Despite the interdependence of intellect and intuition in both Kant's and Bergson's philosophical systems, Bergson had to try to show that Kant ignored intuition in his critical philosophy in order to protect the heart of his own metaphysics—intuition—from neo-Kantian attack.[8]

A brief summary of the Kantian dilemma as it faced Bergson is useful in understanding how Bergson attempted to "bridge the Kantian gap" (Cassedy 1987, 318) between science and metaphysics, or between analytical knowledge and knowledge of the "thing-in-itself."

In 1783 Kant wrote that Hume had awoken him from his "dogmatic slumber" (*Prolegomena*) and as a result had precipitated an entirely new direction in his philosophical searchings. To Kant, the two major lines of philosophical inquiry up to that time—British empiricism, culminating in the thought of Hume, and Continental rationalism, developed by Descartes and Leibniz—had both failed to provide a satisfactory answer as to how one may justify knowledge of the external world. Kant rejected Hume's conclusion (built on the theories of Locke and Berkeley) that true knowledge may be acquired only from experience; if that were true, Kant believed, Newtonian physics would not be able to increase our knowledge of the world, which it evidently did. On the other hand, Kant rejected the rationalist attempt to turn philosophy into geometry, the attempt "to extend our theoretical or scientific knowledge to reality as it is in itself; and [to use] categories having validity only within the phenomenal world to transcend phenomena" (Copleston 1946–53, 4:59). As a result of the impasse Kant considered philosophy to have reached, he proposed a new approach similar to that taken by Copernicus in astronomy, who came to the revolutionary conclusion that the earth revolves around the sun, and not vice versa. Thus, Copernicus reasoned, when we perceive the sun setting, it is actually the spectator, rather than the sun, that is changing position. Kant similarly concluded that our knowledge of external things may depend more on the nature of the observer than on the object being observed, and thus he shifted the general focus of philosophy from knowledge of the external object to knowledge of the self, or subject. Our way of thinking determines the objects of experience, making all knowledge of the external world relative. In this sense Kant considered the intellect the only method of attaining knowledge, but knowledge only of phenomena, things as they appear, and not things-in-themselves, as they really are. Kant placed this latter type of knowledge in the category of faith; thus the impossibility of metaphysics, or of what Kant considered to be scientific proof of that which lies beyond the realm of science.

In each of his major works, Bergson takes issue with the Kantian limitation of man's knowledge to the intellect, arguing instead for "two ways of knowing a thing" (*CM* 159). As one scholar notes:

> Bergson tells us that Kant was wrong, that we have a "way of knowing" which goes beyond the Kantian "island of experience" and gives us knowledge of the self. Bergson takes up the epistemological problem at exactly the point where Kant lays it down. . . . The great difference between Kant and Bergson, thus far discovered, is that the former recognized just the one, the intellectual, way of knowing, whereas Bergson holds that in addition to this Kantian intellec-

> tual way there is another way, the intuitional, which Kant admitted to be necessary (though impossible) for metaphysical knowledge. (Landes 1924, 457 and 459)

Bergson claims that, through the use of intuition, we can both grasp our own inner duration and thus truly know ourselves, as well as come to know another thing's "innermost quality" by entering into "spiritual harmony" with it. Intuition, then, is the bridge, "broken by Kant," that Bergson proposes to reestablish between science and metaphysics, a bridge between the knowing subject's intellect (which can attain only relative knowledge) and the thing-in-itself, of which absolute knowledge may now be possible.[9] While taking a jab at Kant's "critical" philosophy, Bergson writes in his *Introduction to Metaphysics:* "It [dogmatism] was bound to fail. This alone is the impotence which characterizes the skeptical, idealistic and critical doctrines, all those doctrines, in fact, which question our mind's ability to attain the absolute" (*CM* 189).

The notion of intuition as the special faculty for attaining absolute knowledge (that is, perceiving the inner meaning and essence of things) lies at the heart of the Russian conception of art (beauty), perception, and knowledge, all of which come together in the theology of the icon. In examining the Russian intuitivist tradition, which provided such fertile soil for the reception of Bergson's philosophy in Russia, attention should also be focused on such thinkers as Ivan Kireevskii, Aleksei Khomiakov, Vissarion Belinskii, Lev Tolstoy, and Vladimir Solov'ev, some of the main contributors to the Romantic, organicist movement in nineteenth-century Russia.

The icon's importance in Russian culture cannot be overestimated, serving as a reminder of the ever-present divine in the midst of the human sphere that may be immediately apprehended or intuited without recourse to analytical thought (Billington 1970, 35). When the iconoclastic movement was finally and officially rejected at the Second Council of Nicaea (A.D. 787), a momentous statement was made about the nature of Eastern Orthodox perception and its relationship to revelation. The debate over the worship of icons centered on the nature of the icon itself. The iconoclasts argued that the icon was a material representation of the divine, and as such, according to the Old Testament, could not be the object of worship. The iconophiles, on the other hand, argued within the Neoplatonic tradition that one can distinguish between image and prototype (or, in other terms, between phenomenon and noumenon, appearance and the thing-in-itself). According to the iconophiles, the icon is a *revelation* of divine truth, not a representation; thus, by contemplating the icon, the worshipper is able to enter into spiritual "sympathy" with it and thereby gain immediate, noncognitive understanding of reality in its essence. The iconophile victory at Nicaea exemplified an essential aspect of Russian thought, namely the notion that the human being is able to participate in divine reality by the intuitive apprehension of things as they really are (given by grace).

This deep-rooted tradition in Russian thought of what V. V. Zenkovskii (1970) calls Orthodox ontologism (1:196–97)—whereby knowing is not separated from the known and faith informs cognition—is opposed to the traditionally rational emphasis in Western philosophy on an epistemology informed by the dichotomy between knower and object of knowledge. Russian thinkers historically have rebelled against this dichotomy (epitomized by Kant's assertion that it is impossible to know the "thing-in-itself") because it serves to contradict the notion of the world as an organic whole and stifles man's intuitive ability to apprehend and take part in the true nature of reality. Also characteristic of Russian thought is the distrust of pure reason (*rassudok*) in favor of integral reason or understanding (*razum*), which requires not only the intellect but all the human faculties of perception, united in the creative effort to grasp the noumenal world.[10] Thus, in the Russian tradition words themselves are somewhat suspect because of their usual reliance on purely intellectual means of comprehension. A similar problem is faced by Bergson, a philosopher who must use the medium of words to express what cannot be contained in words, the fluid essence of duration. In his discussion of Bergson and modernist poetry, Paul Douglass (1983) asks: "Must not Bergson oppose words themselves as too rigid? . . . It would seem that for Bergson the artist's intuition cannot be cast into words without its fluidity being arrested" (239). Douglass goes on to state, however, that Bergson considered poetry to be born of intuition, and words that were "at first, only signals" are thus "converted into instruments of art." Russian modernists treat words in much the same way: for example, Bely's magical word (*Magiia slov*), Khlebnikov's transrational language, and Kharmsian words that ostensibly mean nothing, and thus bear their absurd meaning.

Interestingly, the nature of the Russian language itself—its use of perfective and imperfective aspect—reflects a very Bergsonian duality between objective and subjective time, or between time considered spatially and time as duration. Boris Gasparov discusses the metaphysical nature of the Russian language in a recent article, wherein he states that the distinction between the two aspectual forms lies not so much in context as in two different world outlooks. The use of the perfective aspect, writes Gasparov (1990), "assumes an external (objective) perspective" of a given situation, which in turn is "perceived as a discrete event and thus singled out from the continuous flow of time. . . . By approaching the reality from this position, the speaker achieves a segmentation of his continuous experience" (194–95). With the imperfective case, however, "the speaker assumes an internal (subjective) perspective in his view of the situation. Such a position projects an 'existential' view of the world; it views life as a continuous experience into which every person (including the speaker) is inextricably immersed" (195). The imperfective aspect of the Russian verb, then, closely corresponds to Bergson's conception of duration as the uninterrupted flow of time, ceaseless movement.

When a speaker uses the imperfective, it is as if he were plunging into this duration through an act of intuition, whereby he becomes "immersed" in it himself. The use of the perfective, on the other hand, reflects the fragmenting, conceptualizing use of the intellect that surveys a situation from the outside, "segmenting" experience into static portions of time. While the Russian language needs both linguistic aspects just as the human mind needs both intellect and intuition, the use of the imperfective reflects the Russian metaphysical need (characteristic of Russian intuitivism) to grasp the inner essence of reality, to plunge into the ceaseless movement and dynamism that is life itself.[11]

On the basis of the Orthodox belief in the intuitive grasp of reality and participation in the divine as accomplished through the veneration of icons, life is seen as organic movement by which one is constantly striving to become closer to the divine. This "flow of life" may be grasped intuitively as one continues to grow spiritually and to become more aware of the divine principle within oneself and the world. The idea of life as movement—a concept central to both the patristic tradition and Russian consciousness in general—reached perhaps its greatest fruition in the reception of German Romanticism in early nineteenth-century Russia. In his discussion of organicism as a central manifestation of German Romantic philosophy, Isaiah Berlin (1978) outlines the nineteenth-century intuitivist answer to the objective excesses of the eighteenth-century Age of Reason:

> The whole notion of organic method militated in favor of supposing that the favorite instrument of the eighteenth century—chemical analysis into constituent bits, into ultimate, irreducible atoms . . . —was an inadequate way of apprehending anything. "Growth" was the great new term—new, that is, in its application far beyond the bounds of scientific biology; and in order to apprehend what growth was, you had to have *a special inner sense capable of apprehending the invisible kingdom, an intuitive grasp of the impalpable principle* in virtue of which a thing grows as it does; grows not simply by successive increments of "dead" parts, but by some kind of occult vital process that needs a quasi-mystical power of vision, *a special sense of the flow of life*, or the forces of history, of the principles at work in nature, in art, in personal relationships, of the creative spirit unknown to empirical science, *to seize upon its essence.* (121; my emphasis)

As in Eastern Orthodoxy, the "organic method" presupposed an intuitive ability to apprehend the "invisible kingdom" (the absolute qualities of things), the "flow of life" (duration), and the "creative spirit" (élan vital) at work in the universe, ever present but simply unseen by the blind analytical eye of the intellect.

As part of the nineteenth-century Romantic, anti-Enlightenment reaction in Russian thought and culture, both Westernizers and Slavophiles alike believed in the power of intuition and the creative spirit at work in the universe, concepts that lie at the heart of Bergson's philosophy. Although the philosopher Petr Chaadaev pre-dated the controversy between Westernizers and Slavophiles and embraced ideas from both groups, he is usually listed as a Westernizer. Chaadaev was one of the first Russian philosophers (if not *the* first) to express his affinity with the idea of duration, a term he uses numerous times in his *Philosophical Letters* (1829–30), originally written in French. "One is lost in the world," writes Chaadaev, "without the sense of a permanent duration (*durée*) guiding one"; furthermore, Chaadaev notes that "the duration in which the eternal designs of divine wisdom are realized cannot be grasped by our limited vision."[12] The Bergsonian notion of duration as "real time" as opposed to the artificial, chronological time of the clock is also represented in the *Letters,* wherein Chaadaev states: "I perceive myself in that limitless duration, which is not divided into days, into hours. . . . [This is] the only real time."[13] Thus, what would become in the early twentieth century some of Bergson's most influential ideas on time were already being written about as early as 1830 by one of Russia's greatest thinkers, who, like Bergson, also happened to be critical of Kant's limitation of human knowledge to that of intellect.[14] Other prominent nineteenth-century Russian intellectuals, including Bakunin, Belinskii, Kireevskii, and Khomiakov, took up the ideas of duration, intuition, and artistic creativity in their Romantic assault on the Enlightenment apotheosis of reason.

Andrzej Walicki (1979) points out that although Mikhail Bakunin thought of himself as a materialist, he and Bergson nonetheless shared the goal of perceiving the inner qualities of things, the "thing-in-itself," which is invisible to the purely analytical eye:

> [Bakunin] rebelled against scientific abstractions in the name of the particular, of the individual flavor that could not be expressed in abstract concepts or explained by theories. This anti-intellectual strand in Bakunin's world view . . . was an interesting anticipation of Bergsonian ideas and the idealistic "philosophy of life." (276)

Like Bergson, Bakunin emphasized the eternally creative spirit at the heart of life, while linking it with the destructive element in the universe: "Let us therefore trust the eternal Spirit which destroys and annihilates only because it is the unfathomable and eternally creative source of all life. The passion for destruction is a creative passion, too."[15] In a 1914 article on Bakunin, one Russian critic notes the similarly prominent role that the creative life force plays for both Bakunin and Bergson: "Life is creation! . . . We have, after all, met with the idea that the entire universe is a product of creation, and that Bakunin attempted to endow the universe with a system of creation . . . 'Life is creation!' Isn't it striking how Bakunin's idea coincides with the central idea of Henri Bergson? With his idea of 'creative evolution?'" (Grossman 1914, 51).

Intuition served an even greater role for Belinskii, who states in "The Idea of Art" (1841) that art is characterized by its "immediacy" (*neposredstvennost'*), which may only be apprehended intuitively: "Art is the *immediate* contemplation of truth."[16] In addition, Belinskii writes about the aesthetic inferiority of pure reason compared to integral reason when it comes to the creation of a work of art.[17] For Belinskii, two worlds exist in conflict with one another: the organic and the mechanistic. Whereas the organic world is marked by movement, freedom, and creativity (what could be called duration or integral reason), the mechanistic realm is one of numbing, static nonfreedom (which could be equated with mathematical time or pure intellectuality). By juxtaposing the organic and the mechanistic realms, Belinskii anticipates the main Bergsonian dualities of intuition/intellect; fluid, dynamic duration/static, segmented time; free will and creative evolution/deterministic nonfreedom; art/symbol. Belinskii (1953–59) states:

> Organism and mechanism, or nature and craft—here are two worlds, aggressively opposed to one another. One is free, continually moving and changing, elusive in its play of colors and tints, loud and sonorous; the other is torpid in its deathly stasis, slavishly proper and lifelessly fixed in unnatural brightness, a counterfeit life, mute and silent. The occurrences of the first world are alive, spontaneous sproutings which may be called inspired or creative, whereas occurrences of the second world are mechanical objects or products of human hands. (596)

The Slavophiles Ivan Kireevskii and Aleksei Khomiakov similarly juxtapose pure and integral reason, denigrating the former as a dangerous construct of Western rationalistic thinkers, beginning with Aristotle, whose philosophical system "broke apart the wholeness of self-consciousness and transferred the root of man's inner beliefs . . . to the intellectual consciousness of abstract reason. The tools by which truth is known [in the Aristotelian system] were limited by the logical activity of the mind."[18] For Kireevskii, rationality or intellect alone distances one from reality, allowing only for the observation of phenomena. For the true apprehension of reality, however, one needs constantly to strive "to elevate reason to the level at which it could sympathize with faith" (1861, 312), or, in other words, to combine intellect with intuition, which is capable of grasping the essential inner meaning of phenomena, or the noumenal quality of a thing.

Khomiakov defines faith as "the contemplation of the unseen fact, manifested in the seen fact," or the "unveiling" (*raskrytie*) of the internal world of phenomena.[19] Furthermore, Khomiakov conceives of phenomena as in constant flux, "a continuous change" (*postoiannoe izmenenie*) during which "this arm, this leg, this blossoming blade of grass, this dried-up hay, all of it, inside and out, is continually decomposing and forming new combinations. . . . There is not one moment of time in which even the minutest particle remains itself. Nothing exists: all is *im Werden* [*sic*]."[20] There are clearly similarities between Bergson's philosophy of the intuition of duration and Khomiakov's conception of faith as the faculty for "unveiling" the hidden essence of life, which is continually "becoming." In a discussion of the similarities between the two thinkers, one Khomiakov scholar notes:

> Duration is at the base of all being, everything flows, everything moves; but nonetheless, within the movement . . . there is something which endures, . . . something which is not a concept, but a reality, a self no less real than the phenomena. . . . There is nothing to suggest that Mr. Bergson knew of Khomiakov. [But] they arrive at the same conclusion, one starting from the analysis of life, the other from the analysis of the entire tradition of humankind, cultivated, guarded and animated by the Church.[21]

Such a statement could also apply to the religious thinkers Losskii and Frank, who, as will be shown, like Khomiakov arrive at the same conclusion as Bergson; life is process, movement, change, a flow that one is capable of penetrating intuitively (being part of it oneself) in order to grasp the absolute nature of both one's own personality and the universe. This task, however, cannot be accomplished by intuition alone but rather requires all of one's faculties, "integral reason," or reason elevated to faith. (This is an important difference from Bergson, who does not touch on questions of religion or faith until his last major published work in 1932, *Two Sources of Morality and Religion*.) Man, according to Kireevskii (1861), should constantly seek in the depths of his soul "that inner root of understanding, where all separate strengths merge into one living and whole vision of the mind" (2:309–10). For a vision of the Whole, the whole human being is necessary.

Like Kireevskii and Khomiakov, Lev Tolstoy conceives of life as movement, a continuous flow of divine energy that encompasses everything in its flux. Immediately following Platon Karataev's death in *War and Peace*, Pierre contemplates this organic principle of movement: "Life is everything. Life is God. Everything shifts and moves, and this movement is God" (1960–65, 7:181). The goal of history, according to Tolstoy (1960–65) is to understand the laws of this continuous motion, but such a task is extremely difficult given that "the absolute continuity of movement is not understandable to the human mind" (6:300). Much of human error results from the arbitrary division of continuous movement into discontinuous parts, the same intellectual process of fragmentation that Bergson describes in his *Introduction to Metaphysics*: "Our mind . . . substitutes for the continuous the discontinuous, for mobility stability" (*CM* 188). Just as Bergson argues for the reverse procedure to take place in order intuitively to grasp reality—namely, for the mind "to seize movement no longer from outside and in its manifold result, but from within and in its tendency towards change, in short, to adopt the mobile continuity of the pattern of things" (*CM* 190)—so Tolstoy states that the only possible way to reach an understanding of the workings of history is to start with the small, seemingly insignificant events of human life (the "inner events" of history), to plunge into the unceasing movement of humanity and to try to apprehend "the pattern of things": "Having permitted ourselves to observe only an infinitely small unit—the differential of history . . . —we can expect to grasp the laws of history" (6:234). Kutuzov, whose motto is "patience and time," has the advantage over Napoleon as military strategist precisely because he is capable of apprehending these laws. Prince Andrei's confidence in Kutuzov is a reflection of this intuitive, as opposed to strictly intellectual, strength:

> The more he saw an absence of everything personal in the old man—in whom it seemed only habitual passions were left, and instead of intellect (grouping events and making conclusions) only the ability to calmly contemplate the course of events—the more he was calmed by the thought that all would be as it should. (153)

Kutuzov does not consider time spatially, as does the Western Napoleonic intellect, but instead contemplates the fluidity of historical movement (duration) and thus apprehends intuitively—in the Russian tradition—the course of events. "'And most importantly,' thought Prince Andrei, 'the reason to believe him is that he is a Russian.'"

Isaiah Berlin (1978) expands on Tolstoy's notion of a historical science while commenting on the similarities with Bergson's later theory of reality as flux:

> How would an ideal historical science operate? By using a kind of calculus whereby . . . the infinitely small human and non-human actions and events would be integrated, and in this way the continuum of history would no longer be distorted by being broken up into arbitrary segments. Henri Bergson, who made his name with his theory of reality as a flux fragmented artificially by the natural sciences, and thereby distorted and robbed of continuity and life, developed a very similar point at infinitely greater length, less clearly, less plausibly, and with an unnecessary parade of terminology. (44)

It should be noted that this "calculus" implies a "reasonable consciousness" similar to the method of cognition that the Slavophiles espoused, or that of "integral reason." In each case, the whole range of one's faculties, including both intellect and intuition, is necessary for the apprehension of the whole flow of life.

In addition, M. O. Gershenzon (1919) makes the interesting observation that Tolstoy's approach to the written word parallels Bergson's approach to philosophy:

> The following lines of Tolstoy are especially interesting because in them he preaches essentially the same method for the study of poetry that Bergson applies to the teachings of philosophers. In 1876, at the height of his artistic creativity, [Tolstoy] wrote to N. N. Strakhov: "In everything, almost in everything that I have written, I have been guided by the need to collect thoughts which

are interconnected in order for me to express myself; but each thought, expressed verbally by itself, loses its meaning, is terribly degraded when it is taken alone, independent of the linkage of which it is a part. The linkage itself is put together not by thought (I believe), but by something else; the basis of this linkage cannot be expressed directly through words but only indirectly, by describing images, actions, situations. . . . Now . . . when art criticism makes up 9/10 of all that is printed, people are needed who would show the senselessness of trying to find separate thoughts in an artistic work and who would constantly guide readers within that endless labyrinth of linkages in which consists the essence of art." (35–36)

The notion of an endless, cohesive linkage of ideas (*stseplenie myslei*) that Tolstoy considers the essence of art may be compared to the Bergsonian concept of duration as the continuous flow of interpenetrating moments of time. To pluck out a single idea from the linkage is just as meaningless for Tolstoy as focusing on one frame of a film strip is for Bergson. Tolstoy believes that this "cohesive linkage" of ideas, while of necessity expressed through the intellectual medium of words, is not put together by thought but by "something else" (*chem-to drugim*), suggesting the more intuitive, unmediated nature of creativity; similarly, Bergson states that only through intuition may the flow of duration be penetrated and grasped, although whatever meaning is apprehended from this intuitive process must be expressed through the intellect by way of concepts.

Vladimir Solov'ev, Russia's first truly original, systematic philosopher, gave voice in the late nineteenth century to many deep-rooted themes in Russian thought, including that of "all-unity" (*vseedinstvo*), which emphasizes the triune nature of goodness, beauty, and truth, as well as the unity of the three modes of knowledge: experience, reason, and intuition. Solov'ev's concept of "all-unity" greatly influenced Russian artists of the early twentieth century and had much in common with the Bergsonian mix of intellect and intuition, the union of science and metaphysics. Although Solov'ev died in 1900, the same year that Bergson's first work was published in Russia, he wrote about many of the same epistemological issues that Bergson would explore and become famous for in Russia and around the world after Solov'ev's death. Solov'ev and Bergson shared a view of life as continually in flux, creative, intuitive, and thus forever in conflict with the stasis of the "dead" material world. As A. F. Losev notes in his introduction to an edition of Solov'ev's collected works: "Bergson's *Creative Evolution* appeared in 1908. But twenty years prior to this work, which is marked by a profound intellectual dramatism, Vladimir Solov'ev had already portrayed the continual *élans vitals* in nature and their struggle, often unsuccessful and fatal, with dead matter" (Solov'ev 1988, 1:19). According to Losev, Bergson's main task is essentially the same as Solov'ev's, noting in one of his own essays that Bergson depicts "the tragic struggle of life for its existence amidst dead, static, lifeless matter."[22] Whereas Bergson conceives of this conflict in primarily secular terms (at least until *Les deux sources de la morale et de la religion*), for Solov'ev the battle between the unceasing life flow in nature and its static, lifeless, material surroundings represents the cosmic struggle for the incarnation of the divine principle in man.

Philosophers who expounded the virtues of intuition in the time of Solov'ev and Bergson were fighting in some way the specter of neo-Kantianism, which was the dominant philosophy in Germany from roughly 1870 to 1920, and which represented to many Russian religious thinkers the bankrupt rationalism of Western analytical systems. In the beginning of the chapter entitled, "What Does the Philosophy of Vladimir Solov'ev Offer to Modern-Day Consciousness?" (Chto daet sovremennomu soznaniiu filosofiia Vladimira Solov'eva?) from his 1903 work, *From Marxism to Idealism* (*Ot marksizma k idealizmu*), Sergei Bulgakov (1903) describes the profound influence of neo-Kantian philosophy on Russian thought at the beginning of the twentieth century:

> At the entrance to the temple of philosophy now stands guard a theory of knowledge from which each philosophical doctrine must receive a residence permit. The permanent significance of Kant in the history of philosophy lies in the fact that, after him, metaphysics (even theology) must be critical; in other words, each philosophical teaching must be prepared at the outset to provide an intelligent answer to the question of the nature of knowledge itself. (198)

Bulgakov goes on to point out that the primary weakness of neo-Kantian philosophy lies in its artificial fragmentation of the inherent unity between subject and object (199). As one of the contributors to the celebrated collection of essays *Signposts* (Vekhi, 1909), Bulgakov (along with six other Russian religious thinkers) descries the spiritual impoverishment of the Russian intelligentsia and calls for the restoration of this unity, of the fully integrated individual whose mind and heart work in organic unison instead of battling divisively for supremacy. Emphasizing the importance of combining the rational and the irrational in the human being (who is "more than just intellect"), Bulgakov and other religious thinkers argue for the "trans-empirical dignity of the self,"[23] a self that is as much of a unified, organic whole as is the world in which it lives.

Bergson, whose most popular book, *Creative Evolution,* also appeared in Russian in 1909, similarly comments in that work upon the necessity of both intellect and intuition in order to apprehend the inner essence of things. Like the contributors to *Vekhi,* Bergson spurned Kantian philosophy, writing that "the criticism of Kant consisted chiefly in limiting the dogmatism of his predecessors, accepting their conception of science and reducing to a minimum the metaphysic it implied. . . . The human intellect is enough: such is precisely the Kantian solution" (*CE* 357). Bergson's call for the union of intellect and intuition, or science and metaphysics, is similar in essence to Solov'ev's doctrine of "all-unity," itself an elaboration of the Slavophile concepts of *sobornost'* and "integral knowledge" (*tsel'noe znanie, tsel'noe poznavanie*). This latter concept, expounded most fully by Ivan Kireevskii, stresses the wholeness of man's cognitive ability—the combination of intellect and intuition—as opposed to the Western emphasis on analytical reason or intellect alone as the key to understanding the world. For the Slavophiles, logic and faith both played necessary roles in "integral knowledge," a reflection of the divine wholeness of man based on both rational and nonrational modes of perception. Building on this concept of "integral knowledge," Solov'ev consistently strove for the organic, logical synthesis of disparate elements, a rational system of "all-unity," one of the clearest illustrations of which may be found in his 1877 work "The Philosophical Principles of Integral Knowledge" (Filosofskie nachala tsel'nogo znaniia).

In this latter work, Solov'ev states that each person is made up of a large number of organic elements, thus giving the individual a "collective" character (*sobiratel'nyi kharakter*). Furthermore, as everyone equally searches for meaning in life, the goal of each person's life is linked (*nerazryvno sviazana*) with the life goal of all others. Man desires three types of societal bonds—economic, political, and spiritual—and three types of knowledge correspond to these bonds: factual material knowledge, formal logical knowledge, and absolute knowledge. Continuing with his trinitarian approach, Solov'ev states that science (*polozhitel'naia nauka*) gives the necessary material foundation to knowledge (the real fact); philosophy gives to knowledge ideal form (the general idea); and theology, or religion, endows knowledge with absolute content or the supreme goal (the absolute essence). Solov'ev (1966) writes: "Only this source (theology) imparts real sense and meaning both to philosophic thought as well as to scientific fact; without theology the former would appear as empty form, and the latter as indifferent matter" (1:260). In the tradition of Schelling, Solov'ev also uses the term "intellectual intuition" (*umstvennoe sozertsanie*) to indicate the "primary form of integral knowledge."[24] Bergson, in criticizing Kant for denying the importance of intellectual intuition in both science and metaphysics, makes a very similar statement in his *Introduction to Metaphysics:* "Because he [Kant] relieved metaphysics and science of their 'intellectual intuition' which gave them their inner weight, science . . . presents to him only an outer wrapping of form, and metaphysics . . . an outer wrapping of matter" (*IM* 195). The central idea is the same for both Solov'ev and Bergson, namely that intellectual intuition unifies science and metaphysics by giving absolute meaning to both.

Before Bergson set about distinguishing the two basic ways of "knowing a thing" (thereby implying that the "thing" has a reality that may be known), Solov'ev was first establishing the fact that the "thing," or "object," exists in its own right, independent of the sensations and thoughts of the cognizing subject. Without such faith in the self-sufficient existence of objects, according to Solov'ev, philosophy would be reduced to solipsism, or at best to a critical Kantian rationalism, wherein "things-in-themselves" are unknowable. Solov'ev (1966) argues this point in the first half of his article, "On the Reality of the External World" (O deistvitel'nosti vneshnego mira), wherein he writes: "Everything that is consists of beings which possess their own inner reality" (219). Solov'ev attacks (as Bergson would later) the metaphysical distinction between appearance and reality, claiming, in a true post-Kantian idealist fashion, that not only the image but also the "thing-in-itself" is knowable to the human mind. In rejecting the primacy of either positivism or rationalism, Solov'ev turns to the third form of knowledge—intuition, or, as he often calls it, faith (*vera*)—as the answer to the epistemological (and for him, ontological) problem. Noumenal knowledge is therefore possible only through an effort of intuition, an effort of disinterested, intellectual sympathy with the inner reality of a given object. While Bergson describes the difference between relative and absolute knowledge as the difference between "going all around" a thing as opposed to "entering into" it, so Solov'ev similarly states that there is "external" as opposed to "internal" knowledge of that which exists:

> 1) In *external* or objective knowledge . . . we have knowledge only of the practical relationships between actual beings, or their *external* interaction.
> 2) With *internal* experience . . . we have knowledge not only of relationships, but of some actual psychological essence, namely our own. Unmediated knowledge of a being is possible only in terms of *internal* experience, or that which I call essential knowledge. (226; my emphasis)

One is reminded here of the Slavophile opposition of external versus internal knowledge, the former allowing only for the observation of phenomena while the latter is capable of grasping essential inner meaning. Bergson's basic juxtaposition of intellect (external knowledge) and intuition (knowledge resulting from a sympathetic "entering into" the object, the apprehension of duration) was not new to a Russian reading public already familiar with Solov'ev's earlier distinction between outer, objective knowledge and inner, unmediated, essential (*sushchestvennoe*) knowledge.

For both Solov'ev and Bergson, intuition is a fundamentally aesthetic phenomenon through which one is able to grasp one's own inner, unique qualities, as well as those qualities of other concrete objects—fluid depths not plumbed by our everyday utilitarian perception, which is limited to static intellectual conceptualization. Bergson states in *Creative Evolution:* "That an effort [of intuition] is not impossible, is proved by the existence in man of an aesthetic faculty along with normal perception" (*CE* 176). Bergson's (1925) clearest definition of art is found in *Laughter,* wherein he observes:

> There is a veil between nature and us . . . a veil which is thick for ordinary men, but thin, almost transparent, for the artist and the poet. . . . Thus, art has no other object than to set aside the practical, useful symbols, the conventionally and socially accepted generalities, in short, all that masks reality from us, in order to place us face to face with reality itself. . . . Art is certainly only a more direct vision of reality. (153 and 160)

The idea that the artist is capable of "removing the veil" between himself and reality, as Bergson states above, has much in common with the Russian Orthodox notion that the divine manifestation of God exists continually in and around us—we just have to *see* it. Such a coincidence of thought reflects one of the many ways in which Bergsonian ideas overlap with Russian philosophy, and suggests how Russian modernism—marked by a neo-Romantic preoccupation with artistic intuition—drew on the intuitivist tradition in Russian Orthodoxy.

Solov'ev's pronouncements on art and intuition are strikingly similar to Bergson's. In "The Philosophical Principles of Integral Knowledge," Solov'ev (1988) claims that "the existence of ideal intuition in general is proven beyond a doubt by the fact of artistic creation" (2:205). In addition, while Bergson claims that one of the most important roles of art is to make us discover the hidden qualities within ourselves, so Solov'ev earlier remarks that "the poet who completely gives himself up to creative work and, so to speak, transfers his inner life to objective artistic creations, not only does not lose by doing so, but on the contrary, affirms in the highest degree and fully realizes his own individuality."[25] According to Solov'ev, the poet realizes himself most fully through the creation of art, an act that affirms his inner, divine essence by mirroring the eternally creative nature of the absolute.

Both Solov'ev and Bergson consider artistic intuition the means by which to achieve clearer perception of things, yet for Solov'ev intuition is a spiritual tool for uncovering the divine element in oneself (and therefore in the world), while for Bergson intuition is simply a method of perception by which objects, including oneself, are "seen" more clearly. As one critic observes: "Art (for Bergson) grasps external reality in felt particles, revealing their unique qualities. This emphasis upon individuality in presentation represents Bergson's revolt against all 'spiritualistic' aesthetic theories. For him art was no 'sensuous manifestation of the Idea'; nor was it 'the perception of the Infinite in the finite'" (Szathmary 1937, 68). Despite their differing emphases (religious versus secular), Solov'ev and Bergson conceive of the balance between intellect and intuition in very similar terms. As Bergson stresses the necessity of the intellect to "furnish the verification" of something just intuited, Solov'ev states that what is given in ideal intuition must be verified analytically: "Only through intellectual intuition may a whole idea be grasped. . . . But once the content of the absolute is given to us in an ideal intuition, it can and must be justified by the reflection of our intellect and brought into a logical system; in other words, the general, logical necessity of that content must be shown" (340). One of the reasons that Bergson appealed to groups with varying ideologies (Symbolists and post-Symbolists alike) was that his philosophy could easily be appropriated to fit different aesthetic agendas. For example, while some students of Bergson might view Bergsonian intuition as a "revolt" against the "spiritualistic" aesthetic theories of Symbolism, others see him as primarily a mystic, his concept of an élan vital, or "vital impulse," approximating that of the divine.[26]

Solov'ev (1994) similarly tried to combine elements of mysticism and materialism in his philosophy, conceiving of man as the material and spiritual bridge between this world and that of the divine: "Man, belonging to both worlds, can and must connect with the divine world through an act of intellectual intuition. . . . In particular, this positive (although incomplete) knowledge of, or penetration into, the reality of the divine world is characteristic of poetic creation" (142). As for Solov'ev, intuition for Bergson is inextricably linked with artistic creation; M. O. Gershenzon (1919) remarks upon this poetic nature of Bergsonian intuition: "At the Congress of Philosophy in Bologna in 1911, Henri Bergson delivered a magnificent speech on philosophical intuition. . . . His profound analysis of philosophical intuition could have been applied in its entirety to poetic vision, because in essence they are identical" (32).

Both Solov'ev and Bergson were interested in artistic intuition as a tool for clearer seeing of an "absolute" reality. Solov'ev's "absolute" equaled knowledge of the divine in the world, while for Bergson the "absolute" indicated the unique quality of a thing, its "living essence," sympathetically perceived in the flux of duration. Both philosophers sought to bridge the Kantian gap between science and metaphysics because they believed in the possibility and necessity of knowing "the-thing-in-itself."[27] While Solov'ev's discussion of the synthesis of rationality and spirituality strongly influenced the Symbolists and the Russian religious philosophers who followed him, it was Bergson's discussion of these themes *and* his examination in secular terms of "real time," or *durée (dlitel'nost'* or *tvorcheskoe izmenenie)* that aligned the French philosopher with Russian modernists who were seeking to supersede the Hegelian model of history (a determined evolution of the one Idea) and reclaim time as a "creative evolution."[28] Bergson's intuitivist philosophy became popular in Russian artistic circles of the early twentieth century not only because it gave philosophical grounding to a certain modernist aesthetic already in the air, but also because it coincided fundamentally with the strong intuitivist tradition in Russian thought given fullest expression by Russia's first systematic philosopher, Vladimir Solov'ev.

Perhaps the most common criticism of Bergson's philosophy is that he rejects science and intellect in favor of the subjective workings of metaphysics and intuition.[29] A closer reading of Bergson reveals, however, that while he does distinguish between the realms and functions of intellect and intuition, he also stresses their interdependence:

> But, in default of knowledge properly so called, reserved to pure intelligence, intuition may enable us to grasp what it is that intelligence fails to give us, and indicate the means of supplementing it. On the one hand, it will utilize the mechanism of intelligence itself to show how intellectual molds cease to be strictly applicable; and on the other hand, by its own work, it will suggest to us the vague feeling, if nothing more, of what must take the place of intellectual molds. Thus, intuition may bring the intellect to recognize that . . . neither mechanical causality nor finality can give a sufficient interpretation of the vital process. Then, by the sympathetic communication which [intuition] establishes between us and the rest of the living, by the expansion of our consciousness which it brings about, it introduces us into life's own domain, which is reciprocal interpenetration, endlessly continued creation. But, though it thereby transcends intelligence, it is from intelligence that has come the push that has made it rise to the point it has reached. Without intelligence, it would have remained in the form of instinct, riveted to the special object of its practical interest. (*CE* 177–78)

What is often perceived as a contradiction in Bergsonian thought—namely that intuition is both separate from and united with intellect—is resolved by examining Bergson's pronouncements on the two modes of knowledge. In Bergson's lexicon intuition implies some element of intellectuality; hence the term "intellectual intuition," which he uses in *Introduction to Metaphysics* and elsewhere. Bergson states that his philosophy is one that "attempts to reabsorb intellect in intuition" (*CE* 270), meaning that once the subject has, through an act of intuition, grasped the essence of the "thing-in-itself," has become one with it in sympathy, then the intellect must come into play in order to give conceptual meaning to what has just been intuited:

> But as soon as we have intuitively perceived the true, our intellect recovers itself, corrects itself, intellectually formulates its error. It has received the suggestion; it furnishes the verification. As the diver feels out the wreck on the sea floor that the aviator has pointed out from the air, so the intellect immersed in the conceptual environment verifies from point to point, by contact, analytically, what has been the object of a synthetic and super-intellectual vision. (*CM* 64)

Far from rejecting intellect, Bergson emphasizes the reciprocal relationship of intellect and intuition necessary for the apprehension and subsequent conceptualization of noumena, the inner workings of things, the wreck at the bottom of the sea.

Such an interdependence of intellect and intuition as put forth by Bergson proved of great importance for Russian modernists, whose Neoplatonic yearning for noncognitive union with an "absolute" reality was always anchored by some sort of intellectual framework. Bergson's use of the term "intellectual intuition" paralleled that of perhaps his closest philosophical predecessor, Friedrich Schelling.[30] Given that Bergson's popularity in early twentieth-century Russia was due in part to the fact that he was considered a "new Schelling" (himself revered by Russian Romantics a century earlier), an examination of the philosophical similarities and differences between Bergson and Schelling will help elucidate the nature of Bergson's reception by Russian modernists.

Schelling was introduced into Russia in the 1820s through the secret society of Wisdom-lovers (Liubomudry), which included Prince Vladimir Odoevskii, Dmitrii Venevitinov, and the future Slavophile, Ivan Kireevskii.[31] The popularity of Schelling in Russia at this time represented a Romantic reaction against Russian Voltaireanism (characterized, in the spirit of the Enlightenment, by a strict reliance on rationalism and reason) in favor of a more mystical, spiritual approach to knowledge, in which intuition played a major role. The warm reception of Bergsonian philosophy in the early twentieth century may similarly be seen as a neo-Romantic reaction against the excessive rationalism that developed in the late nineteenth century when the world was thought to be determined and wholly decipherable by scientific formulae.

As the most Romantic of the post-Kantian idealist philosophers, Schelling not only believed that the subject could fully know the object, but also that the subject identifies itself with the object in self-consciousness; thus the importance of "intellectual intuition," by means of which the essence of the Absolute may be grasped. Along the same lines, Bergson states that "an absolute can only be given in an *intuition,* while all the rest has to do with *analysis*" (*CM* 161). For Schelling, the "Absolute" (capital A) connotes some kind of static, infinite totality, while for Bergson, the "absolute" (small *a*) suggests more of a fluid, cosmic élan vital, a dynamic impulse that serves as the source for the unceasing creative principle in all manifestations of life. More often, however, Bergson uses the term "absolute" to indicate the absolute *quality* of a thing perceived through an act of intuition, as opposed to the relative knowledge of the external world available to the intellect. Stating that "there is no doubt that Bergson continues the heritage of Schelling," one critic goes on to discuss the essential difference between Bergson's "neo-spiritualism" and Schelling's idealism:

> Bergson introduces with decisiveness and consequence his view of intuition as an instrument of the concrete world. Both Schelling's and Bergson's philosophies are oriented towards the absolute. But Schelling prescribes to the absolute its form of being, and yokes it to a closed circle. He prides himself that he succeeded in this. 'A system is complete if it leads back to its initial point of departure' (*Werke* 3:628). Bergson's philosophic faith is the faith in an infinite dynamism of the absolute, that the absolute can only be apprehended in

> its uniquely occurring manifestations. A closed intuitive system of thought, embracing the infinity of the universe is for Bergson an impossibility. His method serves as a task which is ever new, and whose problems are as numerous as births are in organic nature. (Hausheer 1933, 105)

Despite varying conceptions of the absolute, Schelling and Bergson both consider art to be the highest form of human endeavor and artistic intuition the most privileged faculty of man. Bergson states in *Creative Evolution:* "That an effort of [intuition] is not impossible, is proved by the existence in man of an aesthetic faculty along with normal perception" (*CE* 176–77), and in an earlier work he remarks that "art is surely only a more direct vision of reality" (1925, 160). Such an emphasis on art and the creative process as a method of apprehending reality appealed greatly to Russians both of Schelling's and Bergson's generations because of the historical symbiosis of philosophy and art in Russian thought, dating back at least to the theology of the icon.

A vital difference remains, however, between Schelling's and Bergson's conceptions of intuition. Whereas for Schelling intuition is mystically "given" to a passive recipient (such as an artist, who is endowed with the exalted capacity for such heightened awareness), intuition for Bergson represents an active method of cognition that is available to anyone willing and able to sharpen his perception:

> Schelling's intuition is given. In none of its forms is the individual really active. Not we have reason, but reason has us: not we construct, but the absolute constructs in us. Intellectual intuition is an entirely passive and receptive self-surrender to revelation, which the average man cannot attain by effort. . . . For Bergson intuition is acquired and developed. In its origin it is mystical; but as a method its mysticism is almost wholly stripped. Intuitive knowledge is not obtained as an unearned gift. It requires a heightened state of consciousness, a highly tensioned wakefulness. (Hausheer 1993, 101)

Russian Romantics embraced Schelling's philosophy because it offered them a way of self-surrender to the Absolute, a "Truth" that lay not in the material world that seemed so lacking (the world that the French Enlightenment thinkers proclaimed to be ruled by reason), but rather in the higher, more intuitive reaches of culture, art, and religion. The intuitive process, as put forth by Schelling, was a mystical gift that allowed for communion with the Absolute, but it was bestowed only on those select creative spirits who were capable of perceiving the infinite in the finite. Thus, Dmitrii Venevitinov, the foremost poet of the Liubomudry, offers a clear look in his first "Sonet" in 1824 of the Schellingian poet, who acknowledges that he has tried in vain to soar toward the "pure spirit" of the Absolute, the "source of inspiration," but nonetheless entreats his lyre to ring out with hope and love (*Gremi nadezhdoiu, gremi liubov'iu, lira!*). Here, Venevitinov's vision of the poet is of one removed from the cares of everyday life, one who seeks knowledge of and union with the Absolute by looking within his own poetic soul: "I read You in the heartfelt depths" (*Tebia chitaiu ia vo glubine serdechnoi*). Schelling's philosophy provided the Liubomudry, the lovers of divine wisdom, with what they needed, namely a mystical escape to another—better—world. In a sense, this is also what Bergson's philosophy provided Russian modernists nearly a century later: a neo-Romantic escape from the oppressive world of scientific determinism into that of creative evolution, where, by an act of artistic intuition, one could plunge into the flux of life and apprehend the inner reality of things in ceaseless change. (In this sense Bergson falls more within the tradition of German Romanticism than of French Enlightenment thought.)

But modernism did not call for Schelling's mystical transcendence, for a "passive self-surrender to revelation." Rather, following the revolution of 1905 and the death of mystical Symbolism, Russian modernists wanted a more pragmatic way to live in *this* world and an "absolute" that was as fluid and dynamic as twentieth-century quantum mechanics proved reality to be (as opposed to the static, closed system of Schelling's Absolute). Intuition no longer would serve simply as a way to escape into a higher, purer realm of being, but would represent an active means for clearer seeing of reality in duration and would thus help the artist to transform the world. Such was the impetus for both the Pragmatism of William James and Bergson's "creative evolution," as noted by V. M. Khvostov ("Spor o pragmatizme," 1910). "James has in mind the incompleteness of existence itself and endows man with a positive mission in the process of the formation of the world. Here James' ideas come very close to those expressed by Bergson in *Creative Evolution*" (138). The Russian modernist conception of the role of art also expressed the need to strive for the active transformation of reality, a theurgic impulse that motivated all of the artists and thinkers included in this study.

Like Schelling, who came to challenge Hegelian rationalism with his philosophy of revelation, Bergson challenged the neo-Kantians with his intuitive metaphysics. Furthermore, Schelling was eclipsed by Hegel in popularity among Russians in the 1840s primarily because the Russians found in the Hegelian idea of History an inspirational blueprint for social change; a parallel shift in literary sensibility accompanied the philosophical one as the wane of Romantic poetry heralded the dawn of realist prose. In a similar fashion, Bergson's popularity in Russia was cut short by the growing socialist demand, following the revolution of 1917, for materialist philosophies as well as for literature that portrayed reality "in its revolutionary development." Such a transition from a "creative" to a "determined" evolution anticipated the birth of socialist realism in Russian art and the subsequent death of intuition, bringing with it the end of Russian modernism.

Having examined Bergson as a "new Schelling" in early twentieth-century Russia, one must also consider Bergson's place alongside the other major philosophical influences in the modernist period, namely Schopenhauer and Nietzsche. Bergsonian intuition, which allowed for the individual to grasp his inner self in duration and thus enjoy free will, came closer in the Russian philosophical landscape to Nietzsche's Dionysian "will to power" than to Schopenhauer's pessimistic negation or suspension of the will. Bergson's philosophical views on intuition, however, are often difficult to distinguish from Schopenhauer's. As Copleston (1946–53) points out, "there is an obvious analogy" between the two; furthermore,

> for Bergson as for Schopenhauer philosophy involves the interplay of intuition and discursive or conceptual reasoning. . . . The same current or line of thought which found expression in the philosophy of Schopenhauer, when considered under the aspects in question [that is, intuition], reappeared in the thought of Bergson. (7:271)

What does distinguish Bergson from Schopenhauer is a matter of emphasis: Bergson's philosophy of life is optimistic, intuition serving as a mode of cognition by which to see reality more clearly and therefore to live a richer, more meaningful life of "creative evolution." As opposed to Bergsonian optimism and affirmation, Schopenhauer's philosophy is based on pessimism and negation, artistic contemplation or intuition serving as a means by which to deny one's Will and retreat from the world in ascetic renunciation; Ellis, in fact, calls Schopenhauer "the great pessimist" (1909, 61). Denial of Will runs counter to the tradition of Russian religious thought, which encourages the fruitful cultivation of the "whole" human being in the spirit of Solov'ev's "all-unity." While there is no question that Schopenhauer was more popular than Bergson with Russian decadents like Valerii Briusov, the general tenor of Russian modernism as an optimistic scramble oriented toward the future, toward new ways of artistic perception and expression, was more in tune with the self-affirmation inherent in Bergsonian thought (as well as with the Nietzschean "superman") than with the self-denial of Schopenhauer's philosophy.[32]

Nietzsche's influence on Russian thought, which had taken hold in the 1890s, was already starting to wane by the time Bergson's *Creative Evolution* was published in Russia in 1909; Viacheslav Ivanov, for example, proclaimed in 1908: "Dionysus in Russia is dangerous."[33] Following the failed revolutionary attempt of 1905, Nietzsche's vision of a heroic superman fighting for a new order seemed untenable in Russia (Rosenthal 1986, 28). Nietzsche and Bergson shared a worldview based on the individual, freedom, and creativity (the Apollonian/Dionysian dichotomy paralleling in a sense that of mathematical time/the flux of duration). While both Nietzschean and Bergsonian ideas filled the air of Russian modernism, Bergson's philosophy appealed to post-1905 Russian modernists interested less in apocalyptic political upheaval and glorifying the personality than in new modes of artistic perception by which to tap into the élan vital of the Dionysian flux and thus to discover the true essence of life.

Bergson's view of art as only a more direct vision of reality was much more compatible with the Russian modernist faith in art as theurgy than were Nietzsche's many statements on art as illusion.[34] Furthermore, Bergson's notion of duration as a ceaseless process of becoming in which the past is continually merging with the present (not to mention the significance of memory in his metaphysics as a bridge between matter and spirit [see *Matter and Memory*]) was much more relevant to historically minded modernists as diverse as Mandel'shtam and Khlebnikov than was Nietzsche's call for "forgetfulness" of the past.[35] Lastly, while Russian thinkers could attempt to spiritualize Bergsonian thought, positing the artist as (divine) creator and the intuition of the flow of duration as a revelation of the essence of things (that is, of a divine "whole"), no such spiritualization could take place of Nietzsche, the atheistic existentialist, who boldly proclaimed in *The Gay Science* that "God is dead."[36] If Bergson's philosophy is oriented toward the discovery and cultivation of the life force, Nietzsche, according to one critic, ends up destroying "life" as a result of his overemphasis on will: "Nietzsche is not the last of the Romantics, but rather the embodiment of their nightmare; the overwhelming of the ideal by naked instinct—'the triumph of life.' . . . If Nietzsche stands in any relationship at all to the 'organic/vitalist tradition,' he is its betrayer. By the time Nietzsche is through with the word and the concept, 'life' is dead" (Amrine 1992, 144 and 147). Thus, as distinguished from that of Schopenhauer and Nietzsche, Bergson's philosophy may be seen to best embody the modernist ethos, characterized by an unbridled optimism in both art and life, and a belief in the individual's creative power to perceive and participate in a constantly changing, growing, dynamic universe.

Born in the same year that Darwin published his *Origin of Species*, Bergson owed his fame in large part to his critique of neo-Darwinian mechanistic biology in favor of a "creative" evolution. Bergson claimed that species do not evolve arbitrarily, as the Darwinists maintained, but rather that evolution takes place as a result of consciousness, the free, nondeterministic creative impulse in beings (the élan vital) which sparks all growth and change. Such neo-Romantic notions as duration (organicity, interpenetrability, flux) and intuition (introspection, reflection, sympathy) would have appealed to modernists who were interested in breaking free of traditional concepts of time and space, and who sought to reclaim for the individual a direct link with reality, a link that had been usurped by the grandiose claims of rationalism and empiricism. Furthermore, Bergson's emphasis on the importance of art for the clear seeing of reality paralleled the modernist call for new modes of artistic perception and expression. Lastly, Bergson's pointed rejection of static "systems" of philosophic thought, such as Kant's, in favor of a more pragmatic philosophy of life, a "creative evolution," was compatible with the modernist revolt in Russia, Europe, and America against the often dehumanizing philosophical conventions of nineteenth-century scientific determinism.

Chapter One

Russian Religious Thought: The World as Organic Whole

> Bergson undoubtedly thought that the very fate of the spirit was inseparable from the consciousness of its presence and of its universal significance: in this, as in other ways, he crosses paths with religious thought. The meaning of life, beginning with its simplest and most humble manifestations, seemed to him spiritual in the highest degree.
> —Paul Valéry

ALTHOUGH RUSSIAN religious thought does not exactly qualify as "modernist," it nonetheless underlies a central goal of Russian modernism: to uncover new modes of artistic perception and thus to grasp an elusive reality existing beyond the bounds of the intellect alone. For religious thinkers, this "elusive reality" is the reality of the divine existing in and around one. The notion of theurgy—the active transformation of reality through the Logos, or "the Word"—is based on what might seem to the Western mind a fundamental paradox in Russian Orthodoxy, namely, that one continually strives to uncover and to build what is already present all around: the Kingdom of God. The theurgic impulse helped to unify the scattered movements of Russian modernism, the artistic "word" and artistic intuition substituting for the explicitly religious "Logos" as the primary means for modernist artists to grasp and thus creatively to shape the dynamic flow of life; Bergsonian thought—focused on the artistic intuition of duration, and on an active philosophy of living rather than a passive "explanatory idea"—coincided with this theurgic impulse. The study of Bergson and Russian modernism must therefore begin with a discussion of how Bergson was viewed by Russian religious thinkers such as Nikolai Losskii and Semen Frank, the two philosophers who critiqued Bergsonian intuitivism most thoroughly.[1]

Bergson presented Losskii and Frank with a dilemma concerning the question of the "absolute." In Russian religious thought, the "absolute" stands for reality as a living organism, or the divine content realized in the world. The absolute is something whole, complete, unified (*polnoe, vsetseloe*).[2] While

Losskii and Frank presuppose a unified, Platonic "whole" as encompassing all of the "parts" of life (that is, the world as organic whole or as absolute divine essence), Bergson's position regarding the existence of such a unity or absolute is not consistent.

On the one hand, Losskii and Frank were drawn to Bergson's philosophy because they found compelling parallels between Bergsonian intuition and the Orthodox concept of immediate, noncognitive understanding by which man is capable of attaining the absolute. Indeed, much of Bergson's *Introduction to Metaphysics* is devoted to such a discussion of the absolute, with language and imagery often reminiscent of Orthodox theology. After identifying "relative" and "absolute" knowledge as the two basic ways of knowing a thing, Bergson characterizes the former as analytic, static, and external while absolute knowledge is achieved only through intuition, through the active sympathy with the object of knowledge by which it is possible to enter into the fluid reality of the thing itself. Bergson states: "*Symbolic knowledge attained through pre-existing concepts is relative and goes from the fixed to the moving, but not so intuitive knowledge, which penetrates into the moving reality and adopts the life itself of things.* This intuition attains the absolute."[3] In addition, Bergson's definition of "duration" is suggestive of the Russian Orthodox doctrine of *sobornost'*. Taken from the word *sobor,* or cathedral, *sobornost'* originally expressed the theological notion of an organic ecclesiastical consciousness (which characterized the Orthodox Church council) as opposed to the hierarchical structure and mind-set of the Western Catholic Church wherein the Pope holds absolute authority. Linked with the Russian religious conception of the absolute as a unified, organic reality, *sobornost'* suggests the idea of unity in multiplicity, as does Bergsonian duration: "I shall say, for example, that there is, on the one hand, a *multiplicity* of successive states of consciousness and, on the other hand, a *unity* which binds them together. Duration will be the 'synthesis' of this unity and multiplicity" (*CM* 184).[4]

On the other hand, however, Bergson often seems firmly to believe that *if* an absolute exists, it will only be attained through the experience of intuition. In his introduction to *The Creative Mind,* Bergson states:

> [My metaphysics] . . . would not embrace in a single sweep the totality of things; but for each thing it would give an explanation which would fit it exactly, and it alone. It would not begin by defining or describing the systematic unity of the world: who knows if the world is actually one? Experience alone can say, and unity, if it exists, will appear at the end of the search as a result; it is impossible to posit it at the start as a principle. (31)

Here, Bergson prefers only to hold out the *possibility* of an absolute unity that might result from the ceaseless flow of life and experience. It is not surprising, then, that Losskii and Frank were both drawn to Bergson's belief in the ability of intuition to attain the absolute, while at the same time rejecting what they considered to be "Bergson's anti-Platonism" (Losskii 1968, 127).

LOSSKII: EPISTEMOLOGICAL COORDINATION VERSUS EPISTEMOLOGICAL DUALISM

One of the first Russian philosophers actually to have been familiar with Bergson's works was Nikolai Losskii, a self-proclaimed "intuitivist" and therefore especially interested in Bergsonian intuition.[5] In his *Vospominaniia*, Losskii (1968) comments on his acquaintance with Bergson's work:

> I can precisely pinpoint one direct influence on the development of my views. S. A. Alekseev once pointed out during a conversation with me that the link between spiritual and corporeal processes had been examined by the French philosopher Bergson in a spirit favorable for the elaboration of my intuitivism. I immediately sent for "Essai sur les données immédiates de la conscience" [*sic*] and "Matière et mémoire" [*sic*]. (127)

Losskii's best-known writings on intuition include *The Intuitive Basis of Knowledge* (Obosnovanie intuitivizma, 1906) and *The World as an Organic Whole* (Mir kak organicheskoe tseloe, 1915). The two most significant of Losskii's works in terms of his relationship with Bergson, however, are *The Intuitive Philosophy of Bergson* (Intuitivnaia filosofiia Bergsona, 1914) and "Shortcomings of Bergson's Epistemology and Their Influence on his Metaphysics" (Nedostatki gnoseologii Bergsona i vliianie ikh na ego metafiziky, 1913).[6] Losskii had much in common with Bergson, given the "revelatory" similarities between Bergsonian intuition and the intuitivism inherent in Russian religious thought; as the latter title suggests, however, Losskii also was intent on pointing out the shortcomings of Bergson's epistemology. To illustrate more clearly the role Bergson played in twentieth-century Russian religious thought, I shall examine first Losskii's basic philosophical views and then his evaluation of Bergson's philosophy.

Losskii divides the world into two halves, "I" and "non-I" (*ia* and *ne-ia*), distinct but organically interconnected realms. Arguing against Leibniz's conception of "windowless" monads, or units of being, Losskii's monads (or, to use his term, "substantival agents" [*substantsial'nye deiateli*]) *do* have doors and windows; thus they are open and free to interact with each other and to take part in a "creative evolution" on the path toward absolute perfection. In his work, *God and World Evil* (Bog i mirovoe zlo, 1941), Losskii describes this process of substantival evolution as follows: "Every agent strives toward the absolute fullness of life and toward absolute perfection. . . . In this way evolution takes place, that is, the development of the agent by which it is led, if it chooses the right path, toward the threshold of the Kingdom of God. . . . Every step on this path demands a free creative effort"

(341). Whereas Bergson claims that "life in its entirety, regarded as a creative evolution . . . transcends finality, if we understand by finality the realization of an idea conceived or conceivable in advance" (*CE* 224), Losskii's "creative evolution" is informed by the preconceived idea of the Kingdom of God as the one final goal toward which all evolution is oriented.

Losskii's philosophy is based on two interrelated theories: "epistemological coordination" (*gnoseologicheskaia koordinatsiia*) and intuitivism, the latter made possible by the former. Epistemological coordination represents for Losskii the process by which the "I" substantival agent (or simply the cognizing subject) becomes unified with the substance of "non-I" (or the object of knowledge) as parts of the same organic whole of existence. Losskii opposes this latter concept to the Western tradition of epistemological individualism or subordination established by Cartesian rationalism and continued up through Kantian critical philosophy, according to which the subject can never truly know the "thing-in-itself," and the object is thus subordinated to the knowing subject. According to Losskii, the meaning of the external world is not determined by the knowing subject's impressions but rather depends on the "coordination" of subject and object resulting from the closing of the gap between them. Losskii's theory of intuitivism, then, reflects both the immanence of the "thing-in-itself" in knowledge as well as the general organic interconnectedness (*konsubstantsial'nost'*) of the "human I" (*chelovecheskoe ia*) with all the other substantival agents in the world.

One contemporary Russian scholar, in noting Bergson's absence from the 1934 International Philosophical Congress, makes the following comment about the historical significance of both Losskii and Bergson: "Unfortunately not present at the Congress were Bergson and those few thinkers along with whom Losskii turned a new page in the history of philosophy, returning the latter to its preeminent position in the republic of the sciences" (Spektorskii 1976, 128). Losskii and Bergson are here credited for basing their epistemological notions on the ontological, thereby closing the gap between "knowing" and "being." In other words, the essence of that which one truly knows is not valuable simply as a trophy of epistemology, but actually transforms the knowing subject as a living entity. When the "I" is joined to the "non-I" through intuitive knowledge, the "I" starts to exist in a different way, now taking active part in the organic whole that is the world (like the individual in Bergson's philosophy who grasps life more fully having intuitively penetrated the ceaseless flux of duration). This is not, however, a "new page in the history of philosophy" at all, but precisely what Schelling attempted to accomplish in his post-Kantian idealist philosophical revolution. Although Losskii does not give Bergson credit for doing so, both philosophers follow in Schelling's footsteps; in both Bergsonian and Russian intuitivism, epistemology is not a goal in itself but rather serves as a means of addressing ontological questions. In her critical study of Russian intuitivism, I. P. Chueva (1963) observes that

> the intuitivism of Bergson and Russian intuitivism share not only the same name. Supported by the philosophical views of the German Romantics, Schelling and Schopenhauer, as well as by the mysticism and alogicality of the Neoplatonists, they feed, like parasites, on the shortcomings of mechanistic materialism. . . . As is clear from the very name of this trend—"intuitivism"—its representatives devote most of their attention to the working out of a *new method of cognition,* i.e., to questions of *epistemology.* However, for them, epistemology is not a goal but only a means of making a transition from theoretical questions of cognition to *ontological* problems dealing with ethics and religion. (15; my emphasis)

In his work *The Intuitive Basis of Knowledge,* Losskii (1908) criticizes Kant for *subordinating* being to thought rather than *coordinating* the two (355). In stressing the "organic, living unity of the world" and stating that "ontology must grow from the soil of our epistemology" (346), Losskii places himself squarely in the Russian ontological tradition (as outlined by Zenkovskii in his *History of Russian Philosophy*), whereby the theory of knowledge is considered useless when taken in isolation but becomes valuable only when serving as part of our total activity or "being" in the world.[7] Following a study of Losskii's metaphysics, though, we see that Losskii spends much more time on questions of epistemology than on the actual revealing of ontological truths. Nonetheless, Losskii's concept of "coordination," and subsequently his assessment of Bergson's thought, may be elucidated by briefly examining Losskii's rudimentary outline of the historical development of philosophy as put forth in *The Intuitive Basis of Knowledge.*

According to Losskii, the period of Greek philosophy was characterized by the nondifferentiation of subject and transsubjective world, the former "wallowing in the boundless ocean" of the latter. As a result, philosophical systems in the ancient Greek world inevitably took on universalistic traits (350). While not in an absolute sense, the Greek world was characterized by a tendency toward the universal as the "I" subordinated itself to the world of "non-I." With the advent of new European philosophical systems of the seventeenth and eighteenth centuries, Losskii writes, universalism gradually gave way to individualism, which ultimately led to subjective idealism: "The new philosophy of the seventeenth and eighteenth centuries possesses a different character in that the cognizing subject begins to understand itself as a person, as a single psychic (conscious) life, as a spiritual individuality" (350–51). The subjective idealism expressed in European philosophy at this time, in which the "I" begins to assert itself over the world of "non-I," paralleled the similar tendency in general life toward individualism, manifested by the growth of Protestantism and the increasing demand for political and civil freedoms. According to Losskii, the strongest champions of epistemological individualism during this period of "new" philosophy were Leibniz, Hume, and Kant, all of whom subordinated the object to the knowing subject.

Individualist philosophies following Kant in the nineteenth century gradually started to acquire more universalistic traits, not in a rupture with the old but rather in an organic growing out of the past. Losskii notes:

> The thinking individual, delving deep into his own "I," finds the roots of his individual existence in the Absolute, comes to understand other finite individualities through the Absolute and constructs a world view in which the world of "I" and the world of "non-I" are in all respects coordinated . . . not subordinated . . . one to the other. Upon this grounding arises the possibility of creating an organic understanding of the world, combining the universalism of Greek philosophy with the individualism of the new philosophy and thereby freeing each of its one-sidedness. (352)

Thus, the "newest philosophy" (presumably Losskii's own) is able to *coordinate* the universalism of Greek philosophy with the individualism of the "new" philosophy (most important, Kant) in order to attain an organic "higher" level of understanding of the world. It is this concept of coordination that serves as the focal point for Losskii's critique of Bergson. But first we must examine the areas in which Losskii concurred with Bergson's philosophy and then turn to what Losskii perceived as its shortcomings.

Although Losskii devotes most of his time to the study of the nature of knowledge, he cites the need for philosophers to turn their attention more toward the examination of metaphysical questions. In his work *The Intuitive Philosophy of Bergson*, Losskii (1914) considers the popularity of Bergsonian thought to reflect the growing interest in questions of ontology as opposed to epistemology:

> In the second half of the nineteenth century, philosophers focused excessively on issues of epistemology, on the construction of a theory of truth about the world while devoting themselves too little to the task of attaining this truth. In our time the situation is changing: an interest in the world itself is growing once more among philosophers, and research is being undertaken on ontological and metaphysical problems in general. One could consider a symptom of this shift to be the enthusiasm for the philosophy of Henri Bergson, whose influence has spread far beyond the borders of France into Germany, England, and Russia. (3)

Losskii (1914) sides with Bergson when it comes to the latter's conception of life as duration as opposed to mechanism: "Each of us need only delve into our spiritual life in order to be convinced that, in the debate between Bergsonian thought and the mechanistic worldview, the truth lies with Bergson" (13). In addition, Losskii (1914) hails Bergsonian duration as a "*unity of the whole flow of life*" (78; emphasis in original), and states that "one of Bergson's greatest contributions lies in his brilliant research, which has clearly emphasized the organic nature of movement, and which has precisely demonstrated that movement is a whole" (1978, 8). In movement as in life, according to Losskii, unity exists despite an infinite variety of spatial and temporal states; in other words, the whole is greater than the sum of its parts, a position consistent with the notion of *sobornost'* as well as with Losskii's theory of the consubstantiality of substantival agents in the organic Kingdom of God.

In the last major instance of his concurrence with Bergson, Losskii (1917) supports Bergson's idea as expressed in *Matter and Memory* that the body plays an essential role in the life of the spirit (38). Consistent with his belief in the world as organic whole, Losskii writes in his work of the same name that psychological and physical processes in man are "indissolubly linked" (*nerazryvno sviazany*), a "whole" being formed out of spiritual and corporeal elements. While the body is an essential partner of the spirit, however, it is still only the tool by which the door is opened to spiritual truth and understanding. In discussing *Matter and Memory,* much of which Bergson devotes to an exploration of the workings of human perception, Losskii (1968) agrees with Bergson that when it comes to perception the body serves only as a "stimulus" for true spiritual apprehension: "I gladly welcomed and added to the list of theories under my protection Bergson's teaching that . . . physiological processes in nerve centers are in essence not the cause, but only the stimulus which pushes the spiritual 'I' toward perception and recollection" (127). Thus, Losskii agrees with Bergson's philosophy when he finds in it elements of unity and organicity—a unified duration as opposed to mechanism, or the unity of body and soul as a prerequisite for true perception.

Despite what he sees as promising flashes of organicity and unity in Bergsonian thought, Losskii nonetheless is strongly against what he considers to be its thoroughly dualistic nature, or lack of the aforementioned concept of "coordination" so important in Losskii's own epistemology. In his *History of Russian Philosophy* (Istoriia russkoi filosofii), Losskii outlines the essential difference between his own intuitivism and that of Bergson as he defends himself against an attack by an outside critic. Writing about himself in the third person, Losskii (1994b) states:

> Pavlov did not notice the fundamental distinction between Bergson's and Losskii's intuitivism. Bergson's theory of knowledge is dualistic; he thinks that there are two essentially different types of knowledge—intuitive and rationalistic. Intuitive knowledge is the contemplation of a thing in its true, living essence; such is absolute knowledge. On the contrary, rationalistic knowledge, i.e., discursive thinking with the help of concepts, consists, according to Bergson, only of symbols, and therefore has only a relative significance.

> Losskii's theory of knowledge is *monistic* in the sense that he considers all forms of knowledge to be intuitive. (399–400)

Losskii (1914) similarly criticizes what he considers to be an artificial division in Bergson's thought between intellect and intuition: "On this point Bergson is wrong: there is no abyss between intuition and intellect *since intellect itself is intuitive*" (41).[8] Losskii rejects Bergson's "epistemological dualism"[9] and labels him an irrationalist for claiming that intellect can yield only an inferior "symbolic" knowledge as opposed to the "absolute" knowledge resulting from intuition. As opposed to what he (Losskii 1913, 104) considers to be Bergson's subordination of intellect to intuition (the most serious shortcoming of Bergson's epistemology in Losskii's opinion), Losskii believes in the "connectedness, rationality, logos" (1917, 53) of the world wherein even the intellect's symbolic knowledge partakes of the unity of the absolute and is therefore intuitive in nature.

Aside from the charge of dualism, Losskii finds greatest fault with Bergson for the latter's inconsistent position regarding the a priori existence of a universal whole/absolute. Both Losskii and Bergson claim to believe in the unity of science and metaphysics; Losskii, however, cannot accept Bergson's reluctance to posit such a universal whole/absolute at the base of his epistemology and therefore criticizes Bergson for his notion of the unity of intellect and intuition. After Losskii (1913) quotes Bergson's *Introduction to Metaphysics* several times in order to grant that "for [Bergson], as for us, the combination of positive sciences and metaphysics represents the ideal of the development of knowledge" (111), he goes on to qualify this statement by claiming that Bergson's supposed belief in the ideal unity of science and metaphysics is in actuality inauthentic:

> And so, Bergson considers the ideal of knowledge to be the combination of science and metaphysics into one whole. However . . . it is clear that he attempts to attain this goal by banishing from science precisely that which makes [science] scientific—ideas in the Platonic sense of the word. Thus the ideal of unification that he puts forth is just so many words. (112–13)

According to Losskii, Bergson denies the ideal, rational basis (Logos) of the world and thus rejects the objective nature of knowledge that leads one to contemplate the absolute.[10] What Losskii misses—or chooses not to see—is that Bergson often makes explicit statements about the importance of intellect in conceptualizing intuitive knowledge and therefore leading to a true grasp of objective reality. Many such statements are to be found in *Creative Evolution,* a work which Losskii quotes at length in his own book on Bergson's intuitive philosophy and thus must have known well.

While it is true that Bergson's notion of intellect is not equivalent to Losskii's conception of Logos (as representing cosmic laws shared by all metaphysical reality, thus guaranteeing consubstantiality), it is fair to say that

Bergson comes closer to acknowledging the objective nature of knowledge than Losskii gives him credit for.

It is possible that Losskii met Bergson in person, or at least heard him speak, at the Fourth International Congress on Philosophy held in Bologna, Italy, in April 1911. In any case, both philosophers in their talks defended the intuitive theory of knowledge against the dangers of naturalism; nonetheless, it seems as if Bergson was the revered star of the proceedings. In his description of the congress, B. V. Iakovenko notes that perhaps the single redeeming event of the otherwise "boring" and "unpleasant" congress was Bergson's presentation. After indifferently summarizing in a few lines the basic ideas of Losskii's paper, Iakovenko (1912) goes on to devote two dramatic pages to Bergson's discussion of the essence of philosophy:

> The long-awaited Bergson finally appeared at the fourth plenary session. . . . Everyone anticipated new revelations from the remarkable thinker, everyone had the desire to see him in person and have the immediate feeling of the depth of his philosophical experience during his lecture. And those who had gathered were not disappointed in their expectations. How unlikely that anyone could forget that amazing discussion, lasting over an hour, which Bergson held with his audience. Indeed, before us stood a "teacher." (16)

Iakovenko goes on to detail some of Bergson's main points, including his statement that the true spirit of philosophy is found in intuition ("or there, where the human spirit strives to penetrate to the very essence of things, to directly merge with the absolute" [17]). After listening raptly to Bergson's talk, the audience rewarded this "original philosophical spirit" with long, thunderous applause. Finally, noting Kant's inability to decide whether or not anything exists outside of empirical reality, leading to the gap in his philosophy between science and metaphysics, Iakovenko praises Bergson for his "decisive step in establishing a metaphysics of objective reality," in which one is able to grasp the essence of reality by virtue of objective intuition (disinterested intellectual sympathy). According to Iakovenko, "only Bergson accomplished the great deed of giving a full, clear picture of life as a fundamental metaphysical principle, and by doing so he placed his name alongside that of Kant" (20). Although Losskii consistently criticizes Bergson for his lack of "epistemological coordination" (in other words, for his subjective denial of the intellect's ability to apprehend the essence of life), it may be seen from Iakovenko's remarks that Bergson was considered to have "bridged the Kantian gap" between science and philosophy, between the longing for empirical and metaphysical truths, precisely because of the objective nature of his metaphysics.

Of what then does Losskii's intuitivism actually consist? And what role does Bergson play in it? While Losskii goes to great lengths to define his theory of knowledge, which depends primarily on the immanence of all in all, he offers little else in terms of actual "intuitions." Zenkovskii (1953) observes that

> at first glance, it may seem overly paradoxical and implausible that Losskii should have no genuine intuitions of his own, when he has constructed a whole system of intuitivism, but this is actually the case. The fact that a system built on the concept of *intuition* is more convenient and flexible than other systems (this is Losskii's claim) speaks "indirectly" in favor of his metaphysics, but nowhere do we find in him anything analogous to Bergson's remarkable pages in *Time and Free Will.* (661)

Zenkovskii concurs with the sentiment of philosopher L. M. Lopatin, according to whom, Zenkovskii notes, "Losskii's basic mode of proof is to refute other theories rather than to exhibit his own fundamental intuitions" (660). Bergson was therefore very valuable to Losskii as an influential fellow proponent of intuitivism, perhaps most valuable as a prime source for refutation whereby Losskii could bolster his own epistemological constructions. Losskii in fact defines his work through contrast with others. Intuitivists such as Solov'ev and Florenskii, he writes, devote themselves to the study of religious problems; others, such as Bergson, labor strictly on ontological questions; still others, including Losskii himself, concentrate on problems of logical deduction while intentionally failing to "get to the bottom" of the concept of intuition (Losskii 1919, 235).

FRANK: THE MONODUALISM OF LIFE-KNOWLEDGE/THOUGHT-KNOWLEDGE

Like Losskii, S. L. Frank was well acquainted with Bergson's philosophy.[11] Frank, however, generally gave more credit than did Losskii to Bergson's metaphysics because he also held somewhat dualistic views of the nature of knowledge, admitting that, while science and religion are both essential tools of knowledge, the latter yields truths to which the former is blind.[12] Whereas Zenkovskii groups Losskii under the "Neo-Leibnizianism" heading in his *History of Russian Philosophy,* thereby stressing Losskii's preoccupation with the monadology of "substance," Frank is discussed in the "Metaphysics of Total-Unity" chapter in order to emphasize the continuity between Solov'ev's philosophy of all-unity and Frank's metaphysics. In fact, Frank's "system," like Solov'ev's, represents an attempt at an all-encompassing worldview in which the role of intuition is more clearly formulated than in Losskii's "Leibnizian" writings. In order to explore the role played by Bergsonian thought in the formulation of early twentieth-century Russian intuitivism, Frank's evaluation of Bergson as seen in various of his writings must be examined, with special attention given to the article "Pragmatism as Philosophical Teaching" (Pragmatizm, kak filosofskoe uchenie), part of a 1910 debate about the nature of Pragamatism in which Frank presents his most thorough critique of Bergsonian thought. First, however, it will be helpful to begin with a brief discussion of Frank's metaphysics.

Building on the heritage of the Slavophiles ("integral knowledge") and Solov'ev ("all-unity"), Frank conceives of the individual as rooted in the primary reality of the Whole, continually open to, and part of, divine reality (*realnost'*). Frank constructs his metaphysics in opposition to two major assumptions of Western philosophy: first, that logic and reason are the sole means of attaining truth, and second, that an impenetrable wall separates subject and object so that one can never truly know the "thing-in-itself." Whereas Losskii defines his worldview as "monistic" in the sense that he regards all types of knowledge as intuitive, Frank characterizes his metaphysics as "monodualism." As with Bergson, who distinguishes between analytical and intuitive knowledge, Frank states that there are two kinds of knowledge with different functions—thought-knowledge (*znanie-mysl'*) and life-knowledge (*znanie-zhizn'*), with the latter more necessary for grasping the Absolute. Frank, however, stresses that this and every duality is encompassed by a greater unity:

> Every duality, even the most starkly drawn . . . is nonetheless a duality *within the bounds of unity*. . . . The coincidence of "inner" and "outer," "I" and "non-I," while fully preserving the contradictions therein, nonetheless represents the most expressive display of a contradictory unity of two elements; such is the *antinomy of monodualism.*[13]

Unlike Losskii, Frank appreciates Bergson's epistemological dualism—similar to his own—but at the same time finds lacking in Bergson's metaphysics that monistic element of a Whole (*edinstvo*), greater than man, which underlies and unifies all that is in the world.[14]

In his review of Bergson's *The Perception of Change* and *Psychophysiological Parallelism,* Frank (1913) observes that all of Bergson's long works—including *Laughter, Matter and Memory, Time and Free Will,* and *Creative Evolution*—have been published in Russia, as well as his most important articles, such as "Introduction to Metaphysics" and "On Philosophical Intuition." While noting Bergson's widespread popularity as a contemporary thinker, Frank makes it clear that he is not to be labeled as one of the many star-struck admirers of the French philosopher.[15] Seemingly in order to put the Bergson craze in perspective, Frank goes on to remark that, compared to the rich, architectonic complexity of Kant's system of thought, Bergson's conceptions appear one-sided and ideologically impoverished. However, to give Bergson his due, Frank acknowledges Bergson's "outstanding literary and artistic gifts," and states that "the exceptional success of his philosophy lies in the fact that it anticipates the profoundly vital and intense spiritual current of our time, a current directed toward the limitation of the competence of 'intellectual knowledge' and the restoration of the rights of the integral spiritual life" (50). Frank thus sees Bergsonian thought as the embodiment of the "spirit of the age"; although Bergson himself does not explicitly call for the restoration of spiritual life in place of an inadequate rationalism, Frank as religious philosopher interprets what he considers to be Bergson's anti-intellect stance as just such an appeal.

While Losskii strongly criticizes Bergson for placing intuition over intellect as the only true means of grasping the absolute (Losskii arguing that logical thought is equally as viable as intuition in this regard), Frank supports Bergson's position by claiming that a higher objective truth, or knowledge about reality, is to be found only in religion ("the intuition of truth") and not in science. In his article "Pragmatism as Philosophical Teaching," Frank (1910) states: "I hold the viewpoint that scientific knowledge provides a plan, an outline, which may yield genuine truth only after having been filled in with living content; only in intuition is the experience of a higher, objective reality possible" (127). For Frank, as for Bergson, both intellect and intuition are essential tools of knowledge, although operating on different levels. Frank goes on to declare that,

> when considering the question of the relationship between science and religion, one must acknowledge that religion—the intuition of truth—is a higher form of knowledge, which science cannot reach. This, however, does not exclude the self-sufficient significance of science in its own sphere; there must be a truly constitutional government with a strict separation of powers. (127)

As we have already seen, Bergson takes a very similar position, stating that intellect provides the necessary framework for intuition by giving conscious expression to that which has been intuited. In this sense, Frank, like Bergson, attacks the Kantian problem of philosophical subjectivism by attempting to "bridge the gap" between scientific knowledge and religious (or metaphysical, in Bergsonian terms) revelation.

Frank's main criticism of Bergson, as expressed both in *The Soul of Man* (Dusha cheloveka) and *The Object of Knowledge* (Predmet znaniia), concerns the role of the absolute in duration. Losskii's praise for Bergson's organic conception of duration as a reflection of the dynamism and organicity of spiritual life has already been noted. Frank (1939) similarly observes: "As Bergson has so aptly shown, existence in and of itself is essentially a process . . . , it is dynamism, living duration" (137). Like Losskii, Frank equates the dynamism of Bergson's "flow of consciousness" with the creative flow of spiritual life, recommending the reader to Bergson's "brilliant critique of psychological determinism" in the latter's *Time and Free Will* (1917, 242). Frank points out, however, that this flow of the spirit exists *outside* of time, unlike Bergsonian duration, which is rooted in the temporal: "But this dynamism [of spiritual life] is in no way synonymous with change in the literal sense, i.e., with the replacement of one thing by the next (as Bergson recognizes), and therefore is also not synonymous with the stream of time (despite Bergson's opinion)" (105–6). Concurring with Losskii, Frank takes issue with Bergson's refusal to posit a Whole or absolute unity at the base of what he considers duration, uninterrupted change. Rather than define intuition as the subject's fleeting grasp of a moment in this dynamic flow of life, a process of the past continually becoming a creative new present, Frank stresses the *supra*temporality of duration and the unity (absolute) lying at the heart of change. In *The Object of Knowledge,* Frank interprets Bergson's concept of time according to his own metaphysics of "all-unity": "The concept of time which Bergson, in fact, has in mind is not 'experienced time' or time as process, not even time as pure duration, but time as it is given in intuition—time [as] becoming, duration in indissoluble unity with the most supra-temporal unity" (1915, 356).

According to Frank, Bergson's idea of duration is valuable in that it associates the dynamic, creative "moment" in duration with the nature of the absolute (356). But whereas Bergson posits intuition as the means by which to penetrate this uninterrupted flux of becoming and thereby to grasp the essence of the dynamic absolute (while at the same time relegating the notion of "immobility" to the secondary realm of the intellect, that is, static, symbolic knowledge), Frank stresses that the absolute also encompasses permanent immobility and therefore transcends the boundaries of time. Duration, in Frank's conception, must of necessity partake of both becoming and stasis, temporality and supratemporality, rationality and suprarationality; therein lies Frank's belief in "all-unity," as seen in opposition to Bergson's division between the immobile and the fluid, intellect and intuition. "Bergson believes that this moment [of creation in duration] is characteristic of time itself—as becoming or change—whereas a moment of immobility coincides with fragmentation and plurality. It is impossible to agree with this. Continuity is always derived from unity" (356).

Despite sharing, to a certain degree, Bergson's dualistic epistemology and supporting his association of the dynamism and creativity of duration with that of the absolute, Frank generally criticized Bergson for ignoring the essentially timeless nature and all-encompassing unity of the absolute. As one of the leading scholars of Frank observes:

> It is one index of the complexity of Frank's relationship to Bergson, and to "life-philosophy" generally, that the ends he sought to achieve by adopting a Bergsonian dualism were quite different from Bergson's. Bergson believed that intuition yielded a true knowledge of reality as it actually is, but a knowledge which was of no practical use. In his understanding of the character of "relative" knowledge, on the other hand, he was essentially a Pragmatist. For Bergson, the "analytic" approach to objects was the fruit of the human need to render them manipulable, to control them and use them in sustaining man's

> biological life. Frank accepted neither Bergson's teaching concerning the "uselessness" of metaphysics nor his pragmatistic view of common-sense and scientific knowledge. In his maturity, he would insist on the radical distinction between the conceptual and the intuitive apprehension of reality primarily so as to be able to uphold—*against* the American Pragmatists, among others—the *objective validity* of conceptual knowledge in its own proper sphere. (Swoboda 1992, 530)

Perhaps most problematic for Frank in terms of supporting Bergson's thought was the latter's philosophical proximity to Pragmatism, the teachings of which had gained great prominence in Europe and America in the first decade of the twentieth century. In his article devoted to the exploration of Pragmatism, Frank (1910) concedes at the offset (possibly with Bergson in mind) that "the truth of Pragmatism may be found in the fact that it signifies an overcoming of naive *intellectualism,*" but goes on to warn of Pragmatism's subjectivist pitfall:

> The advocacy of Pragmatism poses a great cultural peril. Acknowledging the value of the growing wave of romanticism today as a rebellion against rationalism, it is still necessary to protect the most precious legacy of the rationalistic world view—namely faith in the all-obligatory and supra-human criterion of *objective truth* in the whole sphere of spiritual existence. (119)

Losskii and Frank both stress the objectivity of all forms of knowledge, including both logical thought and intuition, because the single goal of all thought is knowledge of the absolute, the a priori universal truth of the Kingdom of God. Bergson, on the other hand, agreeing with Kant that intellect yields only a subjective, relative knowledge of the external world, believes absolute knowledge of a universal (Neoplatonic) unity, *if* it exists, will result only from those rare moments when one is able to penetrate duration in an effort of intuition (knowledge Kant believed to be impossible). Frank, while not disputing the notion of two types of knowledge, intellect and intuition (or science and religion), with intuition yielding a more direct vision of reality as it really is, still maintains that both types of knowledge are objective insofar as the one true goal of all knowledge is that of the divine—self-evident yet also the endless source of all epistemological strivings (thus Frank's "monodualism"). Bergson, on the other hand, does not posit such a unity or absolute at the base of his philosophy; rather, he makes man the metaphysical center of his system, hinting that perhaps universal truths will be uncovered through the experience of life, the grasping of the forever flowing, creative stream of duration. In *Reality and Man* (*Real'nost' i chelovek*), Frank (1965) comments on this perceived shortcoming of Bergson's:

> An influential tendency in modern thought emphasizes . . . the vital, dynamic, creative character or reality and identifies it with becoming and potentiality. Bergson develops his philosophy of "becoming" as against the old Platonic

> conception of the ontological primacy of the eternal, complete, and immovable being. . . . I am far from sharing this modern trend of thought and indeed altogether disbelieve in the possibility of radically new discoveries in philosophy, subversive of ancient truths. The vital, creative, and dynamic aspect of reality cannot coincide with the abstract idea of becoming, evolution, or temporal process as distinct from eternity, complete finality, and fullness. (76–77)

Losskii and Frank appreciate and share Bergson's stance against Kantian intellect (through which reality was presumed to be constructed) as well as his dynamic, organic concept of duration, opposed to mechanism and analogous in many ways to the spiritual life. However, Bergson falls short in their estimation because of the apparent primacy in his philosophy of man's epistemological journeys over the objective truth of a Platonic Unity greater than man. Bergson is often vague as to his position on Platonism, at one moment claiming that transcendent truths exist and that the duration in which we live represents the absolute unity of being; the next, stating that we must reject any concept of metaphysical unity that is posited as a given at the outset of philosophical inquiry. "In the absolute we live and move and have our being," writes Bergson, but then goes on to say that only "in renouncing the factitious unity that the understanding imposes on nature from the outside, shall we perhaps find its true, inward, and living unity" (*CE* 199). It was this "peut-être" that Russian religious philosophers could not accept, despite their agreement with Bergson on the spiritual nature of duration and the importance of intuition in its apprehension.

Although Losskii and Frank had certain reservations about Bergsonian philosophy, they were nonetheless drawn to a type of religious optimism inherent in his thought (if not expressed in religious terms). Such optimism also motivated other Russian modernists in their search for revelation, or a positive means of intuiting (divine) reality. Bergson perfectly accommodated the theurgic impulse in Russian thought, the almost spiritual need of the modernist artist to feel himself or herself an active participant in—and creator of—the world as organic Whole.

Chapter Two

Symbolism

> The most essential characteristics of the contemporary lyric known as *Symbolism* reflect the workings of Bergsonian thought to such a degree that to define one is to speak of the other.
> —Tancrède de Visan

AT FIRST GLANCE Bergsonian thought and Russian Symbolism might seem to represent diametrically opposed philosophies. While Bergson states triumphantly in 1903 that "metaphysics is the science which claims to dispense with symbols" (*CM* 162), Andrei Bely writes in 1909 that "to define the Symbol in metaphysical terms is our most immediate task."[1] Bergson equates symbolic representation with the workings of science whereby objects are reduced to already recognizable elements in order to be analyzed and compared. For Bergson, a "symbol" is nothing more than a static concept constructed by the analytical intellect in order to make reality more intelligible to the human mind (*CE* 160). In order to possess reality *absolutely*, on the other hand, "having the intuition of it instead of making the analysis of it" through symbolic representation (*CM* 162), metaphysics becomes the means of grasping the inner, fluid meaning of phenomena. Rather than juxtapose static symbols and intuitive metaphysics as does Bergson, Bely conceives of the Symbol as itself the metaphysical embodiment of movement, the unity of Apollonian form and Dionysian content, the dynamic Word as flesh.[2] Instead of focusing on the exteriors of objects, the artistic Symbol for Bely is the musical inner essence of the image in flux, reflecting the ceaselessly dynamic process by which the world of phenomena strives to approach the divine world of noumena.

Despite these differing notions of "symbol," some very convincing parallels may be drawn between Bergson's philosophy and Symbolism. Tancrède de Visan (1911) made a comparative study of Bergsonian thought and French Symbolist aesthetics, wherein he lists several characteristics common to both, including the following: first, a reaction against nineteenth-century mechanism; second, the rejection of overintellectualism and abstraction in favor of the richer, more dynamic interior life of the fundamental self; and third, the embrace of intuition as the method of creation. Visan remarks that "the task of the symbolists consisted precisely in the establishment of a lyric of intuition" (453), a statement endorsed by the Russian Symbolist poet Fedor Sologub, who notes that "every art is symbolic in essence since it is intuitive knowledge. . . . We apprehend the world of essences not intellectually or empirically, but only intuitively" (1915, 44–45). "Symbolism," therefore, is, in a sense, a misleading label; while connoting a system of external signs of things that yields only relative knowledge of the world, the term "Symbolism" is thus seen to represent exactly the opposite of the true goal of Symbolist art, which is to penetrate the exterior, phenomenal world in order to grasp reality in its essence—the absolute. In this sense, writes Visan, "the symbolist esthetic, like Bergsonian philosophy, is that which claims to *dispense with symbols*" (455).

Both French and Russian Symbolists held the Romantic belief in the nonrationality of art and in the poet as intuitive seer of the eternal in the ephemeral (Donchin 1958, 93). Russian Symbolism, however, by virtue of its inherently mystical and religious nature, comes closer to the Bergsonian conceptions of artistic intuition and the élan vital than does French Symbolism, the latter being more concerned with the formal aspects of aesthetics than with religion.[3] Closely linked to the religious renaissance of the modernist period, Russian Symbolism coincided with the Bergsonian "revolution" in philosophy as a spiritualistic, neo-Romantic reaction against the positivism and realism of the nineteenth century.

In his article "Contemporary Art" (Iskusstvo nashikh dnei), Sologub (1915) observes that Symbolism, like artistic intuition in Bergson's terms, allows one to penetrate the static, relative forms of things, constructed by the intellect, in order to apprehend the absolute connections between all that exists, the divine source or élan vital: "Symbolism always gives us the sense of universal connection; it attributes all phenomena to one source and, like religion, strives to penetrate to the meaning of life" (61). Russian Symbolism and Bergsonian thought are, respectively, more than just an artistic movement and a philosophical system; each ultimately represents a theory of being (ontology) based on a way of knowing (epistemology), art serving as the prism through which the mysteries of life may intuitively be grasped. The artist may thus creatively transform life by hearing the flowing notes of the world orchestra (to borrow from Blok) and adding some of his own,[4] the essence of the theurgic impulse that so motivated Russian modernists in general. Bergson's concept of the artistic intuition of duration parallels the Symbolist worship of music as the means by which to grasp and actively shape spiritual reality, the inner dynamism of life, as opposed to the passive analysis of the phenomena of empirical reality. Bergson's statement in *Time and Free Will* equating duration, or the ceaseless flow of reality, with the flowing notes of a melody would have appealed greatly to Russian Symbolists drawn to music as the expression of life's inner essence. As Georges Sorel wrote to Benedetto Croce in March 1920: "Music is the art of all creation, and Bergson understands it the best" (quoted in Grogin 1988, 86).

Whereas Nietzsche exerted a clear and well-documented influence on writers such as Dmitrii Merezhkovskii, Konstantin Bal'mont, Andrei Bely, Viacheslav Ivanov, and Aleksandr Blok,[5] it is more difficult to establish such influence when it comes to Bergson. While Georgette Donchin (1958) states that "Baudelaire was certainly the only important influence that France exerted on Bal'mont" (25), Czech scholar Danuse Kšicová considers Bal'mont's poetry to be based on "Wagner's pan-aestheticism, Nietzsche's philosophy of Life and the principle of continuous movement in the philosophical system of A. Bergson" (1988, 115). In fact, flashes of this possible Bergsonian subtext of duration may be found in some of Bal'mont's notebooks from 1904 to 1923 held in the Bibliothèque Nationale in Paris. For example, Bal'mont (1904) writes: "I go, I go, I expand, I don't slow down, I change things, and am myself changed. I give myself up to the moment, and over and over again it opens up to me new horizons. And new flowers are eternally blossoming." Furthermore:

> Cities will burn down, forests will burn down, but in the places where they stirred and then fell, new rustlings, caresses and smiles will originate, eternal Life. . . . I know that there are two gods: the god of Rest and the god of Movement. I love them both, but shall not tarry long with the former. I served him once. No longer. (2–3)

As for Ivanov, James West (1970) remarks that the poet was primarily influenced by Nietzsche, applying the Nietzschean concept of myth to aesthetic creation; however, it is very likely that Ivanov was familiar with Bergson's philosophy even though he never mentioned Bergson in his writings (100). In fact, a compatibility with Bergsonian thought may be seen in some of Ivanov's statements on art and the artist. For example, in *Testaments of Symbolism* (*Zavety simvolizma,* 1910), Ivanov (1916) states that myth endows the otherwise static form of the symbol with an inner, dynamic duration: "Myth is the dynamic aspect (modus) [*sic*] of a symbol, the symbol apprehended as movement and motive force, as action and active force" (129–30). Although Ivanov's aesthetic reflects Bergsonian thought to a certain degree, West notes that one would expect Ivanov to have rejected Bergson given the latter's de-emphasis of the act of will in aesthetic experience (100).

The Symbolists' dualistic, yet fundamentally organic, conception of the world as consisting of phenomenal and noumenal realms (with the artistic intuition of the symbol as the bridge between the two) may be seen to coincide in large part with the Bergsonian juxtaposition of static, "outer" form and fluid, "inner" duration, intuition alone capable of penetrating to the inner, dynamic, ceaseless flow of life. While Russian Symbolism comprised diverse trends and interests, the intuition of the continuous creative flow of life (duration)—Bergson's leading idea—served as a common thread.[6]

By the time educated Russians started talking about Bergson around 1909, Russian Symbolism as an artistic movement had just about run its course. Andrei Bely and Zinaida Hippius—the only two Russian Symbolists who actually mention Bergson by name in their writings—continued nonetheless to write in the Symbolist tradition well beyond this date. Attention should therefore be focused on Bely and Hippius in order to examine the ways in which Bergsonian thought might be reflected in their Symbolist art.

BELY: THE MUSIC OF BERGSONIAN DURATION

More than one scholar has noted the difficulty in pinpointing Andrei Bely's philosophical influences given his many inconsistent statements on the philosophy of art, and the question of Bergsonian influence on Bely is no exception. In an outline of Bely's intellectual heritage, Steven Cassedy (1987) lists as influences on Bely the neo-Kantian school, Hegel, Schopenhauer, Nietzsche, Husserl, Bergson, "and many, many others" (319). James West (1970) explains in his introduction that the main reason he did not choose Bely as the focal point of his work on Russian Symbolism was that, in contrast to Ivanov's "coherent aesthetic," Bely's excursions into the philosophy of art are "inconsistent and sometimes hardly coherent" (48). In further treating the often difficult question of philosophical influence on Bely, West (1991) offers the following useful prescription:

> The lesson to be learned here is that questions about Bely's use of his philosophical sources can often only be answered in a way that is dictated by his methods: by drawing broad analogies, by identifying apparent instances of paraphrase, by reading between the lines of his shorthand references to individuals, and (perhaps most importantly) by tracing Bely's use of key words that attach to certain ideas. (99)

Through an examination of the philosophical ground shared by Bely and Bergson, and subsequently by "reading between the lines" as West suggests, a possible Bergsonian undercurrent in Bely's theory of Symbolism may be discerned. Certain Bergsonian themes in Bely's *Second Symphony* reappear in later prose works such as *Peterburg* and *Kotik Letaev,* allowing for the possibility that Bergsonian thought may ultimately have been as compatible a model for Bely as were the philosophies of neo-Kantianism, Schopenhauer, and Nietzsche.[7]

In many respects, Bely and Bergson share a philosophical vision based on the intuition of a musical type of duration as the means by which to grasp the essence of reality. One of the central slogans of the Symbolist movement in both France and Russia was Verlaine's decree from his *Art Poétique* (1884): "De la musique avant toute chose!"[8] Russian Symbolists (most notably Blok and Bely) adopted Schopenhauer's belief in music as the highest art form due to its lack of any true external form, as, for example, painting and sculpture possess: "Music deepens everything it touches," writes Bely. "Music is the soul of all the arts" ("Printsip formy v estetike," in Bely 1969, 179). Music thus represents pure movement, the pure inner essence that runs through all static, outer forms.[9] In a letter to Bely in 1903 praising the musicality of the latter's Symphonies, Blok notes that "the inner depths of music and its *lack of any external reality* suggests the notion of its noumenal quality; music explains the mystery of movement, the mystery of *existence.*"[10]

Bergson, who often in his works employs musical metaphors for the dynamic flux of life, compares "pure duration" to "the notes of a tune, melting, so to speak, into one another" (*TFW* 100); elsewhere Bergson states that, living as we ordinarily do by our intellect alone in the practical world of spatialized time, "we have no interest in listening to the uninterrupted humming of life's depths. And yet, that is where real duration is" (*CM* 149–50).[11] Only through intuition may one grasp the continuous movement, duration, at the heart of reality: "Intuition starts from movement, posits it, or rather perceives it as reality itself. . . . Intuition is what attains the spirit, duration, pure change" (*CM* 33–34). Bely's literary Symphonies manifest the same insistence on sound, and the intuitive act of hearing it, as the bridge between the phenomenal and noumenal worlds;[12] such an interconnection among music, time, and the continuous movement of duration is vital to both Bely's and Bergson's metaphysics.[13]

Trotsky, a critic of Bely's prose, notes that Bely fails in his musical literary attempts to reveal the dynamism at the heart of his literary images: "His rhythmical prose is terrible. The phrase does not obey the inner movement of the image but rather its outer metrics" (1923, 39). Trotsky's opinion of Bely is valuable in this case only to elucidate Bely's aesthetic intention, successful or not, regarding musicality and literary inner movement. It should be remembered, however, that Bely's intentions were not strictly aesthetic but oriented toward the active transformation of the world. John Elsworth, in remarking upon Solov'ev's influence on Bely, has noted Bely's primary belief in art as theurgy: "Art has the ultimate purpose of serving as an active force in the process of reuniting the fallen world with God, and in Bely's view it is through its gravitation toward music that this will be fulfilled."[14] Bely himself states that art has no other true meaning except for a religious one ("Smysl iskusstva," in Bely 1969, 224). For Bely, movement in art (or what Bergson might call artistic duration) represents the continuous movement of everyone and everything toward the divine. Whereas Bergson resists the presupposition of a divine Whole at the base of the ceaseless movement of duration (although it could be argued that some of his statements regarding the élan vital speak to just such a presupposition), Bely conceives of movement in precisely such a religious, teleological framework.

Although Bely may have been familiar with Bergson's first major work, *Time and Free Will* (published in Paris in 1889) as early as 1902 when he was a student at Moscow University and had started writing his Symphonies, there is no concrete evidence to suggest that this was so; it is thus impossible to speak of a definitive Bergsonian "influence" on Bely during his student years. Nonetheless, both Bely and Bergson at this time were arguing against the nineteenth-century belief in rigid scientific models as the key to understanding man and nature; as a result, both were exploring more intuitive pathways to understanding time. Bely's conception of time as it relates to music and movement in his first creative work to be published, the *Second Symphony* (1902),[15] parallels in many respects Bergsonian duration (characterized in *Time and Free Will* as a flowing of musical notes one into the next) and is thus worthy of attention.

As Danuše Kšicová points out in her article on Russian "Secession" poetry, there is some philosophical compatibility between Bely's Symphonies and Bergson's concept of time as a dynamic, nonlinear flow that is impossible to analyze spatially:

> It is interesting to observe that Bely, who in his collection of articles on Symbolism amply alludes to philosophical literature, nowhere mentions H. Bergson, whom he must have considered a kindred spirit because of the similarly high esteem for the genre of symphony they both shared. It is, however, Bergson's concept of time as an autonomous philosophical category which must be studied independently of space that constitutes the philosophical basis of Bely's Symphonies.[16]

Furthermore, Kšicová states:

> The style of Andrei Bely's Symphonies, deliberately arranged according to the structure of the eponymous musical genre, is characterized by an intentional decomposition of the plot into a series of details at times linked together only by the location of the plot or a mutual temporal level. . . . From the point of view of Symbolist poetics and the poetry of Secession, Bergson's term for duration, "la durée," which classifies the intrinsically experienced dynamic movement of life, is the philosophical platform for registering reality as a sequence of individual events, images or metaphors. (67–68)[17]

Bely associates music with noncausal, inner connections between phenomena, the dynamism of life, much as Bergson defines duration as the nonspatial flow of "real time," the organic interpenetration of past and present. (Music comes to play just such a role for Kotik Letaev: "Music is the dissolving of the shells of memory and the free passage into another world" [Bely 1964, 184].)

K. Mochul'skii has observed that in the *Second Symphony,* Bely attempts to create a new literary form by "tear[ing] apart the traditional structure of narrative—the sequential flow of events joined by a causal and temporal link" (33; quoted in Carden 1976, 53). Bely's protagonist in the *Second Symphony,* the young philosopher, Sergei Musatov, similarly aims to escape the steel rails of time that determine the progression of his own life "narrative"; Musatov is driven mad by the contemplation of traditional a priori notions of time and space as put forth by Kant and seeks to "tear them apart" in the hopes of discovering some kind of transcendent spiritual truth. Bely writes of Musatov in the first instance in which the young philosopher is seen to be reading Kant:

> Thus, having read about time and space as a priori forms of cognition, he began to think whether he might be able to conceal himself with screens that would hide him from both time and space, to leave them behind and go off into the fathomless distance. . . . To distract himself, he approached the broken piano. He sat down on the stool and opened the lid. . . . And blows followed blows. And the philosopher's servant plugged her ears with cotton wool even though she was in the kitchen and all the doors were shut. And this horror . . . he called *improvisation.*[18]

Musatov (later described as the "insane melancholic" who "felt loathsomely subservient to time" [116]), turns to music in his existential despair, but significantly he improvises at the piano, playing notes in an unconventional order rather than adhere to the "traditional structure" of the melody. Musatov's musical improvisation may serve as a metaphor for the way in which both he and Bely seek to conceive of time: creatively, qualitatively, musically, rather than in the traditional sense of chronological sequence. Thus, one of Bely's most pervasive leitmotifs in the *Second Symphony* is that of the ceaseless flow of time, often associated with sound: "And time flowed without stopping" (97, 116); "Sounds ran together with minutes . . . Time flowed without stopping" (119); "Time flew over the melancholy trees in a howling stream" (166). Such an approach to time closely parallels that of Bergson, who conceived of a musical, pure (that is, nonspatial) duration that is based on the principle of "inner" connection and characterized by the continual flux of interpenetrating moments. Whereas Mochul'skii considers Bely's images of time to represent the author's fear of Nietzchean nontranscendence, "the senselessness of time" (35), it could also be argued that time appears "senseless" only to one bereft of the intuitive capacity to hear the musicality of time as duration—the ceaseless flow of reality—that holds the rich promise of transcendence and noumenal knowledge for one able to grasp its mellifluous song. Bely, who believed that "he who is not musical will understand nothing" (1994b, 246), would likely have agreed with Bergson's characterization of consciousness as "an invisible musician playing behind the scenes" (*TFW* 147).[19]

Like Bergson, Bely sought to "bridge the Kantian gap" between the phenomenal and noumenal worlds, between the intellect (capable of apprehending the former) and intuition (capable of grasping the latter). Bely (1969) introduces this problem of philosophical reconciliation in part 1 of his *Second Symphony* by depicting Musatov's dilemma as that which involves the seemingly impossible synthesis of relative Kantian intellect with absolute Platonic a priori knowledge: "And he woke up; and his first thought was the thought of the impossibility of uniting the teachings of Kant and Plato; and he lifted his head from the crumpled pillows; and he shuddered from the evening cold" (94). In each Symphony—but especially in the Second and Third (*Vozvrat*)—Bely grapples with what for him are two interrelated impasses in philosophy: first, the relativity of Kantian knowledge, which seemingly excludes metaphysical knowledge of the noumenal world; and second, the Nietzschean concept of "eternal return," which, as Roger Keys (1987) states, represents

> the possibility despondently raised by Schopenhauer and joyfully affirmed by Nietzsche that there is no ultimate reality beyond that of the life force, that the only transcendent truth is that there is no transcendence—nothing to hope for but an eternity of meaningless repetitions of the phenomenal world. (52)

Thus in the *Second Symphony* Bely describes a room marked by "the horror of absence and nonexistence" in which lies Kant's *Critique of Pure Reason* and in which hangs an enormous mirror, eternally reflecting the same things (94). This stifling room of "nonexistence" (death by Kantian rationality) and nontranscendence (the eternal, horrifying Nietzschean reflection of "one and the same") becomes later, in *Kotik Letaev*, an airy, open room of music and meaning, transcendence made possible on the wings of sound: "Toys are chords; we walk on chords; by means of chords we enter: *into secret rooms of meaning.* Raisa Ivanovna and I fearlessly open all doors, and as we walked through all the *sound-rooms,* doors were opening for us" (Bely 1964, 205). Music for Kotik allows for movement, freedom, and mystery, entrance to a realm where the doors open of their own accord rather than lie in wait for the approach of a familiar hand.

In his 1922 article on Bely's creative work, S. A. Askol'dov characterizes Bely's primary artistic concern in the Symphonies as that of combining in a single melody both the seen and unseen worlds, a musical synthesis grasped only by artistic intuition (75–76).[20] In the same way that Bergsonian intuition allows one to hear the notes of time melting one into the next, so too for Bely the harmonious melody of both the external and internal realms of life may be heard through an act of intuition. In Bely's metaphysics, intuition allows one to hear the Word of God, which unites form and content, Sophia and Logos, and which is spoken *shumom vremeni* (1965, 49); thus the conflict throughout the *Second Symphony* between the leitmotif of flowing sound/time, beckoning to a world of greater noumenal meaning hidden within that of phenomena, and references to Kant's *Critique of Pure Reason,* the embodiment of spiritual death at the hands of nontranscendent reason that ultimately drives Musatov into a mental asylum: "'Who is sitting in that affected pose?' 'That's a former Kantian, disillusioned with his ideals. . . . A searcher of truth who spent a little time in the lunatic asylum, but even there didn't find it'" (1969, 172).

According to Zinaida Hippius (1951), Bely spent the year 1906–7 living not far from the Merezhkovskiis in Paris and saw Hippius every day (170–71). Given that during this time Hippius was acquainted with Bergson, among other French modernists,[21] it seems likely that Bely also became familiar (or more familiar) with Bergson's thought, if not with the philosopher himself. Bely never lists Bergson as a philosophical mentor, although in his commentary to the essay "Problemy kul'tury" (1910), Bely notes in regard to the slogan "creation over cognition" (*primat tvorchestva nad poznaniem*), a theory that plays a major role in *Peterburg:* "We see the same thing in Bergson (*Creative Evolution*)" (1994b, 24). Although Bely's conception of language in *Peterburg* has traditionally been linked to the ideas of Nietzsche and Potebnia,[22] it is possible that the appearance of Shishnarfne—the "word as music" that "sounds with Dionysian force (Anschuetz 1983, 150)—represents in some sense a Bergsonian approach to language based on the ideas expressed in *Creative Evolution.* The mechanism of habitual cognition would therefore parallel the mechanism of Darwinian evolution, neither process yielding any true meaning about the inner essence of word or organism. What is needed, according to Bely, is a more intuitive approach to language whereby meaning is created (not cognized) from the "word as music." Similarly, in *Creative Evolution,* Bergson praises Lamarck for taking a more intuitive approach to the evolutionary process than Darwin and for finding that variation in species results not from accident, but from "the very effort of the living being to adapt itself to the circumstances of its existence" (76); such an effort "may imply consciousness" and an "internal principle of development" (77), thus freeing evolution from the mechanism of arbitrary natural selection and making it truly "creative." Bely's approach to language may thus be seen as "Lamarckian" in much the same sense that Bergson applies the term to the study of evolution.

Elsewhere, Bely associates his conception of intuition with that of Bergson. In his 1928 work, *Pochemu ia stal simvolistom,* Bely (1982) relates a particular conversation he once had with Rudolf Steiner about metaphysics: "Steiner once commented on my meditative works: 'YOUR INTUITIONS ARE PREFECTLY CORRECT,'" and in a footnote to the word "intuitions," Bely states: "Of course Steiner here used the expression 'intuitions' not in the technically spiritual sense (for in that sense 'intuition' suggests 'the end of the line') but, for example, in the Bergsonian, 'pan-cultural' sense" (123). The suggestion that Bely may have been drawn to a type of Bergsonian intuition is intriguing, and leads one to wonder whether Bergsonian philosophy played a greater role in Bely's Symbolist aesthetic than Bely would have one believe. The notion of a "pan-cultural" intuition, as opposed to an intuition limited to a single, complete act of cognition (*venets puti*), suggests that Bely's "Bergsonian" intuition was geared more toward the subversion of traditional categories of time and space, and thus more toward the notion of "creation" than "cognition."

The dual horrors of Kantian rationality and Nietzschean eternal return as expressed in the *Second Symphony* reappear under the heading of neo-Kantianism—or contemporary philosophy—in Bely's 1912 "Krugovoe dvizhenie." Neo-Kantianism, according to Bely, represents "circular movement" whereby "over-refined reason" (*slishkom ochishchennyi razum*) turns back on itself (eternally returns); Reason (*Razum*) thus becomes "Nosaer" (*Amuzar*) and no meaning is gained. In their discussion of the genesis of *Peterburg*, Maguire and Malmstad point to Bely's article (Bely 1912, 56) as a particularly important source and quote one passage that helps to elucidate Bely's use of the term "Nosaer":

> its name is contemporary philosophy, where over-refined reason—Kantian reason, in which almost nothing of Kant has remained—hurls itself into the abyss, taking with it the modernist philosopher; the modernist falls headfirst; along with him goes *The Critique of Pure Reason*, which he continues to read upside down and right to left: instead of *Reason* he reads some Eastern nonsense, provided it is not some Eastern incantation, for he reads *Nosaer*. (Maguire and Malmstad 1987, 122)

This passage is reminiscent of Musatov, the "modernist philosopher" in the *Second Symphony*, who similarly falls into the abyss of insanity while reading Kant's *Critique*. According to Maguire and Malmstad (1987), the above quotation suggests Bely's point in *Peterburg* that modern philosophy combines both Kant and Eastern thought, and thus the line separating the rational from the irrational is erased (123). In support of this idea, *Peterburg* ends with Nikolai Apollonovich, the former Kantian ("Kant? Kant is forgotten"), reading Skovoroda, just as Bely concludes the earlier *Second Symphony* in the Novodevichy Convent, where the recently deceased Solov'ev has been seen "riding in a cab in a fur hat and with a turned-up collar!" (169). Although Nikolai Apollonovich has evolved further in his spiritual awareness than has Musatov, who in his disillusioned flight from Moscow seems far from pulling himself out of the Kantian abyss, Bely seems to suggest in both the *Second Symphony* and *Peterburg* the possibility of arriving at some type of "total-unity" in philosophical inquiry whereby the notes of empirical and spiritual reality could join together in what Askol'dov calls "one harmonious chord."[23]

Bergson strives to attain a similar type of unity through his conception of musical duration.

Rudolf Steiner's anthroposophy is generally believed to play a significant role in Bely's metaphysics (see Anschuetz 1976; Janecek 1976; Malmstad 1987), and it is therefore interesting to examine the similarities between Steiner's and Bergson's thought. Bely's mention of "Henri Besançon" in *Peterburg* (which Maguire and Malmstad [1987] suggest represents a clear reference to both the theosophist Annie Besant and the philosopher Bergson) might be seen as an attempt on Bely's part to unite certain aspects of Steiner's and Bergson's philosophies. Although Bely himself does not make the connection explicit, he nonetheless writes to his friend E. Metner in 1913 that "there is talk of *Steinerism* . . . from the point of view of James and Bergson."[24]

As Gerald Janecek (1974) states, the organization of *Kotik Letaev* might, in one sense, be described within the framework of anthroposophy as "an ascending of the 'stages of higher knowledge'" (253). Bely's article "O smysle poznaniia" (1916) was written one year after Bely participated in Steiner's anthroposophical circle in Switzerland and the same year that he finished work on *Kotik Letaev*. In the article, much of which is devoted to Steiner's teachings, Bely concludes that truth is to be found only in what the Slavophiles called *razum*, or integral knowledge, uniting, as Bergson sought to do, the intellect and intuition as interdependent partners in the search for meaning: "Imagination, inspiration, and intuition are the three zones of cognition united in Reason" (47). Steiner himself (1991) considers intuition to be the third and highest mode of cognition (integrating imagination and inspiration, the first two stages) by means of which spiritual reality might be apprehended: "Through such a higher consciousness—an imaginative, inspired, and intuitive consciousness—we can see ourselves apart from the intellect as members of the suprasensible world" (11). Furthermore, Steiner states that this spiritual reality—like Bergson's concept of duration—is characterized by movement, creativity, continuous change: "In the spiritual world all is in perpetual, mobile activity, in the process of ceaseless creating" (1946, 146). Bely begins "O smysle poznaniia" by defining an act of cognition (*akt poznavaniia*) as inherently intuitive (*vne-rassudochen*) and goes on to describe the intuitive cognitive act in terms very reminiscent of both Steiner and Bergson: "Cognition is limitless, it has no boundaries; the flow of streams is boundless, formless. The cognitive act is a stream" (39).

The Bergsonian notion of the ceaseless flow of forever-changing reality plays a major role in the developing consciousness of Kotik Letaev, whose earliest childhood memories focus on perceptions of a world in flux: "My first childish tremblings: . . . tremblings of the formation of flowing worlds. . . . My first childish tremblings surprise me; everything surprises me: that it is what it is; why is it not flowing?" (60). Like the *Second Symphony* and *Peterburg*, Bely's *Kotik Letaev* deals with the struggle to bridge the gap between intellect and intuition; however, whereas the first two works focus on a young adult philosopher's struggle to synthesize the worlds of phenomena and noumena, in *Kotik Letaev* the conflict between these worlds is reduced to its most fundamental level as a child's inherent intuitive capability is gradually and inevitably weakened through conformity to the practical world of ticking clocks and rigid forms.

In *Kotik Letaev,* Bely focuses on the "immediate data of consciousness," the attempt to grasp duration and thus one's "fundamental self." Bergson states in *Time and Free Will* that "we reach [the fundamental self] by deep introspection, which leads us to grasp our inner states as living things, constantly *becoming,* as states not amenable to measurement, which permeate one another" (231). The thirty-five-year-old Kotik is plunged into just such "deep introspection" at the beginning of his autobiographical exploration of his first years of life: "Here, on the sharply slicing line, I throw long, mute glances into the past. . . . I am thirty-five: self-consciousness has burst open my brain and rushed into childhood" (9). Kotik's early childhood is marked by the gradual loss of his intuitive sense of fluid reality (or time as duration) and subsequent submission to the world of intellect and chronological time, or that of "inflexible forms" (*strogie stroi*):

> I began to live . . . in that which *has become* (as formerly I had lived in *becoming*); . . .
>
> —I am to live according to the law; and—in regulation: near the corner there is a small trunk by the clock; I am to listen to the faint ticking; that is, to live in inflexible forms; not to pull the small chains behind the weight; not to stop the ticking; not to search out new rooms. (62, 84–85)

Bely would not, however, ultimately surrender to "the law" of intellect, or "inflexible forms," but would instead strive through heightened self-consciousness, through an intuitive grasp of duration or constant "becoming," to discover the "new rooms" of creativity and transcendence in which to transform himself and the world. "At that time," writes Bely in the epilogue, referring to the anticipated moment of Kotik's crucifixion when the bridge between human and divine will be accomplished, his childhood self-consciousness and intuition returned to him, "I will be born again; the ice of concepts, words, meanings—is breaking" (292).

In his 1941 book *Le Symbole littéraire,* Eméric Fiser places Bergsonian thought at the heart of the Symbolist aesthetic, stating that Bergson's conception of artistic intuition was "the key to [his] esthetic as well as to the esthetic of the symbolist movement. It is difficult to speak of direct influence. These are the leading ideas of an epoch" (Pilkington 1976, 222). More a part of the German Romantic philosophical tradition than the French classical tradition, Bergson joined Kant, Schopenhauer, and Nietzsche as one of the philosophical guiding lights for the so-called second generation of Russian Symbolists who were interested more in religious mysticism than in the aestheticism of the "first generation" of Russian "Decadent" poets. As Asmus (1926) points out, the philosophical roots of Russian Symbolism grew primarily from two sources: Solov'ev's view of the theurgical role of the artist and the neo-Kantian critique of science as the sole means of grasping reality (28). Although some Russian Symbolists went through a phase of neo-Kantianism (Bely grappled with Kant throughout his life),[25] neo-Kantian philosophy, which was considered to be inherently hostile to metaphysics, did not go far enough for Bely and other modernists in promoting intuition as a viable means of attaining knowledge. Bergsonian philosophy, in attempting to "bridge the Kantian gap" between science and metaphysics by means of intuition, was therefore more in accord with Symbolist aesthetic concerns than was that of the neo-Kantians. The reaction of A. F. Losev—although himself not a Symbolist—to both Bergson and the neo-Kantians serves as a good example of the Russian modernists' deeper attraction to the former than to the latter:

> In those times [1910–20] Bergson's name resounded throughout the world. How could I not study Bergson in those times? I was never a Bergsonian and even criticized Bergson in many respects. But his book *Creative Evolution* made an impression on me that lasted my entire life. In my opinion, Bergson's is not even a philosophy but some kind of tense drama depicting the tragic struggle of life for its existence amid dead, static, inert matter. . . . The neo-Kantians, whose teachings also resounded throughout the world in those times, similarly could not escape my attention. However, I never sympathized with the logical monism of the neo-Kantians and therefore always fought with them.[26]

The accuracy of Losev's, as well as Bergson's, reading of Kant (or creative "misreading," as Bloom might call it) is less important than the fact that many Russian modernists, beginning with the Symbolists, found neo-Kantianism lacking; in some significant way, its "logical monism" did not satisfy a fundamental Russian need for knowledge of the "thing-in-itself." Schopenhauer's philosophy of intuition attracted Russian Symbolists in the waning years of the nineteenth century, and Bely also gravitated toward him as an alternative to Kant, a shift clearly outlined in "Krititsizm i simvolizm" (1904). Bely seems to conclude, however, that even Schopenhauer is an insufficient guide for Russian modernists, and one is left to speculate as to whether Bely considered Bergsonian thought to be more in accord with his own Symbolist vision.

Only after *The Critique of Pure Reason,* writes Bely (1904), was thought finally separated from feeling, criticism from dogmatic empiricism; only then did it become possible to discuss levels of consciousness nondogmatically. As a result, all Symbolists owe Kant a debt of gratitude for clearing the way for free philosophical discourse: "We, the Symbolists, consider ourselves . . . the lawful descendants of the great Königsberg philosopher" (3). But this separation of thought and feeling (*raskol mezhdu rassudkom i chuvstvom*) created its own problems in terms of the individual's ability to grasp "the essence of things":

> Kant admitted to the absolute impossibility of knowing the world in its essence. . . . If, according to Kant, we are not capable of penetrating to the essence of things by means of inner feeling, then we are even less capable of doing so by way of thought. . . . And here, Kant's negative thinking may be likened to a man who has fallen into a swamp. (6–7)

Bely argues that the only way out of this Kantian swamp is through Schopenhauer (the transition figure between Criticism and Symbolism [9]), and more specifically through his concept of intuition, whereby one is able to apprehend the Platonic Ideas within phenomenal forms—the "thing-in-itself." Such a method of intuition represents not a contradiction or elimination of intellect but rather a broadening (*rasshirenie*) of knowledge in general: "This [intuitive] knowledge unites reason and emotion in something different from each, shielding them both. This is why intuitive knowledge is necessary for the cognition of ideas" (11). Marked by intuitive knowledge, Symbolism, "born of Criticism and opposed to it," thus becomes more than just an artistic school or theory, but an actual mode of living in the world—a "living method" (*zhiznennyi metod*).

Bely, however, ends his article with a paean to decadence, wherein the artist does not in fact engage in the life-affirming method of Symbolism, as he had just described it, but rather retreats from life in aesthetic transcendence: "We are 'decadents' because we renounce a civilization with no God and with no revelation. . . . Through foggy life we are moving toward the drunken azure" (13). It thus becomes clear that Schopenhauer cannot accompany Symbolism beyond its decadent phase, cannot be the source of philosophical inspiration for Symbolism as a "living method" because Schopenhauer advocates the renunciation as opposed to the engagement of life. Nietzsche's "nontranscendence" was equally unsatisfying for Bely, who sought to combine in symphonic harmony the chords from both the noumenal and phenomenal worlds. Only Bergson, who argues for the intuitive penetration of the ceaseless flow of reality in order to better grasp one's own identity and one's own niche in the creative, organic flux of the universe, could offer Bely the symphony he desired. Bergson, in contrast to both Schopenhauer and Nietzsche, is both life-affirming and life-engaging in the fullest sense, offering a type of transcendence without renunciation, and thus would seem to provide a more compatible model for what Bely calls the theurgic role of art: the unveiling of the divine essence in all worldly manifestations, including the self, in order to bring about the spiritual transformation of reality.

HIPPIUS: *L'IMPRÉVISIBILITÉ* OF TIME AND LOVE

In her study of the poet Zinaida Hippius, Olga Matich (1972) claims that if one must classify Hippius according to one literary grouping, she should be considered along with the second generation of Russian Symbolists, "who in contrast to the decadents associate their art with religion rather than pure aestheticism" (15). Despite having gone through an early decadent period herself,[27] Hippius ultimately denounced the so-called decadents for what she considered to be an individualist approach to poetry and literature, one that lacked any sense of a common human spirituality or the organic dynamism of life and thought. In her essay "Decadence and Community" (Dekadentsvo i obshchestvennost', 1915), Hippius (1970) remarks: "The decadent . . . has no feeling of community or connection—not in the least. He simply has no inkling that others exist besides himself" (339), and furthermore: "Almost all poetry and literature—insofar as it is decadent—exists outside the movement of history, of humanity, outside the struggle between 'we' and 'I'; this literature has no relationship to the movement of life and thought, nor is life related to it" (343). Hippius's comments regarding the shortcomings of the decadent aesthetic reveal much of her own poetic vision. First, art must be dynamic in that it should tap into the continuous movement of life and love (*vliublennost'*), within which man is forever striving to come closer to the divine. Second, the artist must be aware of the organic connections linking all of God's creations in the dynamic flux of time, for this is the essence of faith. As with Solov'ev, love plays an especially important role in Hippius's worldview as it embodies movement, the ceaseless human striving to reach new heights of spiritual understanding and closeness to God.

Although Hippius's emphasis on will and spiritual strength has been associated with the "all-pervading turn-of-the-century Nietzscheanism" (Matich 1972, 54), and Hippius's contention that "the man of the future would be a visionary, endowed with . . . rational powers and artistic prowess" has also been attributed to a Nietzschean influence (Pachmuss, 1971, 20), there is much to be said for Hippius's attraction to Bergsonian thought as well. Writing of her first lengthy stay in Paris from March 1906 to July 1908 with her husband, Dmitrii Merezhkovskii, Hippius (1951) notes that "at that time in Paris . . . we knew, of those belonging to the modernist movement, very few: Le Roy [*sic*], Bergson" (167). Whether Hippius knew Bergson or his work prior to 1906 is unclear, although given her interest in the international modernist movement and the fact that she and Merezhkovskii often traveled to Europe following their marriage in 1889, it seems likely that she was at least familiar with some of Bergson's main ideas regarding time and intuition as expressed in his works *Time and Free Will* (1889) and *Introduction to Metaphysics* (1903). After 1908, Hippius (1970) was especially drawn to Bergson's philosophical conceptions of time as duration, and intuition as the only means by which to grasp reality in its essence, as an organic, inner (*vnutrennii*) process as opposed to the mechanistic, outer (*vneshnie*) forms of life crystallized in everyday existence ("Vse protiv vsekh," 316).

In her profile of the poet, Temira Pachmuss (1971) comments on one of the philosophical links between Hippius and Bergson, namely, their common conception of "real time" or duration as constituting the essence of (spiritual) reality, unattainable through rational knowledge:

> As Hippius herself admitted, her concept of Time approaches one of Bergson's philosophical ideas, that ultimate spiritual reality can be grasped only by man's metaphysical intuition. Spiritual reality constitutes the essence of real events and these events can be experienced only by human irrational, intuitive knowledge. "Real events" are "real moments" of "real time" (*la durée réelle*) or duration. (80)

In her introduction to the reprint of Hippius's collection of stories, *New People* (*Novye liudi,* 1896), Pachmuss further states that

> like Henri Bergson, Hippius differentiated between *la durée réelle* and physical time. . . . Physical time is only able to represent symbolically each moment in the temporal process as a distinct, concrete form. It disregards both the specific, unique attributes of individual moments and their inner relation. It obscures the nature of "real love." (Hippius 1973, xvii)

As an example of Hippius's "Bergsonian" distinction between static physical time and the duration of "real time," Pachmuss points to one of Hippius's earliest short stories, "Humility" (Smirenie, in Hippius 1973), which concludes with the main character, Zatenin, pondering the nature of "real beauty" as he gazes at the sea from his window: "Immutable forms, motionless beauty—such is not beauty. The beauty that I know, by which I live, is contained not in this dead, 'eternal' art but in continuous movement . . . [in beauty which is] unexpected, fleeting" (202–3). A picture similar to that which A. F. Losev saw in both Solov'ev's and Bergson's worldview—one of "continual élans vitals (*zhiznennye poryvy*) in nature and their struggle . . . with dead matter" (introduction to Solov'ev, 1988, 19)—may also be seen in Hippius's conception of the conflict between the dynamic movement of "real time," or real beauty, and the static, "dead" forms of physical time and so-called eternal beauty.

According to Pachmuss (1977), this Bergsonian interpretation of "real time" informs many of Hippius's works, perhaps most notably among her poems "The Unforeseeable" (L'Imprévisibilité [*sic*], 1914):

> По слову извечно Сущего,
> Бессменен поток времен,
> Чую лишь ветер грядущего,
> Нового мига звон.
>
> С паденьем идет, с победою?
> Оливу несет иль меч?
> Лица его я не ведаю,
> Знаю лишь ветер встреч.

Летят нездешними птицами,
В кольцо бытия, вперед,
    Миги с закрытыми лицами,
    Как удержу их лет?

И в тесности, в перекрестности,
Хочу, не хочу ли я—
    Черную топь неизвестности

    Режет моя ладья.

(January 1914, Saint Petersburg)

Upon the ancient word of the Absolute,
The stream of time is continuous,
    I sense only the wind of the future,
    the sound of a moment being born.

Does it come in degradation or victory?
Carrying olive branch or sword?
    Its face is unfamiliar to me,
    But not the breeze of our encounters.

Moments with hidden faces,
Like unearthly birds, fly
    Into the ring of existence;
    How can I clip their wings?

Both in closeness and crossing,
Whether I want it or not—
    My boat cuts through
    The black bog of the unknown.

Hippius's mention of a "continuous stream of time"—although a concept fundamentally religious in nature ("upon the ancient word of the Absolute")—may be seen as a reference to Bergsonian duration, the ceaseless stream of time that makes up the essence of life's flowing reality. The marsh of uncertainty through which the poet's boat inevitably ("whether I want it or not") cuts, is made up of ever-new, interwoven moments with hidden faces that cannot be separated or categorized into recognizable, distinct elements, representing the poet's experience not of physical time but the "real time" of duration. The unforeseeability of the ceaseless flow of new moments is unsettling ("the black bog of the unknown") but in a deeper sense exhilarating for Hippius, who senses the divine nature of duration (as do Losskii and Frank) and is unable (and seemingly unwilling) to cage the dynamic moment in flight.

Hippius expresses this enjoyment of the *imprévisibilité* of "real time" in her introduction to the *Blue Book* (*Siniaia kniga*) collection of her poetry wherein she associates the nature of the *Journal* (*Dnevnik*) with duration, "real time" or the flow of life, while memoirs (*vospominaniia*) are characterized by the static predictability of physical time: "A Journal is not an orderly 'narrative about life' wherein one describes today already knowing what tomorrow will hold, already knowing how it all turns out. A Journal represents the *very flow of life*. . . . 'Memoirs' can provide an image of time, but only a Journal can show time in its duration" (1929, 5–6). In a much later poem, "Trembling Eternity" (Eternité Frémissante [*sic*], 1938), Hippius combines the idea of an absolute "real time" with one of her other major poetic concerns, namely the eternal, absolute nature of real love:[28]

В. С. Варшавскому

Моя любовь одна, одна,
Но все же плачу, негодуя:
Одна,—и тем разделена,
Что разделенное люблю я.

О Время! Я люблю твой ход,
Порывистость и равномерность.
Люблю игры твоей полет,
Твою изменчивую верность.
Но как не полюбить я мог
Другое радостное чудо:
Безвременья живой поток,
Огонь, дыхание «оттуда»?

Увы, разделены они—
Безвременность и Человечность.
Но будет день: совьются дни
В одну—Трепещущую Вечность.

To V. S. Varshavsky

My love is one, one,
But I cry anyway, indignant:
One—and thus divided,
That which is divided love I.

O Time! I love your *élan*,
Your impetuosity and uniformity,
I love the flight of your fancy,
Your fickle faithfulness.
But how could I not fall in love
With another joyous miracle:
The living stream of timelessness,
The fire, the breath of "the Beyond"?

Alas, they are divided—
Timelessness and Humanity.
But the day will come when the days will entwine
Into one—Trembling Eternity.

When Hippius sent this poem in French to her friend, Greta Gerell, she translated the line "O Vremia! Ia liubliu tvoi khod" as follows: "O durée! Il est beau ton témeraire élan" (1972, 253). It is interesting that Hippius chooses the words *durée* and *élan,* two very Bergsonian terms, to serve as equivalents for the Russian *vremia* and *khod.* Furthermore, in 1930 Paris, Hippius explains how her life has changed from pre-Revolutionary days by writing: "Our present *durée,* everyone and everything in it, is quite different from the *durée* of our past" (1975, 295). By distinguishing between "past" and "present" *durée,* Hippius obscures the true Bergsonian sense of the term as the indivisible, ceaseless flow of reality, "succession without distinction" (*TFW* 101).

Hippius's overall characterization of indivisible, unified love in "Eternité Frémissante," however, faithfully approximates the nature of Bergsonian duration. As Pachmuss (1971) notes, Hippius "agreed with Vladimir Solovyov that real love is beyond the realm of physical time and death. Love has its true foundation in one eternal 'present'. . . . It is higher than rational consciousness" (63). In "Eternité Frémissante," Hippius's love is both one (*odna*) and divided (*razdelena*), in the same way that there is both durational, eternal time (*bezvremen'ia zhivoi potok*) with its source "from Beyond," as well as the divided time of humanity's physical world. Hippius concludes the poem with the assertion that one day humanity will come to live in "real time," time that transcends death, and thus will enjoy a "trembling eternity." For Hippius, absolute love is what allows one to partake of absolute time, or eternity; although love does not play a role in Bergson's vision of time, Hippius applies the principles of ceaseless flow and indivisibility that characterize Bergsonian duration to her own metaphysics of love and time.

Like many previous Russian thinkers (the Slavophiles, Tolstoy and Solov'ev, to name a few), Hippius believed that time is movement, duration, and as such must be "felt" or intuited rather than analyzed. For example, in her 1908 preface to her *Literary Journal* (*Literaturnyi dnevnik,* 1899–1907), Hippius (1970) states that, in one sense, the idea of a collection (*sbornik*) is meaningless: by collecting disconnected, individual pieces, separated by time and putting them all together in one collection, "the perspective is destroyed, the dynamism is violently transformed into stasis, the image is distorted—there is nothing." But, if one assumes the proper perspective on the collection, if one can plunge into the flow of time of which the collection is a reflection and actually feel the ceaseless movement of duration, then a true grasp of the essence of the collection may be attained. "But there is another, more accurate view of the 'collection': the historical view. One must be able to feel time; one must remember that history is everywhere, and that everything in history is in movement" (iii).

Last, in one of the essays in her *Literary Journal,* "Daily Routine and Events" (Byt i sobytiia, 1904), Hippius (1970) makes what could be seen as a Bergsonian distinction between the novelty of life (intuition) and everyday habit (intellect), the former characterized by fluidity, dynamism, creativity, while the latter embodies stasis, routine, practicality. Hippius writes: "Life is an event, whereas daily routine [*byt*] is only eternal repetition, the reinforcement or preservation of these events in an encrusted, static form. The daily routine represents the crystallization of life. Therefore, it is precisely life—that is, movement forward, the layering of ever-new events—life alone is creation" (288). It is such fluid creativity and organic growth of the ever-new, manifested in loving relationships between people and ultimately with God, that endows life with a musical (fluid), as opposed to architectonic (static), nature: "Human relationships create a real, daily, *vital* atmosphere for life, its color, its . . . not architecture, but music" (303). Although architectonic motifs would become popular with the Acmeists (see, for example, Mandel'shtam's first collection of poetry, *Stone* [*Kamen'*]), music remained for Hippius and other Symbolists the representation of dynamic duration, the stream of life that organically unites all of God's creatures in its fluid course of movement toward the divine.

Chapter Three

Post-Symbolism

Breaking out beyond the limits of the cognizable toward a strange, other-worldly element, the ecstasy of suprasensible intuition . . . —all of this represents the source of Russian Symbolism. The Symbolists were the first to speak of intuition, and therein lies their greatest contribution, but somehow intuition got fatally . . . lost in dead, abstract, generalized concepts.
—Viktor Khovin

If I ask myself why bodies or minds exist rather than nothing, I find no answer: but that a logical principle, such as A = A, should have the power of creating itself, triumphing over the nought throughout eternity, seems to me natural.
—Henri Bergson

A = A: what an excellent theme for poetry! Symbolism languished and yearned for the law of identity. Acmeism made it its slogan.
—Osip Mandel'shtam

The attempt—undertaken by Bergson in his intuitive philosophy—to apprehend the true essence and reality of the world as distinct from simple appearance is strongly reflected in every aspect of modern art and lies at the foundation of Futurism.
—I. Rozenfel'd

OUT OF THE ASHES of Symbolism around 1910 arose a new generation of poets and artists who rejected what they considered to be "the dead, abstract, and general concepts" of their predecessors and instead proclaimed a new allegiance to the dynamism and uniqueness of things in the everyday world in which they lived. If the Symbolists worshiped music as the mystical bridge between the phenomenal and noumenal worlds, Acmeists and Futurists turned to "the word" (and Suprematist artists to the geometric form) as the key element in expressing the vitality of, and creative potential for, a daily reality reinvigorated from static Symbolist abstraction. Members of both the Symbolist and post-Symbolist worlds, however, were drawn to Bergson, although the nature of his appeal varied along with aesthetic outlook. Whereas the Symbolist Hippius, for example, saw in Bergsonian duration a model for the continuous human striving toward the divine, the Acmeist Osip Mandel'shtam[1] saw in this same duration an organic "system of phenomena" that reestablished the link between himself and the "domestic utensils" of everyday reality, thus "humanizing and warming the surrounding world" ("On the Nature of the Word"). Despite their divergent artistic and ideological emphases, both Hippius and Mandel'shtam (as well as Bely, Khlebnikov, and Malevich) were driven by a dedication to theurgy, the belief that higher levels of cognition are achieved through art, and that once Truth about existence has been intuited, the artist may then facilitate its realization in the world (thus, in a sense, "creating" reality). Symbolists and post-Symbolists alike could find in Bergson an optimistic, dynamic philosophy of artistic intuition and active participation in existence that seemed to encourage the theurgic impulse. In addition, Bergson hinted at an ideal Platonic Whole at the base of existence without any explicit declaration of such (the "peut-être" that so bothered Losskii and Frank), and thus Bergsonian thought was versatile enough to be appropriated by artists with very different views of how to define the "Whole," how best to catch a glimpse of it, and how then to help bring it about through their art.

Acmeists and Futurists are often characterized as being metaphysically at odds: the former typically concerned with linking the present to the past; the latter, with pushing the present into the future, jettisoning the past in the process. Mandel'shtam and Khlebnikov, however, shared an artistic preoccupation with the themes of language and time, both turning to the past for an organic "system" of language (Mandel'shtam to the "Hellenistic Russian word," Khlebnikov to the archaic system of Slavic roots) that might bring meaning to their present. Each poet sought unity and connection through "the word" in a world seemingly overcome by chaotic historical forces beyond human control. In general, the post-Symbolists embraced the modernist goal of escaping time through art,[2] and hoped to discover some type of temporal unity that is based on an intellectual "system." This unity, they felt, may be apprehended only through intuition, an unmediated grasp of the inner essence of the word, of phenomena, of time itself. The primary methods of accomplishing this goal differed among the post-Symbolists, yet Bergson's pronouncements on intuition seemed to provide a compatible model for their worldview and art that sought a new, "modern" way of looking at and participating in a dynamic, organic world.

Like the religious thinkers, Losskii and Frank, who always sought to include the intellect in any discussion of intuition (since the two are inseparable according to Solov'ev's philosophy of "all-unity"), as well as the Symbolist Bely, who yearned for a philosophical synthesis of Kant and Plato, Russian post-Symbolists desired both "system" and revelation.[3] In each case, be it Mandel'shtam's interest in the Hellenistic nature of the Russian language, Khlebnikov's passion for etymology, or Malevich's geometric brushstrokes, some type of intellectual framework anchors their post-Symbolist attraction to a Bergsonian type of artistic intuition.

MANDEL'SHTAM: THE TIMELESS WORD AS BERGSONIAN "SYSTEM"

It seems likely that Osip Mandel'shtam was familiar with Bergson's works prior to his 1922 essay "On the Nature of the Word" (O prirode slova), as Mandel'shtam studied in Paris in 1907–8 and could have been exposed to Bergsonian philosophy at that time. In addition, Georgii Ivanov (1952) notes that Mandel'shtam, returning to Petersburg in the fall of 1910 from abroad, had lost a suitcase containing a work of Bergson's: "Besides a toothbrush and a work of Bergson's, there was also a tattered notebook of poetry in the lost . . . suitcase. The toothbrush, however, was the only real loss—he knew both his own poetry and the Bergson by heart" (113).

Of all Russian modernist thinkers, Mandel'shtam's relationship with Bergson has been the most widely explored (see especially C. Brown 1973; Harris 1979, 1982, 1988; Rusinko 1982; and Freidin 1978). Clarence Brown, one of the first to comment on Mandel'shtam's invocation of Bergson in "On the Nature of the Word," writes of the poet's "enormous debt to Bergson" and of how "Bergson's very style has been absorbed into [Mandel'shtam's] depiction of the [Russian] language, a kind of *durée* made palpable and present" (1973, 154). Gregory Freidin takes note of the Bergsonian quality to *The Egyptian Stamp,* wherein "the reader is plunged into the almost pure *durée* of the author's consciousness" (1978, 433), and Jane Gary Harris focuses on the Bergsonian influence found in Mandel'shtam's *The Noise of Time,* arguing that Mandel'shtam creatively interprets Bergson on time and space in order "to translate [Bergson's] theoretical principle of the unity and interconnectedness of phenomena into literary prose" (1982, 116).

Like Bely, who, according to Rudolf Steiner, used the word "intuition" in his Symbolist metaphysics in the "Bergsonian, pan-cultural sense," Mandel'shtam comes to define Acmeism as "the longing for world culture" (quoted in N. Mandel'shtam 1972, 555), suggesting a similar attraction on his part to the Bergsonian belief in the noncausal inner connection of phenomena considered outside of time and space. As Harris (1982) observes, Mandel'shtam's belief that the meaning of history lies in the philologic consciousness may be seen to reflect Bergson's conception of time as duration (116, 128). Mandel'shtam's attraction to organic noncausality (in many ways the essence of duration) is evident in his praise for what he terms the Hellenistic nature of the Russian language, or the "Hellenic philologic culture." Mandel'shtam uses the term "Hellenism" in "On the Nature of the Word" to express the "system" by which man becomes a participant in the continuous unfolding of inner connections among phenomena:

> Hellenism is the conscious surrounding of man with domestic utensils instead of impersonal objects; the transformation of impersonal objects into domestic utensils; and the humanizing and warming of the surrounding world with the most delicate teleological warmth. Hellenism is any kind of stove near which a man sits, treasuring its heat as something akin to his own internal body heat. . . . Hellenism is a system, in the Bergsonian sense of the term, which man unfolds around himself, like a fan of phenomena freed of their temporal dependence, phenomena subjected through the human "I" to an inner connection. (Harris 1979, 127–28)

Thus, when Mandel'shtam writes of the Hellenistic nature of the Russian word, he is referring to the way in which language connects us to the world in which we live, connects our "here and now" to what has already been, in the same way that duration is the means by which the past is preserved in the present. Through both the Hellenistic word and the intuition of duration, one is able to attain a more unified vision of the self in the world, and therefore in time.

A brief examination of the similarities of Bergson's and Mandel'shtam's worldviews will help to establish the post-Symbolist context in which Mandel'shtam embraced certain aspects of Bergsonian thought. Bergson insists on an "active principle" as the only way of approaching an understanding of reality and rejects any simple "explanatory idea" that passively conceptualizes and blindly affirms absolute truth, such as "the Substance of Spinoza, the Ego of Fichte, the Absolute of Schelling, the Idea of Hegel, or the Will of Schopenhauer" (*CM* 48). Bergson's "system" is continually creating itself, just as reality, he believed, is constantly evolving. "Let us have done with great systems embracing all the possible, and sometimes even the impossible! Let us be content with the real, mind and matter" (*CM* 66). Bergson's call to embrace the "real" over the abstract is echoed by Mandel'shtam, who rejects the "abstract aesthetics of the word" in favor of a "living poetry," writing in "On the Nature of the Word": "'Long live the living rose!'—such was [Acmeism's] original slogan" (Harris 1979, 130, 132). Like Bergson, who attempts to bring philosophy back to "this world" as a means by which to explore man's rich, continuous reality, Mandel'shtam emphasizes "the living rose" in his Acmeist poetics, rejecting the Symbolist abstract conception of the rose's otherworldly significance. Both Bergson and Mandel'shtam thus long for the vital law of identity, where "A," simply and beautifully, equals "A."[4]

Like Bergson in the realm of philosophy, Mandel'shtam seeks to establish a new kind of humanism in art whereby the "infinite complexity" of the human being's "divine physiology" takes center stage in the quest for meaning ("Morning of Acmeism," in Harris 1979, 63). In his study of Mandel'shtam, Clarence Brown (1973) emphasizes this same humanism at the center of Mandel'shtam's Acmeist aesthetics:

> The doctrine of man, and of man in society, is a background to the kind of poetry that Acmeists wish to write. . . . What is important in a man is not his individuality in the sense of what is special and different about him, but his individual share in what is common to all men: his participation in existence. Man is a system of functioning parts and is the essential reality of a larger system of functioning parts, society. (148)

Such "participation in existence," so important to Mandel'shtam, may be seen to represent the Bergsonian "active principle" by which "the unity of our reality" (*CM* 55) may be discovered. In his essays, Mandel'shtam explores this "active principle" on a variety of levels—including the Gothic (organic, fluid, architectonic balance), "the word," Lamarckian evolutionism, and Dante's poetry—in order to reach an understanding of the self in history. In each case, the Bergsonian "active principle" in Mandel'shtam's work is manifested through an artistic, organic, moral "system," existing in duration and therefore timeless and indivisible.

In his early essay, "François Villon" (Fransua Villon, 1910), Mandel'shtam introduces the theme of the Gothic, which would develop into his mature aesthetic vision of a "system of phenomena" informed by Bergson in "On the Nature of the Word." Mandel'shtam defines Villon's worldview, as well as his poetry, in terms of Gothic architecture:

> Gothic physiology (and such it was; the Middle Ages was in essence a physiologically brilliant era) took the place of a world outlook for Villon. . . . People ask: what do the magnificent rhythms of the *Testaments* . . . have in common with the skillful craftsmanship of Gothic architects? But is not Gothic architecture the triumph of dynamics? . . . What, if not architectonics, explains the miraculous equilibrium of the stanzas in which Villon entrusted his soul to the Trinity through the Virgin Mary? . . . This is no anemic flight on the waxen wings of immortality; it is an architecturally founded Ascension, corresponding to the tiers in the Gothic cathedral. (Harris 1979, 59)

Through his denunciation of the Symbolist "anemic flight" to some otherworldly realm and praise for Villon's concrete, organic, Gothic poetics, Mandel'shtam reinforces a central theme of his own Acmeist aesthetics (that which is also central to Bergson's philosophy); namely, the importance of a living poetics that is constructed, as Bergson would say, from "the real, mind and matter." In the rhetorical question, "Which is more mobile, which is more fluid—a Gothic cathedral or an ocean wave?" Mandel'shtam stresses the necessity of artistic movement and dynamism, anchored by the Gothic "feeling of architectonics," a dynamism that may be compared to Bergsonian duration, the dynamic stream of life always anchored by intellectual verification (the diver exploring the wreck at the bottom of the sea).[5] Having praised the Gothic physiology of Villon's verse, Mandel'shtam subsequently proclaims his newly founded literary school, Acmeism, to be characterized by the same Gothic ideal of the "physiologically brilliant Middle Ages"; that is, "love for the organism and for organization" (Harris 1979, 63). Mandel'shtam embraces the Gothic as a harmonious, organic model for his poetics and world outlook, each based on a unified system of phenomena.

Shortly after his essay on Villon, Mandel'shtam devoted three poems to architectural monuments—"Hagia Sophia" (Aiia-Sofiia, 1912), "Notre-Dame" (1912), and "The Admiralty" (Admiralteistvo, 1913)—all of which exemplify the Gothic characteristics of organicity, structure, balance, and mobility that Mandel'shtam so admired in Villon's poetics. In "Hagia Sophia," for example, Mandel'shtam describes a "glorious temple, swimming in the world" (*Prekrasen khram, kupaiushchiisia v mire*), thus emphasizing the fluidity of form. But Hagia Sophia is part not only of the earthly realm, for its dome extends, "as if by a chain, toward the heavens" (*Ved' kupol tvoi . . . / Kak na tsepi, podveshen k nebesam*). The organicity of Hagia Sophia—through which land, sea, and sky all come together in a balanced, dynamic architectonic whole—is reflected in "Notre-Dame" on a more physiological level as Mandel'shtam compares the Gothic cathedral (with its "monstrous ribs"—*chudovishchnye rebra*) to the body of Adam:

Где римский судия судил чужой народ,
Стоит базилика—и, радостный и первый,
Как некогда Адам, распластывая нервы,
Играет мышцами крестовый легкий свод.

Where a Roman once judged a foreign people,
A basilica stands, and joyous and original,
Like once Adam did, stretching every nerve,
The light archway flexes its muscles.

Despite having solid archways and vaults, Gothic architecture is not static but dynamic, just as the human body continues to undergo ceaseless change. As Clare Cavanagh (1995) has observed,

> Notre Dame as Adam is . . . mobile and growing. It stretches its nerves to uncover or expand their limits; it plays with its muscles and tests the strength of its new form. Such energy and incompletion actually characterize Gothic building as much as they do Adam's, or the poet's body. . . . The human body "makes itself or it unmakes itself, but it is never something made," in Henri Bergson's phrase. (83)

Through "Hagia Sophia" and "Notre-Dame," Mandel'shtam illustrates the same Gothic characteristics of equilibrium and dynamism that he admiringly saw embodied in the poetry of Villon. This Gothic ideal also served as the first example of what Mandel'shtam later would call a Bergsonian "system of phenomena" whereby a "fourth dimension" of reality might be discovered. In "The Admiralty," Mandel'shtam devotes less attention to the physical description of the architecture than to the more abstract exposition of its ontological significance, concluding: "The shackles of our three-dimensional world have split, / And the world seas are opening for us" (*I vot razorvany trekh izmerenii uzy / I otkryvaiutsia vsemirnye moria*). Thus, the feeling of architectonics is equivalent to a type of intuition of duration, or the sense that time is more fluid and dynamic than is indicated by the motion of hands on a clock or the progression of a filmstrip across a screen. The feeling of architectonics allows for a new dimension of experiencing life and time, a dimension in which the seas of the world open for us a richer human existence by opening our eyes to the organicity, dynamism, and essential unity of life's phenomena.

Mandel'shtam's admiration for Villon was based in large part on the latter's poetic, "Bergsonian" ability to preserve the seamlessness of time:

> The reader can imagine himself using the data and therefore feels as if he were one of the poet's contemporaries. The passing moment can thus endure the pressure of centuries and preserve itself intact, remaining forever the same "here and now." One need only know how to extract that "here and now" from the soil of Time without harming its roots, or it will wither and die. Villon knew how to extract it. (Harris 1979, 58)

Concerned with the indivisibility of time, Mandel'shtam openly embraces Bergson's "system of phenomena" in his essay, "On the Nature of the Word" (in a "creative" interpretation, as Jane Gary Harris [1979] rightly notes). With Bergson as his guiding light, Mandel'shtam rejects causality in history in favor of duration, whereby the past forever remains "intact." At the outset of the essay, Mandel'shtam asks: "If Russian literature is always of one and the same essence, what constitutes its unity, what is its essential principle?" (Harris 1979, 117), and he turns to Bergsonian duration for the answer:

> To preserve the principle of unity amidst the vortex of changes and the unceasing flood of phenomena, contemporary philosophy in the person of Bergson . . . offers us a theory of the system of phenomena. Bergson does not consider phenomena according to the way they submit to the law of temporal succession, but rather according to their spatial extension. He is interested exclusively in the internal connection among phenomena. He liberates this connection from time and considers it independently. Phenomena thus connected to one another form, as it were, a kind of fan whose folds can be opened up in time; however, this fan may also be closed up in a way intelligible to the human mind.

> To compare phenomena united in time to form such a fan emphasizes only their internal connection. Thus, instead of the problem of causality (which has for so long dominated the minds of European logicians), [Bergson] poses the problem of the connection alone. . . . A science based on the principle of connection rather than causality saves us from the bad infinity of evolutionary theory, not to mention its vulgarized corollary—the theory of progress. (Harris 1979, 117–18)

Mandel'shtam here grasps the essence of Bergsonian anticausality, but his interpretation of Bergson is not entirely accurate.[6] The "connection among phenomena" that Bergson considers, while "liberated" from *linear* time, gains its very essence and unity within what Bergson terms *real* time, or the indivisible time of duration. While Mandel'shtam redresses this inaccuracy in the following paragraph when he speaks of the internal connection of "phenomena united in time," it is important to keep in mind his former tendency to appropriate Bergsonian philosophy as a means of escaping time altogether, a central concern of Russian modernists in general.

After beginning "On the Nature of the Word" with the question of the unity of Russian literature, Mandel'shtam turns to the larger question of time: How does one live in history and preserve a unified vision? Mandel'shtam's need to battle the divisiveness of linear time (or in Bergson's terminology, "spatialized time," implying a rigid succession of states) is expressed through his abhorrence of formlessness and emptiness—thus his great admiration for architectural achievements like Hagia Sophia and Notre Dame, which fill space with soaring, balanced tiers, and his respect for the architect who crafts such unified structures. Mandel'shtam identifies the Hellenistic Russian language as the building material of this unified architecture that does battle with time:

> We have no Acropolis. Even today our culture is still wandering and not finding its walls. Nevertheless, each word in Dal's dictionary is a kernel of the Acropolis, a small Kremlin, a winged fortress of nominalism, rigged out in the Hellenic spirit for the relentless battle against the formless element, against non-existence, which threatens our history from every side. (Harris 1979, 126)

Respect for the Hellenistic Russian word is central to Mandel'shtam's conception of unity in history. Mandel'shtam scorns Bely for his neologistic experimentation, or lack of respect for the Hellenistic nature of the word as a historical phenomenon. Writers like Bely, according to Mandel'shtam, sacrifice the "organic wholeness and active equilibrium" of the Russian word for the sake of "a momentary display of fireworks" (Harris 1979, 121).

Mandel'shtam's concept of Hellenism, which implies the unity of man and the phenomena of his domestic world, parallels Bergson's call for a philosophy that will approach "the unity of continuity, the unity of our reality, and not that abstract and empty unity . . . which could just as well be that of any possible world whatsoever" (*CM* 35). Bergson strives to liberate philosophy from the empty, abstract generalizations of his predecessors and transform it into an active principle, a "domestic utensil" of man, through which to seek unity within the rich, continuous stream of everyday reality. Mandel'shtam similarly seeks to liberate "the word" from the abstractions of the Symbolists that had made it hostile to man by attaching meanings to it completely foreign to his reality:

> Let's take for example a rose and the sun, a dove and a girl. For the Symbolist, not one of these images is interesting in itself: the rose is a likeness of the sun, the sun is a likeness of a rose, a dove—of a girl, and a girl—of a dove. Images are gutted like scarecrows and packed with foreign content. . . . This is where professional Symbolism leads. Perception is demoralized. Nothing is real, genuine. Nothing is left but a terrifying quadrille of "correspondences," all nodding to one another. (Harris 1979, 128)

In such a "symbolic" world, according to Mandel'shtam,

> a man was no longer master in his own house. He had to live either in a church or in a sacred grove of the Druids; a man could not rest his eyes for there was no place for him to seek peace. The domestic utensils all rose in rebellion. The broom begged for the Sabbath; the kettle refused to boil and demanded an absolute significance for itself. (Harris 1979, 129)[7]

By returning to "the word" its Hellenistic nature (that is, respecting the word as historical bearer of stable meaning), Mandel'shtam believed that the Symbolist divide separating man and word would be bridged, and man once more could depend on words as helpful tools by which to feel more a part of the world around him, once more to become "master in his own house." (The Symbolists, meanwhile, believed that they *had,* in fact, bridged the temporal and eternal realms through the musical, abstract word, and that divesting the word of its symbolic import would bring about the same type of divide for which Mandel'shtam held Symbolism accountable.) In the attempt to open the "sealed up" liturgical words of the Symbolists, Mandel'shtam places the word (as he does Notre Dame) on the same physiological level as man, as human organs "just like the liver or the heart." Thus Mandel'shtam envisions the creation of an organic, biological poetics that would preserve the organism's "internal unity" (Harris 1979, 130).

Mandel'shtam's conception of the Hellenistic word as Bergsonian "system" becomes clearer when examined in the context of both his autobiographical prose work *The Noise of Time* (*Shum vremeni,* 1923–24) and his poem, "January 1, 1924," as well as in relation to the nineteenth-century metaphysical rantings of Dostoevsky's Underground Man. To begin with the latter, Mandel'shtam and the Underground Man each claim to be marked by the twin afflictions of sickness and spite. "I am a sick man . . . I am a spiteful [*zloi*] man" proclaims the Underground Man in the first line of *Notes from Underground.* In Mandel'shtam's poem "January 1, 1924," the poet calls himself a "sick son" of the age (1993, 2:51), and "literary spite" (*zlost'* variously translated as spite, malicious anger, fury, rage) serves as the concluding motif of *The Noise of Time.* Jane Gary Harris (1982) has suggested that this *literaturnaia zlost'* may be seen to animate what Mandel'shtam calls "the beast of literature," the kind of literature that exists unbound by Time as the irreverent protest of a *raznochinets,* or rootless intellectual (122–23), who defies conventional social and aesthetic categories. In a more basic sense, Mandel'shtam's illness of spite seems to be fueled by fundamentally the same factors as is the Underground Man's: both Mandel'shtam and the Underground Man are figures who feel like misfits, lacking connection with the world, without a sense of self or place in time. Both feel oppressed by the "universal laws" of nature. The Underground Man battles furiously against the oppressive dicta of science and utilitarianism that demand that twice two is four, and that one must be happy in the Crystal Palace because it is in one's best interest to be so; Mandel'shtam, while claiming in "On the Nature of the Word" that "Utilitarianism in any form is a mortal sin against the Hellenistic nature of the Russian language" (Harris 1979, 121), is most specifically troubled by time.

As is the case with the Underground Man's relationship to science, time oppresses Mandel'shtam with its brutal, anonymous laws that leave one powerless but to comply ("And there is nowhere for me to run from the sovereign age" [*I nekuda bezhat' ot veka-vlastelina*]),[8] and furthermore, time/history does not offer a warm, welcoming embrace for one who is lost ("between myself and the age there is a gap, a ditch, filled with the noise of time").[9] Rudderless amid a swirling chaos of clamorous time, Mandel'shtam comes to rely on "the word," on literature, as his anchor, finding in Bergsonian philosophy a "system of phenomena" whereby a unity of both language and time may be achieved. "The word" thus serves as Mandel'shtam's connection to history, his personal means of creating a temporal unity out of a fragmented life and identity. Mandel'shtam's embrace of the "philological consciousness," or the Hellenistic nature of the word in his 1922 essay "On the Nature of the Word" represents the poet's attempt at forging such a unity through language.

Despite the "noises of time" that permeate Mandel'shtam's autobiographical memoir—the music in Pavlovsk, the locomotive whistles, the clatter of crockery, to name only a few—it is the noise of language that remains most powerful in Mandel'shtam's memory and that in general holds the greatest significance for him. "We learned not to speak, but to babble—and only by listening to the swelling noise of the age . . . did we acquire a language."[10] It is not surprising that perhaps the richest recollection of his mother and father in *The Noise of Time* focuses on his parents' use of language:

> The speech of a father and the speech of a mother—isn't our language nourished all its long life by the blending of these two, don't they compose its character? The speech of my mother was clear and sonorous, without the slightest foreign touch, with a few broadened and excessively open vowels, the speech of literary Great Russia; her vocabulary was limited and condensed, her turns of phrases always the same,—but it was a language, in it was something rooted and certain. Mother loved to speak and took joy in the roots and sounds of her Great Russian speech, made poorer when spoken by the intelligentsia. Was she not the first in our family to grasp these pure and clear Russian sounds? My father had absolutely no language. . . . Was it the Russian speech of a Polish Jew?—No. The speech of a German Jew?—Again no. . . . It was a completely abstract, invented language . . . where ordinary words were all mixed up with philosophical terms from Herder, Leibniz and Spinoza, the odd syntax of a Talmudist. (361–62)

Like Babel, Mandel'shtam rebels against his Jewish identity, yet whereas Babel longs to replace his calm, reflective Jewish rationality with a violent chaos, to partake of the Dionysian abandon of his Cossack comrades as depicted in his stories from *Red Cavalry,* Mandel'shtam is repelled by what he terms "Judaic Chaos" in *The Noise of Time* (360). Instead of the chaos epitomized by his father's "odd" Talmudic syntax, Mandel'shtam seems comforted by what is rooted and secure in the Great Russian language of his mother, by a system of the word through which he is able to feel some rootedness and certainty in his own sense of self.

To use Lev Shestov's well-known juxtaposition, Mandel'shtam prefers the classical order of Athens to the mystical chaos of Jerusalem; as a result, however, he is left lacking faith as is the Underground Man, who appropriates the role of the divine in a pathetic attempt to assert his importance in the universe. Mandel'shtam's "literary spite," his rage, like the Underground Man's, is almost a joyful one, the joy of finally wielding a weapon against a bully (that is, time/universal laws) rather than forever cowering helplessly in fear of a figurative, if not literal, oblivion. The Underground Man proclaims that it is out of spite that he does not seek medical attention: "If my liver hurts, then let it hurt even more!" (Dostoevsky 1979, 2:288). In response to the injustice of (his) suffering, he seeks to exacerbate it in a willful contradiction to the utilitarian tenet that one always seeks pleasure rather than pain. In *The Noise of Time,* Mandel'shtam invokes literary spite in a similar joyful rage at the injustice of the oppressive flow of time:

> Literary spite! If it weren't for you, with what would I eat the salt of the earth? You are the seasoning in the unleavened bread of understanding, you are the joyful consciousness of injustice, you are the conspiratorial salt which is passed from decade to decade with a malicious bow, in a cut-glass salt-cellar, wrapped in a towel! (387)

If the Underground Man must look to faith, to a divine Whole greater than himself, in order to be freed from his self-destructive cellar,[11] the spiritually searching Mandel'shtam looks to the word as Bergsonian system—a secular, linguistic means of attaining faith in some type of unity, a Whole that exists outside of time.

In his essay "On the Nature of the Word," Mandel'shtam considers Acmeism to be "a social as well as literary phenomenon," a "moral force," suggesting that he turned to Bergsonian philosophy in large part to satisfy his theurgic impulse to transform the world through his art. Mandel'shtam thus does not stew in the same spiteful cellar as does the Underground Man, but rather appropriates his spite in his moral mission to return Man to the center of the universe. If Bely's theurgy is based on the magic of words, the notion that a nonsense sound or articulation has the power to alter reality (for example, "enfranshish" in *Peterburg*, the word that finally compels Dudkin to act and kill Lippanchenko), Mandel'shtam's theurgy is much more grounded on respect for the Hellenistic nature of the word, the word in its historical, organic context. Whereas Bely depicts the Revolution in *Peterburg* as a mystical howl expressed through the symbolic sound of "oooo," Mandel'shtam's conception of the Revolution in *The Noise of Time* relies on speech, the utterance of concrete words: "'For me, for me, for me,' says the Revolution. 'On your own, on your own, on your own,' answers the world" (385). If sound, color, symbol and incantation serve as Bely's theurgic tools, the means by which a synthesis of the phenomenal and noumenal realms may somehow be accomplished, Mandel'shtam is only interested in finding a home, a safe place, a haven in this world of time, death, change—thus his attempt to return "the word" from far-flung symbolic reaches to its rightful place, within the domestic hearth as a "domestic tool" by which to understand and shape the world.

In addition to Villon and the Hellenistic Russian word, Mandel'shtam viewed Lamarck—the proponent of a type of biological, organic poetics of evolution—as the embodiment of an organic "system" in the Bergsonian sense. While Darwin "used nature as one would use an enormous, highly systematized card catalogue,"[12] Lamarck, as Mandel'shtam notes in his *Journey to Armenia* (*Puteshestvie v Armeniu,* 1931–32), "cried his eyes out over his magnifying glass. He is the only Shakespearean figure in the natural sciences" (Harris 1979, 367). Although greatly impressed by the "brilliant clarity" of Darwin's scientific prose, Mandel'shtam was drawn instead to Lamarck, whose sympathy with nature allowed him to transcend Darwin's utilitarian card-catalogue approach to the natural world in order to hear "the pauses and syncopes in the evolutionary line." In Bergsonian terms, Mandel'shtam admired Lamarck's ability to pierce the veil interposed between nature and ourselves, thereby being able to hear "the strains of our inner life's unbroken melody—a music that is . . . always original" (Bergson 1925, 150). Mandel'shtam opens his 1932 poem, "Lamarck," with a paean to his scientific role model:

> Был старик, застенчивый, как мальчик,
> Неуклюжий, робкий патриарх . . .
> Кто за честь природы фехтовальщик?
> Ну, конечно, пламенный Ламарк.
>
> There once was an old man, shy as a boy,
> A clumsy, timid patriarch . . .
> Who is a fencer in honor of nature?
> Why, of course, the ardent Lamarck.

As opposed to Darwin's cold, mechanical approach to the study of nature, Lamarck fights for its honor, and thus for the honor of man, who, Mandel'shtam believed, must be considered the center of the created universe.

Mandel'shtam's preference for Lamarck over Darwin may be seen to reflect Mandel'shtam's attraction to Bergsonian thought on two interrelated levels. First, Lamarck's "sympathy with nature" is an illustration of the Bergsonian concept of poetic intuition. Bergson remarks upon the link between sympathy and intuition in *Creative Evolution:* "Intuition seeks to recapture, to get back the movement and rhythm of the composition, to live again creative evolution by being one with it in sympathy" (*CE* 102). Like the poet in Mandel'shtam's essay "Word and Culture" who can hear "the sound of the inner image" of the poem, its "ringing mold of form" before a single word is written down, Lamarck similarly can hear the inner melody of the evolutionary line. It is such intuitive sympathy with the material of his craft as well as with humanity in general that Darwin lacks in his purely scientific approach, and with which the "Shakespearean" Lamarck is endowed.

This leads to the second, more fundamental reason why Mandel'shtam is drawn to Lamarck over Darwin: while Darwin's theory of evolution reflects an external, mechanistic process of nature (natural selection representing a mechanistic drive toward perfection in a species), Lamarck's theory of evolution is characterized by the idea of freedom in nature, some internal principle within the organism effecting the course of its evolutionary development. This "inner principle" (one could say élan vital) represents the essence of Bergson's creative evolution.[13] In discussing the "convergence of effects" in different organisms that are "differently situated, differently constituted, meant normally for different functions," Bergson states:

> Whether we will or no, we must appeal to some inner directing principle in order to account for this convergence of effects. Such convergence does not appear possible in the Darwinian, and especially the neo-Darwinian, theory of insensible accidental variations. . . . So we come to the only one of the present forms of evolution which remains for us to mention, viz., neo-Lamarckism. . . .

> The variation that results in a new species is not, [the neo-Lamarckians] believe, merely an accidental variation. . . . *It springs from the very effort of the living being to adapt itself to the circumstances of its existence.* The effort may indeed be only the mechanical exercise of certain organs, mechanically elicited by the pressure of external circumstances. *But it may also imply consciousness.* . . . Neo-Lamarckism is therefore, of all the later forms of evolutionism, the only one capable of admitting an *internal . . . principle of development.* (*CE* 76–77; my emphasis)

In *Journey to Armenia,* Mandel'shtam's own view of nature—like Lamarck's—reflects an aversion to the "vulgarized corollary" of evolutionary theory: the theory of progress. In the spirit of Bergsonian creative evolution, whereby change is seen as an organic, continuous phenomenon rather than as a form of deterministic "progress," Mandel'shtam observes that a plant is "an event, a happening, . . . hardly some boring, bearded 'development'!" (Harris 1979, 358). In the same way that Hippius distinguishes between the routine of daily life and an "event" (*byt i sobytie*), favoring the latter as the essence of life's fluid novelty, so Mandel'shtam comes to see nature as a continuous series of "events" rather than as a manifestation of determined evolutionary progress.

Perhaps in an attempt to find connections between such "events" in nature as well as in his own life, Mandel'shtam focuses in Armenia (the outpost of the historical world)[14] on what he calls "organic thinking," introduced to him by natural scientists, which might be compared to an intuitive—rather than strictly action-oriented—approach to the world: "We approached the mysteries of organic life. Indeed, the most difficult thing for an adult is making the transition from inorganic thinking (the mode in which we have been trained during the most active period of our lives, when thought is but an adjunct to action) to organic thinking" (Harris 1979, 389). Bergson frames an almost identical dilemma while discussing the difficulty in developing an intuitive mode of perception: "Originally, we think only in order to act. Our intellect has been cast in the mold of action" (*CE* 44). Bergson continues in *The Creative Mind:* "How can we uproot so profound an inclination? How can we bring the human mind to reverse the direction of its customary way of operating, beginning with change and movement, envisaged as reality itself, and no longer to see in halts or states mere snapshots taken of what is moving reality?" (82). For Bergson, as we have seen, the answer to his rhetorical question lies in the artistic intuition of duration. Mandel'shtam's effort to think "organically" reflects the Bergsonian desire to conceive of reality not in broken pieces or "snapshots," but in its essence—as a fluid, dynamic, interpenetrating continuum. Such a way of thinking demands a similar type of art, and Mandel'shtam found the ideal model in what he considered to be the organic poetry of Dante.

Mandel'shtam constructs his most complete aesthetic vision in his last major prose work, "Conversation about Dante" (Razgovor o Dante, 1933).

To all the "systems, in the Bergsonian sense" reflected in his earlier essays—the Gothic, Hellenism, and "the word"—Mandel'shtam now adds Dante and his Italian language:

> Would you like to become acquainted with the dictionary of Italian rhymes? Take the entire Italian dictionary and leaf through it as you will. Here every word rhymes. Every word begs to enter into *concordanza*. . . . Dante's creation is above all the entrance of the Italian language of his day onto the world stage, its entrance as a totality, as a *system*. (Harris 1979, 399–400; my emphasis)

Having once elevated the Shakespearean Lamarck over the mechanistic Darwin because of the former's ability to hear "the pauses and syncopes of the evolutionary line," Mandel'shtam turns to Dante with the same kind of respectful praise: "Everything mechanical is alien to him. He is disgusted by the idea of causality" (Harris 1979, 439). Like the almost melodic "creative evolution" to which Lamarck was so exquisitely attuned, Dante's art is also characterized by a type of artistic "duration," a dynamic flow of interpenetrating notes and motifs that belies any facile attempt at classification on the part of the intellect:

> If we could learn to hear Dante, we would hear the ripening of the clarinet and the trombone, we could hear the transformation of the viola into a violin and the lengthening of the valve on the French horn. And we would also be able to hear the formation around the lute and the theorbo of the nebulous nucleus of the future homophonic three-part orchestra. Furthermore, if we could hear Dante, we would be unexpectedly plunged into a power flow, known now in its totality as a "composition." (Harris 1979, 402)

Mandel'shtam admired Dante's ability to combine form and "power flow," much as he admired Bergson's ability to provide a philosophical "system" of dynamic duration, an "active principle" (as opposed to "explanatory idea") by which one might live. "For the Acmeists," notes one Mandel'shtam scholar, "the poetic word was far more than a literary phenomenon: it was a social, creative, metaphysical force. Bergsonian philosophy points up this original contribution of Acmeism" (Rusinko 1982, 510). For Mandel'shtam, such a philosophy of movement and engagement entailed a certain moral responsibility, a new type of humanism whereby man's active participation in the world as "master of his own house" triumphed over the petrified immobilization engendered by Symbolist metaphysics. Mandel'shtam observes that "in Dante, philosophy and poetry are constantly on the go, perpetually on their feet. Even a stop is but a variety of accumulated movement." Furthermore, "both the *Inferno,* and, in particular, the *Purgatorio* glorify the human gait, the measure and rhythm of walking" (Harris 1979, 400). Bergson similarly outlines how philosophy should serve as a humanistic guide to "the art of living" by empowering one to participate in existence:

> Philosophy stands to gain in finding some absolute in the moving world of phenomena. But we shall gain also in our feeling of greater joy and strength. Greater joy because the reality invented before our eyes will give each one of us, unceasingly, certain of the satisfactions that art at rare intervals procures for the privileged; it will reveal to us, beyond the fixity and monotony which our senses, hypnotized by our constant needs, at first perceived in it, ever recurring novelty, the moving originality of things. But above all we shall have greater strength, for we shall feel we are participating, creators of ourselves, in the great work of creation which is the origin of all things, and which goes on before our eyes. . . . Humbled heretofore in an attitude of obedience, slaves of certain vaguely-felt natural necessities, we shall once more stand erect, masters associated with a greater Master. To such a conclusion will our study bring us. In this speculation on the relation between the possible and the real, let us guard against seeing a simple game. It can be a preparation for the art of living. (*CM* 124)

Mandel'shtam embraces both Dante and Bergson because each provides a system for "the art of living," a basis for the theurgic transformation of life through art. In her second volume of memoirs, *Hope Abandoned* (Vtoraia kniga), Nadezhda Mandel'shtam states that "reading *The Divine Comedy* was an act of worship and communion" (274) for her husband. Undoubtedly, this was because Dante was able to "combine the uncombinable"—the moral, the intellectual, the aesthetic—by virtue of the (Bergsonian) "power flow" that ran continuously and indivisibly through his poetry. Such masterful organicity served as Mandel'shtam's highest artistic model and own lifelong pursuit.

KHLEBNIKOV, MALEVICH: THE TRANSRATIONAL WORD AND IMAGE

As noted earlier, it is often difficult to distinguish between Nietzschean and Bergsonian influence on Russian modernism given that the ideas of both philosophers permeated Russian society at roughly the same time and occasionally in much the same way. Bernice Glatzer Rosenthal (1991) has observed that, although "contemporaries regarded futurism as a Nietzschean phenomenon," the Russian Futurist conception of the word derived from many sources, including the philosophy of Bergson (225, 221). Therefore, the statement that the Futurists celebrated Dionysian movement, constant change, and ceaseless flux (Rosenthal 1991, 240) could just as easily be seen to suggest the Futurist embrace of Bergsonian duration as it could of Nietzschean thought. In her study of Italian Futurism, Rosa Trillo Clough (1961) notes that Italian Futurist critics "quoted freely from Bergson, Nietzsche, and Croce" (67). While Russian Futurists like Mikhail Larionov and Velimir Khlebnikov sought to distance themselves from Marinetti and their other Italian counterparts, Bergsonian intuition may well have inspired both groups, although first invoked by the Italians. Charlotte Douglas (1976) states in her discussion of Kazimir Malevich (Futurist, and later Suprematist, painter) that "the Italian Futurists had applied Bergson's discussion of intuition and analysis, time and duration to their own painting and theories, and Malevich knew these very well" (55). The world of Russian Futurism being very close-knit, Khlebnikov probably was also familiar with the invocation of Bergson by some Italian Futurists. Given his impassioned nationalism—as well as his insistence before Marinetti that Russian Futurism was an original phenomenon rather than a mere copy of the Italian version—it is understandable that Khlebnikov would not proclaim a similar sympathy with Bergsonian intuition, although it seems likely that the latter played some role in Khlebnikov's conception of a transrational language.[15]

In "Intuitivism and Futurism" (Intuitivizm i futurizm), I. Rozenfel'd (1913–14) notes that the concept of reality as "constant movement" (20, 21) is central to both Bergsonian philosophy and Futurism, the former lying at the base of the latter, "which attempts, through the representation of the dynamic process . . . intuitively to grasp and artistically to depict its uninterrupted change and synthetic wholeness" (19). Both Khlebnikov's transrational language (*zaumnyi iazyk*) and Malevich's transrational realism (*zaumnyi realizm*) were intended to create a fresh reality free of conventional modes of perception;[16] as a result, both thinkers would have appreciated Bergson's contrast between the practically oriented, external knowledge of phenomena governed by intellect or reason and the inner realm of duration lying beyond the grasp of reason, penetrated only by intuition. By examining some of the ways in which Bergson's concept of intuition may have played a role in the aesthetics of Khlebnikov and Malevich, yet another of Russian Futurism's varied sources and inspirations may be offered for further study.

It should be remembered that the Futurists, like the religious thinkers Losskii and Frank, conceived of intellect as a vital and active component of intuition. In other words, intuition for the Futurists in the form of "beyond reason" or transrational art resembled the integral reason of the Slavophiles, which broadened—but did not reject—analytical reason to include all human faculties of perception. In her description of Malevich's use of intuition, Charlotte Douglas (1976) provides a useful qualification of the term for Khlebnikov as well:

> Malevich did not advocate intuition as a kind of passive, anti-intellectual approach to art. It is definitely not instinct. He advanced intuition as an active creative principle which is lawful; in this it was quite similar to the original principle of *zaum* [*sic*]. For while it rejects analytical logic alone as too limiting, it certainly includes analytical logic and demands of the intellect the greatest effort. Indeed, Malevich often called this intuition "intuitive reason" or "intuitive will." (54)

Douglas goes on to note that "it would be hard to conclude that Malevich's intuition derived from any other source" than Bergson, for whom intuition, or "intellectual sympathy," also included an analytical component. Khlebnikov's brand of intuition in the form of transrational language, also based on firm intellectual ground, could similarly have been influenced by Bergson.

While many Russian modernists make at least one substantive comment about Bergson at some point in their writings, Khlebnikov does not. It is known that Khlebnikov was reading Baudelaire and Verlaine in 1907, the year Bergson's *Creative Evolution* was published in Paris (Khardzhiev 1975, 6). In 1914, the year the last volume of Bergson's collected works was published in Russia, Khlebnikov (1928–33) makes a humorous aside in his diary to Bergson's "cabby" (*izvozchik Bergsona*) (5:329), and in a 1916 essay Khlebnikov stresses the necessity of an independent State of time, unconnected to the spatial realm (*nezavisimoe gosudarstvo vremeni* [*lishenoe prostranstva*]),[17] echoing Bergson's belief in the necessity of considering time, or duration, separately from space (Bergson criticizes Kant "because he did not attribute to duration an absolute existence, having put time, *a priori,* on the same plane as space" [*CE* 206]). Although Khlebnikov was perhaps drawn most to Leibniz, whose "alphabet of thought"—the attempt to reduce all of human thought to certain numbers and signs—was similar in essence to his own effort to create one universal language based on common semantic units, Khlebnikov rarely mentions any philosopher in his theoretical writings. Indeed, his only remark about Nietzsche is that "both Nietzsche and Bismarck are notably non-German," and his longest, clearest statement about Kant reads: "Kant, who had wanted to define the boundaries of human reason, ended up defining the boundaries of German reason. What an absent-minded professor."[18] Given the paucity of philosophical references in Khlebnikov's work, even a passing mention of Bergson is significant, especially when considering the focus in Khlebnikov's *zaum'* art on the epistemological realm "beyond reason."

A brief look at Khlebnikov's theory of language suggests a possible connection to Bergsonian thought. As Raymond Cooke (1979) points out in his study of the poet, Khlebnikov is often identified as "a leading exponent of that cornerstone of Russian Cubo-Futurist aesthetics, the 'self-sufficient word' (*samovitoye slovo*)" (67) or the word held up as form, texture, and sound rather than as conveyer of meaning. Whereas in Kruchenykh's case this may often be true,[19] Khlebnikov's conception of "the word," according to Cooke, went far beyond the neologistic as he sought to create a transrational, Slavonic "universal language" based on archaisms and a system of roots.[20] In this sense, although Mandel'shtam's and Khlebnikov's *practical* application of language differed considerably, their *theoretical* approach to "the word" was actually quite similar; each turned to language as the embodiment of history, a unifying force of humankind and thus a weapon against the oppressive flow of historical time. Like Mandel'shtam, who considered the Hellenistic Russian word to be "a system, in the Bergsonian sense of the term" whereby the past might be preserved in the present, Khlebnikov similarly sought to create a scientific system of word formation[21] and writes in his "supertale" *Zangezi* of the theurgic ability of the artist to (re)create the wor(l)d: "Let the mists of time be dispersed by the prophetic sounds of universal language. It is like light."[22] Khlebnikov, however, was less interested in preserving the Moment than in discovering the stable Laws of Time, the mathematical equations that he was convinced lay at the center of the universe.[23] Although Khlebnikov's attempts to systematize the flow of time are highly rational and scientific, a Bergsonian subtext may be found in his approach to language, characterized by what he considers to be the intuitive, or transrational, apprehension of meaning.

Like Bergson, who states that art is only a more direct vision of reality, an intuitive grasp of duration or the inner essence of reality that is beyond the bounds of practically oriented intellect, Khlebnikov places language on a new level "beyond reason" (*zaum'*) and thus beyond the automated habitual response to words that he felt had destroyed the essence of their true meaning. Having compared everyday language to playing with dolls, Khlebnikov defines transrational language as consisting of those words that exist outside the rules of the game and thus are "free" enough from conventional communication as to offer some sort of essential meaning:

> But since they don't provide anything directly to the consciousness (are not suited for playing with dolls), these free combinations . . . are called transrational language. Transrational language exists beyond the boundaries of reason. . . . Such words don't belong to any language, but at the same time they say something, something elusive but, nonetheless, something that exists.[24]

While Khlebnikov calls his language "transrational," it ultimately represents a very intellectual, almost mathematical, system of semantic organization; for example, part of a "rational" narrative such as: "[The hordes], spilling out into the Steppes and filling up its emptiness, dispersed into a multitude of bands, stopped and rested on their land" becomes in Khlebnikov's transrational language: "[*S*]*o mo ve + ka so, lo sha* the Steppes + *cha*."[25] Khlebnikov seeks to create a "science of word creation" (*nauka slovotvorchestva*) through which the intuitive grasp of the "self-sufficient word" may be accomplished,[26] intuition thus relying, in a sense, on intellect in a way similar to that seen in Bergson's metaphysics, wherein intellect must "verify" that which intuition reveals. Although Khlebnikov does not use the word "intuition" in his theoretical writings, he describes the apprehension of the inner meaning of transrational language in terms of emotion rather than reason: "If a distinction is made in the soul between the government of intellect and the raucous people of feeling, then . . . transrational language is the appeal, over the head of the government, directly to the people of feeling; it is the direct call to the twilight of the soul."[27] Khlebnikov again identifies "twilight" with the pure essence of the word when offering a distinction between the "pure" (*chistoe*) and "everyday" (*bytovoe*) word:

> The word is divided into the pure and the everyday. It could be said that both nocturnal or starlit, and daylight or sunlit, types of reason are concealed in the word. This is because any single, everyday meaning of a word obscures all its remaining meanings, just as all the luminaries in the starlit night disappear during the day. . . . The self-sufficient word renounces the phantoms of given, everyday circumstances, and in place of the self-evident lie creates a starlit twilight.[28]

Bergson's distinction between intellect and intuition could be seen as a significant source for Khlebnikov's concern (and the modernist concern in general) with the pure, inner essence of language, the "self-sufficient word," as opposed to the external, ossified *bytovoe slovo*.[29]

As shown through their 1913 collaboration on the Futurist opera, *Victory Over the Sun* (Pobeda nad solntsem), and through the very term "Cubo-Futurist," the Futurist word and image as expressed by Khlebnikov and Malevich were originally very closely linked. In her introduction to a recent collection of David Burliuk's reminiscences, N. Zubkova observes:

> Painting greatly influenced literature at the beginning of the twentieth century. . . . The Futurists adopted in their literature the painterly devices of displacing time, meaning, and plot, [devices] which had made their creations more difficult [to understand]. From this arose the theory of the word "as such." If in painting color, line and plane became goals in themselves, so in literature the word lost its former, sensible meaning. (Sazhin 1994, 3–4)

Despite the early kinship of the Futurist word and image in the spirit of "self-sufficient" art, Malevich soon came to distance himself from his Futurist beginnings. By 1916, in his attempt to establish the independence of the new art form of Suprematism, Malevich was already "spit[ting] at the altar" of Futurist art.[30]

Similarities nonetheless remained between the transrational art of Khlebnikov and Malevich, such as their common reliance on an intuitive approach to form. As Paul Schmidt notes in his introduction to *The King of Time,* a study of Khlebnikov's thought and art: "This notion of Khlebnikov's, that stable units of sound material could be uncovered beneath the seemingly disorganized surface variety of language, was a vital and immediate contribution to Malevich's Suprematist style of abstract painting" (Khlebnikov 1985, 3). Like Khlebnikov's intuitively mined semantic units that would scientifically combine to form one transrational language for all people, Malevich considers his minimal black *Square* to be the creation of "intuitive reason."[31]

Charlotte Douglas (1976) argues convincingly that Malevich's writings on the creative tension in art between intellect and intuition (or between "utilitarian" and "intuitive" reason) often parallel Bergson's discussion of the same, and concludes that "although Bergson is not explicitly mentioned by name in Malevich's writings, his concepts are present throughout. . . . Malevich often echoed Bergson when he spoke of the 'inner struggle' between the two modes of reason" (55–56). Douglas goes on to state that there was "one important problem" for the Suprematists in regard to Bergson: How might a representative image on material canvas allow for the Bergsonian intuition of flux, reality as ceaseless movement and change? The solution, suggests Douglas, may lie in the fact that Malevich's "image" was never meant to be a static *representation of* movement (as was, for example, a Cubist painting), but was *itself* dynamic essence: "Malevich produced his square as a visible unit of sensation in the new objectless consciousness. On the canvas it was not intended to be an 'image' of anything, but a 'living form.'"[32] Cubist art also aimed for the expression of dynamism, yet, as Malevich notes, unfortunately destroyed the object in the process. Describing the fatal flaw of Cubism, Malevich writes: "In the depiction of movement, the wholeness of things *vanished* as their flashing particles hid themselves among other running bodies. . . . In our era of Cubism the artist has destroyed objects together with their meaning, essence and purpose."[33] In opposition to the Cubists, Malevich sought to create art of "dynamic form" in which the object—such as the square—preserves and asserts its essential "meaning, essence and purpose" by preserving its wholeness and purity of form. Suprematist form, writes Malevich, represents both "the acting force of utilitarian perfection in a coming concrete world" as well as serving as "a state of dynamism."[34] Malevich's definition of his art as an "acting force" recalls Bergson's invocation of an "active principle" over an "explanatory idea" in the realm of philosophy; with both the Suprematist form and the philosophical word, the artist/thinker is acting upon and thus transforming reality, the essence of the theurgic project. To add to Douglas's comments on the Bergsonian undercurrent in Malevich's thoughts on intuition, I would suggest that Malevich's whole idea of "form" as pure, dynamic essence, at once intellectual and intuitive, may be related to Bergson's discussion in *Creative Evolution* of form as "logical essence," a dynamic principle that intellectually opens the way for a more intuitive approach to reality. (Such was precisely the principle at work in Khlebnikov's scientific attempt to create a universal language based on transrational semantic units.)

As we have seen, Bergson conceives of evolution in terms of duration—the ceaseless flow of interpenetrating moments of time in which new forms are constantly being created: "The more we study the nature of time, the more we shall comprehend that duration means invention, the *creation of forms,* the continual elaboration of the absolutely new" (*CE* 11; my emphasis). Malevich similarly states in his essay "From Cubism and Futurism to Suprematism": "Creating means living, eternally creating newer and newer forms" (24), the Suprematist square, however, serving as the emblem of the new age and leading the rush toward the future: "And we declare our time to be the square of our age on which we shall spread out our forms."[35] Malevich uses the term "duration"—meant by Bergson to describe "succession without distinction" (*TFW* 101)—precisely to distinguish the "new" art form, Suprematism, from the "old" schools of Cubism and Futurism. "We must recognize 'short duration' as being the sharp distinction between our epoch and the past—the moment of creative impetus, the *speedy displacement in forms;* there is no stagnation—only tempestuous movement."[36] As noted earlier, Hippius creatively misuses the Bergsonian term "duration" to distinguish between past and present, writing to a friend in 1930: "Our present *durée,* everyone and everything in it, is quite different from the *durée* of our past." Whereas Hippius preserves the original French term, thereby making a connection to Bergsonian *durée* likely, Malevich uses the Russian *nedolgovremennost'* to indicate a "short duration,"[37] thus making more difficult a similar connection to Bergson (the traditional Russian translation of *durée* being *dlitel'nost'*). Although Malevich's *vremennost'* is quite similar in meaning to *dlitel'nost',* his use of the term to indicate temporal succession is, like Hippius's usage, fundamentally opposed to the Bergsonian meaning. Given the tumultuous historical period in which Hippius and Malevich lived, it is perhaps not surprising that they would endow Bergsonian duration with the sense of succession rather than indivisibility; any conception of historical unity was obscured by rapid social, political, and cultural shifts, including the birth of Malevich's Suprematist art movement "from Cubism and Futurism," as well as the onset of the repressive 1930s, which Hippius laments in the aforementioned quotation.

After stating that evolution is defined by the continuous creation of new forms, both Bergson and Malevich go on to admit that, while form is necessary to depict change, in actuality there is no such thing as form because the nature of life is constant flux. While Bergson writes in *Creative Evolution* that "there is no form, since form is immobile and the reality is movement," Malevich similarly states that "form is a condition and . . . in reality form does not exist,"[38] yet "in order to depict the movement of modern life, one must operate with its forms."[39] By examining some of Bergson's statements on the essence of form as conquering the "nought" of existence, a possible model is provided for Malevich's notion of the Suprematist form as pure essence, a product of Intuitive Reason, created "from nothing."

Bergson devotes several passages of *Creative Evolution* to the philosophical problem of "nothingness," or "nought," and questions how one may justify the existence of anything in the universe. Bergson states:

> Philosophers have paid little attention to the idea of the nought. And yet it is often the hidden spring, the invisible mover of philosophical thinking. . . . Whence comes it, and how can it be understood, that anything exists? . . . Existence appears to me like a conquest over nought. . . . In short, I cannot get rid of the idea that the full is an embroidery on the canvas of the void, that being is superimposed on nothing. (*CE* 275–76)

Bergson wonders how to make things "self-sufficient," how to affirm the existence of things-in-themselves instead of simply accepting them as an alternative to nothing; his answer: through the *logical* existence of a thing rather than through its psychological or physical existence:

> A circle drawn with chalk on a blackboard is a thing which needs explanation: this entirely physical existence has not by itself wherewith to vanquish non-existence. But the "logical essence" of the circle, that is to say, the possibility of drawing it according to a certain law—in short, its definition—is a thing which appears to me eternal. (*CE* 277)

Although Bergson uses the example of a circle and Malevich devotes the majority of his theoretical remarks to the square, the principle of the form's "logical essence" remains unchanged. Malevich observes in his essay "Suprematism" that the square represents not the end of art but "the beginning of true essence."[40] In addition, just as Bergson stresses the importance of following a "certain law" for the construction of the circle so that it can endure, Malevich states that "in constructing painterly forms it is essential to have a system for their construction, a law."[41] If the circle may be seen to endure by virtue of its "logical essence" and the "intellectual prejudices" associated with the concept of the eternal are thus eliminated, Bergson believes "the road would be cleared for a philosophy more nearly approaching intuition" (*CE* 277). In the same way that intellect and intuition work together in Bergson's philosophy to create and apprehend the "logical essence" of self-sufficient form, which then "vanquishes non-existence" ("In fact, each of these two lines of thought [intuition and intelligence] leads to the other; they form a circle" [*CE* 178]), so in Malevich's metaphysics, both "the naught" and "Intuitive Reason" play central roles for Suprematist form:

> I consider that it was necessary to understand the intuitive in art as the aim of our selective feeling towards objects. And it followed a purely conscious path, decisively forcing its way through the artist. . . . The forms of Suprematism, the new realism in painting, are already proof of the construction of forms from nothing, discovered by Intuitive Reason.[42]

Although there is no evidence to indicate that Malevich was familiar with the text of *Creative Evolution,* Bergson's collected works were published in Russian translation in 1913–14, and Bergson's philosophy was thus at the height of its popularity in Russia at the very time that Malevich was formulating his main theory of Suprematism. In addition, Malevich was very familiar with the Italian Futurists' application of Bergsonian thought to their aesthetics.[43] It is very possible, therefore, that Bergsonian philosophy played some role in the formulation of Malevich's thoughts on Intuitive Reason and the essence of form.

Bergson's philosophy of form lent itself to two different, yet interrelated, interpretations by Russian modernists. On the one hand, Russian religious thinkers and Symbolists believed that within external, static forms perceived by the intellect flowed the spiritual essence of reality waiting to be apprehended by those capable of intuitive vision. Such a position is consistent with Bergson's numerous statements regarding the role of intellect as "dislik[ing] what is fluid, and solidif[ying] everything it touches" (*CE* 48), as well as his emphasis on the importance of apprehending the dynamic reality flowing within the static forms of practical perception. Thus, in accord with this first, and most significant, way of interpreting Bergson, Frank distinguishes between the outer, more practically oriented "thought-knowledge" and the deeper, more organic "life-knowledge"; Hippius defines art as seeing the invisible within the visible and emphasizes the dynamic, fluid "event" hidden within external "everyday routine"; Bely asserts in his essay "The Forms of Art" that music is the highest art form because, unlike architecture and painting, it has no external form and thus is concerned solely with the artistic expression of inner movement; Mandel'shtam praises the dynamic "inner form" of Dante's *Inferno,* and Khlebnikov proclaims the inner, essential, pure (*chistoe*) word more meaningful than its conventional, everyday (*bytovoe*) exterior. In addition, the Futurist composer and artist, Mikhail Matiushin (a co-collaborator with Khlebnikov, Kruchenykh, and Malevich on *Victory Over the Sun*) criticizes Italian Futurism for focusing on the outer movement expressed by skyscrapers and automobiles rather than on the "true, inner affirmation of this movement." Matiushin writes: "The mistake of the Italian Futurists lay in their obligatory expression of outward movement"; in contrast he praises Russian Futurism, which "reveals the inner world of all appearances and gives shape to that which the ordinary eye does not see or apprehend."[44] Lastly, in writing about Matiushin's wife, Elena Guro, as an ideal model of the new age of Futurist poetry, Viktor Khovin (1916) uses very Bergsonian imagery in his description of how Guro strives in her art "to penetrate to the inner object . . . to merge with the stream of continuous, uninterrupted creative change, the flow of life" (10).

Already with Mandel'shtam, however, who considers the Gothic cathedral to be as fluid as an ocean wave, there is a shift toward a different appropriation of Bergson's philosophy of form; form begins to gain meaning in and of itself rather than serve as a static shell for a dynamic, noumenal core. Vasilii Kandinsky may be thought of as another such transition figure between the two modernist conceptions of form as posited by Bergson. Although Kandinsky played a pivotal role in advancing modern art toward the abstract, he consistently writes of the "inner appeal of form" in *Concerning the Spiritual in Art,* and in another essay states: "As a means of expression, therefore, the artist's emotional vibration must find a material form capable of being perceived. This material form is the second element . . . of a work of art."[45] For Malevich, however, form no longer hides content; it *is* content. In this second way of appropriating Bergson's comments on form, form becomes "self-sufficient," no longer the veil obscuring some hidden inner essence; inner becomes outer, like "milk without the bottle, living by itself under its own aspect, leading its own life independently from the shape of the bottle which does not express its essence, sensations and taste."[46] Like Bergson's axiom "A = A," the "logical essence" of the circle that vanquishes nonexistence by virtue of its definition as itself, Malevich's *Black Square* (or *Black Circle,* for that matter) is created "from nothing" as a dynamic expression only of itself.

This application of the Bergsonian principle of pure form as "logical essence," along with the first interpretation of form *versus* essence, are fundamentally interrelated viewpoints, both stemming from Bergson's self-styled Neoplatonism and thus attractive to Russian thinkers steeped in the tradition of Platonic idealism. In *Creative Evolution,* Bergson outlines how, according to ancient Greek philosophy, the philosophy of Forms was synonymous with the philosophy of Ideas:

> As becoming shocks the habits of thought and fits ill into the molds of language, [the Greek philosophers] declared it unreal. In spatial movement and in change in general they saw only pure illusion. This conclusion could be softened down without changing the premises, by saying that the reality changes, but that it *ought not* to change. Experience confronts us with becoming: that it is *sensible* reality. But the *intelligible* reality, that which *ought* to be, is more real still, and that reality does not change. Beneath the qualitative becoming, beneath the evolutionary becoming, beneath the extensive becoming, the mind must seek that which defies change, the definable quality, the form or essence, the end. Such was the fundamental principle of philosophy which developed throughout the classic age, the philosophy of Forms, or . . . the philosophy of Ideas. (*CE* 314)

This statement of Bergson's illustrates the complex nature of his attitude toward Neoplatonism. On the one hand, although he does not explicitly state it, Bergson supports the Platonic notion that beneath the process of becoming the mind seeks "the definable quality, the form or essence" of things; such, after all, is what he means by the "logical essence" of the circle (or the "Idea" of the circle) that attains the eternal because it is drawn "according to a certain law—in short, its definition." But somehow Bergson resists positing this "logical essence" at the base of duration as a preexisting Idea, the "end" product already established outside of the flux of time and change, and it is in this sense that Bergson considers the philosophy of Ideas inadequate:

> [The Idea] is a stable view taken of the instability of things. . . . To reduce things to Ideas is therefore to resolve becoming into its principal moments, each of these being . . . screened from the laws of time, and, as it were, plucked out of eternity. That is to say that we end in the philosophy of Ideas when we apply the cinematographical mechanism of intellect to the analysis of the real. (*CE* 315)

Instead of beginning the metaphysical search for "the definable quality, the form or essence" in the dynamic flow of becoming, "the philosophy of Ideas follows the inverse direction. It starts from the Form; it sees in the Form the very essence of reality. It does not take Form as a snapshot of becoming; it posits Forms in the eternal; of this motionless eternity, then, duration and becoming are supposed to be only the degradation" (*CE* 318). Thus, while Bergson may believe in Platonic Ideas, a realm of absolute definitions, his philosophy proceeds in the opposite direction from Plato's, starting in the essence of becoming or duration and moving toward the eternal, the circle's "logical essence." Bergson states along these lines that "in renouncing the factitious unity which the understanding imposes on nature from outside, we shall perhaps find its true, inward and living unity" (*CE* 199).

It is impossible, Bergson maintains, to posit such stable "snapshots" of reality at the start, "plucked out of eternity," for then life would be ruled by intellect alone and the rich experience of living, the intuition of our duration, would be denied us. Russian modernists were concerned primarily with the freedom of the creative act as well as with the discovery of something eternal in the fragmentation of modern life (Russian modernism itself being a loose coalition of many separate elements). Bergson offered a tantalizing hint of the eternal, the absolute, the Platonic Idea, as perhaps the immutable form of the continuous, all-important flux of life, the realm of pure creativity and art. Like the ancient Greek philosophers, Russian modernists all sought the "black square" in life, a "logical essence" that is eternal and can thus conquer the "nought" of existence, but unlike them (and like Bergson) they felt the flux of becoming must be posited as the primary reality because in this duration is the freedom from oppressive "Ideas" that repress the creative impulse for novelty.[47] As long as the universe remains continuously in flux, the artist retains the capability of transforming it—again, the theurgic impulse inextricably linked with the modernist project. Whether the Symbolists conceived of form as hiding the true, dynamic essence of life, or whether

Malevich posits the geometric shape as true essence itself, both viewpoints are based on the Bergsonian notion that the reality is movement and that form is only a "snapshot" of this continuous change; form, if it does exist, can only be apprehended through the prism of fluid becoming, the realm of freedom, creativity, and art.

Chapter Four

The Kharmsian Absurd: Against Kant and Causality

> Of course, *absurdity* in and of itself is not an indication that something belongs to the realm of *noumena.* But belonging to the realm of noumena will certainly be expressed for us through absurdity.
> —P. D. Uspenskii

P. D. USPENSKII'S NOTION of a fourth dimension (*chetvertoe izmerenie*) where time is extended into unknown space is expressed both in his 1909 work of the same name (itself a popularization of the Englishman Charles Howard Hinton's 1904 work *The Fourth Dimension*), as well as in *Tertium Organum* (1911). The artists Kazimir Malevich and Mikhail Matiushin were particularly interested in discovering the fourth dimension in the aesthetic realm, as were other Russian modernists who considered art to embody fresh insight into the noumenal world, free of the confines of three-dimensional reality.[1] Like Bergson, Uspenskii rejects the Kantian limitation of knowledge to intellect and turns to intuition (the "third organ"—*tertium organum*—of thought) as the means of penetrating beyond the three-dimensional world to the realm of noumena, or "things-in-themselves." In his article "On Life and Poetry" (O zhizni i poezii, 1918), transrational poet Aleksandr Tufanov (one of Daniil Kharms's first poetic role models) links Bergson's concept of "real time" to Uspenskii's idea of the fourth dimension. Claiming that time for Kant is quantitatively one-dimensional and therefore not "real," Tufanov looks to Bergsonian philosophy ("And what does time mean in Bergson's conception?") and finds that time is "not quantity but quality"; as a result, Tufanov embraces Bergson's concept of the artist whose creativity lies outside of three-dimensional space, "in the fourth dimension, in real time."[2]

The OBERIU (Ob"edinenie Real'nogo Iskusstva—The Association for Real Art)[3]—a literary group active mainly from 1928 to 1930 and thus considered by some to be "the last flare-up in Russian modernism before it was suffocated by Stalinist socialist realism" (Gibian 1987, 31)—was founded in 1927 by Kharms, who earlier that year had been given by his friend Malevich a copy of the latter's book, *God Is Not Cast Down* (*Bog ne skinut,* 1921) with the inscription, "Go and put a stop to progress" (*Idite i ostanavlivaite progress*).[4] In the spirit of Malevich's inscription, one of Kharms's main artistic concerns from his days as a member of the OBERIU through the 1930s was the escape from causal systems of meaning that defined the traditional three-dimensional world, the rejection of the so-called logical chain of events that informed the deterministic conception of socialist "progress." Near the end of his life, Kharms (1991) wrote that the primary impulse behind his creativity lay in the renunciation of the logical, practical world in favor of life in all of its absurdity: "I am interested in . . . only that which possesses no practical meaning. I am interested in life only in terms of its absurd manifestation" (134). In their Manifesto published in 1928, the Oberiuty defend their "real" art precisely because of its lack of logic (that is, its absurdity), a quality they felt essential to reveal the essence of things: "Perhaps you will assert that our subjects are 'unreal' or 'illogical'? . . . Art has its own logic that does not destroy the object but rather helps to recognize it."[5] In outlining the major characteristics of Kharms's absurdist art, Jean-Philippe Jaccard (1985) emphasizes the rupture of cause and effect in Kharms's prose as traditional expectations of plot development are replaced by "a completely distorted causal chain where nothing explains anything"; instead, Kharms endows a story with its "own logic" based in part on the absence of logical cause, thematic and verbal incoherence, and arbitrary associations (297, 299). In this sense, Kharms's art may be seen to reflect life in a society characterized by arbitrary brutality and the "illogical" disappearance of people in the middle of the night, a fate that would ultimately befall Kharms himself.[6]

Both Kharms's poetic and prosaic absurd rely on the subversion of logic and causality, and aim for the creation of "a new sensation of life and of its objects."[7] The basic goals of these two categories of the absurd, however, ultimately diverge. In her examination of Kharms's poetic system, Nina Perlina (1991) lists two of the most prominent features of Kharms's poetics as "the conscious and consistent substitution of synchrony for diachrony on all levels of the text"; and a "new correlation between text and context," according to which "key words are *a priori* made equal to all other semantic components of the text"; this leads to the "introduction of re-accentuated, semantically enriched and restructured discrete elements of the cultural chaos into the poetically organised structure, i.e. into the texts of his poems" (175, 176–77). Thus, in his poetic absurd, Kharms plays with traditional semantic and etymological constructions while exploding any sense of a causal context. Literary associations are made simultaneously on various levels, noncausal juxtapositions that Perlina suggests lie at the heart of Bergson's philosophy as well (188).

Kharms's prosaic absurd, while also violating logical and causal contextual norms, is fundamentally concerned with the thematic expression of the absurd split between man and his surrounding world (Jaccard 1985, 285). Jaccard (1991b) points out that transrational poetry such as Kharms's "is above all an attempt to discover meaning by new means, and not the account of a fracturing of the world" as is found in absurdist prose (55). The shift in Kharms's artistic career from the more aesthetic (his absurdist poetry of the OBERIU period) to the more existential (his absurdist miniprose works of the 1930s) opened the way for greater parallels to the philosophy of Bergson, whose *Le rire* deals with the role of laughter in society and its implications for human activity and consciousness. Kharms's prosaic absurd is meant to reflect the alienation of man in society, the decomposition of language and subsequent failure of communication, and the general incoherence of a world plunged into the madness of Stalinism—a notion of the absurd that differs significantly from the much more optimistic, Western, Bergsonian conception of the comic, but that, as we shall see, shares several key characteristics with the latter.

After several evenings of performance art (the last of which took place in a student dormitory at Leningrad State University in April 1930 when Kharms and others showed up in typical comic garb, wearing signs that read, for example: "We are not pies!" (*My ne pirogi*),[8] the Oberiuty came under attack as "class enemies" and "counterrevolutionaries." An article appeared in the Petersburg newspaper *Change* (Smena) shortly after what would be their final performance in which L. Nil'vich wrote of the Oberiuty: "*Their withdrawal from life, their senseless poetry, their transrational sleight-of-hand* [zaumnoe zhonglerstvo]—*all of this represents a protest against the dictatorship of the proletariat. Therefore their poetry is counterrevolutionary. It is the poetry of people alien to us, the poetry of a class enemy.*"[9] This article marked the end both of the OBERIU and, it might be said, of Russian modernism itself, as efforts accelerated toward making socialist realism official Soviet policy for literature.[10] Kharms was arrested in 1931, briefly exiled, and then allowed to return to Saint Petersburg in 1932. Despite the increasing repression and misery of the 1930s (detailed in Kharms's diary entries during this time), Kharms still managed to produce some of his best work, including the cycle of stories *Happenings* (Sluchai, 1933–39) and the short story "The Old Woman" (Starukha, 1939). As with almost all his work for adults, however, Kharms was never to see either published; rearrested in 1941, he died in a psychiatric hospital in February 1942.

Accused in the infamous 1930 *Change* article of "transrational sleight-of-hand," Kharms in his absurdist prose does share ground with the transrational or "nonsense" poetry of Khlebnikov in that both artists sought to subvert the conventional meaning and logic of the everyday in order to apprehend the pure essence of word and object, inaccessible to analytical reason. Mikhail Meilakh notes that Khlebnikov played a formative role in Kharms's creative development as is clear from one of Kharms's diary entries.[11] In fact,

Kharms's often dreamlike (or nightmarish) plots, which lack the "logical" connections found in wakeful activity, may be seen to reflect the same type of absurdity found in Khlebnikov's verses. Nikolai Gumilev (1911) states that absurdity (*nelepost'*) and incoherence (*bessviaznost'*)—two of the main elements of Kharms's prose—similarly characterize the dreamlike poetry of Khlebnikov: "V. Khlebnikov is a visionary. His images are convincing in their absurdity, his thoughts in their paradoxical quality. It seems that he sees his verses first in a dream and then writes them down, preserving all the incoherence of the dreamlike course of events" (77). Both Khlebnikov and Kharms reject the conventional, "logical" relationship between cause and effect in their work, embracing instead a more intuitive, or dreamlike, approach to reality; in this way they create an artistic vision of the world free of the symbols of everyday life which they felt obscured the essence of things. Bergson's notion of art represents a similar setting aside of meaningless, conventional concepts that are ground in the practical workings of the intellect so that the true, fluid nature of reality might be revealed. According to Bergson (1925), art "has no other object than to set aside the practical, useful symbols, the conventionally and socially accepted generalities, in short, all that masks reality from us, in order to place us face to face with reality itself" (160). Furthermore, Bergson (1925) remarks that a "special logic" akin to that of dreams informs the absurd, and he therefore concludes that "comic absurdity is of the same nature as dreams" (188, 190). With many of his prose works focused on the related themes of sleeping/dreaming/waking, Kharms would seem to concur with Bergson's statement linking the nature of the absurd with that of dreams.

Just as there is "sense" to Khlebnikov's "nonsense" (the goal of creating a scientific system of word formation), so there is "sense" to Kharms's notion of the absurd—the attempt to depict a reality marked by incoherence, alienation, and senseless suffering.[12] For Kharms, that which defies conventional understanding is that which actually bears the most meaning. As with the interplay of intellect and intuition in Bergson's metaphysics (or in the Slavophile concept of Integral Reason, Khlebnikov's transrational poetry and Malevich's Intuitive Reason), Kharms similarly attempts to broaden the traditional concept of reason or logic in his art through the use of the absurd. While Bergson points to the "logical essence" of the circle as something eternal, thus clearing the way for a more intuitive approach to reality, Kharms also comments on the eternal, ideal nature of the circle: "The most exact, incomprehensible, infinite and ideal closed curve is the CIRCLE."[13] As an "ideal" form, the circle is by implication logical, yet it is also "incomprehensible" (*nepostizhimoe*), much as in Russian religious thought the concept of the divine is both ideal and ultimately unknowable (see, for example, Pseudo-Dionysus's apophatic writings or Frank's *Nepostizhimoe*). Thus Kharms's artistic vision of reality relies on both intellect and intuition, the incomprehensible logic of the circle.

When considering the possible affinity between Kharms and the transrational poet Kruchenykh, however, the common ground of "meaningful illogicality" shared by Kharms and Khlebnikov disappears. In one of her many articles on Russian post-Symbolism, Charlotte Douglas (1995b) comments on the nature of the absurd in Kruchenykh's poetry:

> The absurdity of Kruchenykh's works was a very specific *zaum* [*sic*] behavior; it was different from the *seemingly* absurd with a hidden message, an apparent lack of sense which disappears when the right key or keys are found, different even from the "surreal" type of subconscious associations. This absurdity was a pointless, mindless, stubbornly senseless, irresolvable condition. (361)

According to Douglas's breakdown of types of absurdity, Kharms's aesthetic would fit the category of "seemingly absurd" rather than of the "pointless, mindless" variety characterizing Kruchenykh's poetry. The "keys" to Kharms's prose by which one may decipher the apparent incoherence of his sketches and stories include the environment of Stalinist Russia in the 1930s, Kharms's polemic with the Russian literary tradition (in particular with Dostoevsky and Chekhov),[14] as well as the general context of the Surreal and European Absurdist movements, which began in the 1920s with Breton and Kafka and continued long after the demise of the OBERIU primarily with Camus, Beckett, and Ionesco.[15] As A. A. Aleksandrov notes, Kharms's "illogical, inside-out artistic world" makes sense to the reader who is attentive and "sensitive to the paradoxes of social life and to the mysteries of human psychology" (introduction to Kharms 1990, 5). The absurd in Kharms's work is not, as in Kruchenykh's poetry, meant to create a stable "simultaneous universe," but rather is oriented toward the simple yet tragic comprehension of the real world in which Kharms lived, in all its fearful uncertainty and disorder. "Absurd laughter is thus, above all else, the result of a *tragic lucidity*" (Jaccard 1985, 298).

Like other Russian modernists who, in the spirit of Bergsonian philosophy, reached beyond the confines of the intellect to intuition in order to apprehend connections among phenomena—for example, between the human and divine realms (Bely's symphonies), between past and present (Mandel'shtam's Hellenistic "word"), or between varied Slavic roots and peoples (Khlebnikov's transrational language)—Kharms also sought meaning outside of everyday (*zhiteiskaia*) logic. However, his goal was not so much the discovery of connections but rather the defiant, poststructuralist denial of the same.[16] For Kharms, the proposition of a world that is "whole" denies the essential role played by its "parts": "The world, consisting of something whole, uniform and unbroken, cannot be seen to exist, because in such a world there are no parts, and once there are no parts, then there is also no whole."[17] It was the part rather than the whole that interested Kharms, who felt that objects would be reborn "in all the purity of their concrete, masculine forms"[18] if the habitual connections linking them to the world were dissolved. In this sense, Kharms shared in the theurgic project of his fellow Russian modernists by envisioning a newly created world emerging from his art, from the OBERIU "word."

In the same way that Malevich in his Suprematism turns away from the Cubists because they "destroyed" the object, the Oberiuty reject the *zaumniki* (transrational poets) for destroying the word, stating in their Manifesto: "There is no school more hostile to us than *zaum'*. We—real people who are concrete to the core—are the worst enemies of those who castrate the word and turn it into a weak, useless mongrel. In our creative work, we broaden and deepen the meaning of the object and the word; in no way do we destroy it."[19] Nonetheless, like the *zaumniki,* the Oberiuty still subscribed to the formalist "peeling away" of the word's "literary and everyday skin" in order to make it "self-sufficient." A. A. Kobrinskii comments on this aspect of OBERIU poetry: "This was indeed 'real' poetry: the reader and listener were invited to forget things familiar to them and, in renouncing habitual associations in life and literature, to appreciate 'the word as such' and the autonomous essence of objects" (introduction to Kharms 1991, 10). It was in this latter spirit of affinity with the principles of transrational poetry that Kharms began his literary career in 1925 by joining a group of young Leningrad poets headed by Aleksandr Tufanov, the so-called radical transrational poet who sought to create a type of phonetic music in his verse and named himself "Velimir II" after his inspirational model, Khlebnikov.[20] Tufanov also happened to be an especially interested student of Bergson, writing in his 1925 autobiography: "Closest of all to me now is Bergson."[21]

Like Khlebnikov, Tufanov believed that time must be considered outside of space, a concept that lies at the base of Bergsonian duration. Thus, Tufanov (1924) states in *Towards the Transrational* (K zaumi): "People have divided the whole earth into spatial States [*gosudarstva*]. But my State lies outside of spatial apprehension; it is in time" (25). Whereas Khlebnikov makes no mention of Bergson in regard to his "independent State of Time" (*nezavisimoe Gosudarstvo Vremeni*), Tufanov equates consciousness—the "flowing State of Time" (*tekuchee Gosudarstvo Vremeni*)—with the Bergsonian notion of duration (a link Bergson himself makes), both consciousness and duration representing the qualitative, immeasurable, fluid interpenetration of moments and states as opposed to the quantitative, immobile aggregate of juxtaposed elements:[22]

> In our conception, the condition of consciousness . . . is marked not by quantity but by quality; it is immeasurable and can only be apprehended; it consists of a multitude of alternating elements, interpenetrating one another, insepa-

> rable, indistinguishable, incalculable. . . . *Time, in our conception, is a successive and qualitative multitude* (Bergson). (Tufanov 1924, 25)

Tufanov goes on to distinguish between the individual's "external" existence in the spatial realm and life in "the land of Time," wherein one's true, dynamic self is free:

> In the land of Time, our dynamic "I" is freed from all the projections of the external world when, by means of deep introspection, we are allowed to grasp our inner states as living, constantly developing beings, as states that cannot be measured, which permeate one another and of which the succession in duration has nothing in common with juxtaposition in homogeneous space. (26)

This latter quotation from Tufanov appears to be an unacknowledged translation of a passage from Bergson's *Time and Free Will* in which Bergson discusses the "duration of consciousness": "We reach [the fundamental self] by deep introspection, which leads us to grasp our inner states as living things, constantly *becoming*, as states not amenable to measure, which permeate one another and of which the succession in duration has nothing in common with juxtaposition in homogeneous space" (*TFW* 231).

Tufanov ultimately applies Bergsonian philosophy to his notion of a phonetic-based transrational poetry. After criticizing "applied" (*prikladnoi*) lyricism for being preoccupied with literary meaning and imagery (in this sense appealing to spatial apprehension), Tufanov praises "immediate" (*neposredstvennyi*) lyricism, consisting of pure sound (*fonema*) and "always proceeding from the élan vital."[23] Meaning is thus conveyed fluidly and "immediately" from sound, uncategorized and thus unsullied by analytical reason. By using the Russian equivalent for Bergson's élan vital (*zhiznennyi poryv*), Tufanov stresses that transrational poetry is a Lamarckian rather than Darwinian manifestation (to use a Mandel'shtamian metaphor), poetic expression characterized by an inner dynamism, fueled by sound and movement, which is absent in the purely spatial apprehension of the "applied" word: "From phonemes, colors, lines, tones, sounds and movements, we create music that is incomprehensible in terms of spatial perception but rich in the realm of feeling."[24] Tufanov's conception of a phonetics of "transsense" thus could be seen as a blend of Bely's and Khlebnikov's aesthetics—the music of the transrational word—proceeding from the Bergsonian élan vital and in essence mirroring the qualitative nature of Bergsonian duration.

In 1925–26 Kharms appeared together with Tufanov at literary gatherings, and as Aleksandrov notes, Kharms "without a doubt learned much from his older, erudite colleague."[25] Whether Kharms became interested in Bergson before his association with Tufanov or afterward is unknown; what *is* known is that in a diary entry for June–July 1925 Kharms lists all of Bergson's major works among those books he has recently taken out of the library.[26] Perhaps most significant is that Kharms lists Bergson's *Le rire* (Smekh) twice, including the first edition to be translated and published in Russia in 1900 as well as the second edition included in the fifth and last volume of Bergson's *Collected Works,* published in 1913–14. It therefore appears that Bergson's short work on laughter held particular interest for Kharms, and in fact much of Bergson's discussion on the nature of the comic is reflected in Kharms's aesthetic of the absurd. Aside from Perlina (1991), who draws a loose parallel between Bergson and Kharms (188), scholars seem to have overlooked the possible influence of Bergson on Kharms's prose. Given Kharms's documented early interest in Bergson, it seems that Bergsonian thought as expressed in *Le rire* could be considered yet another "key" to the genesis of the Kharmsian absurd. Because Kharms's theory of the absurd is based, in large part, on his aversion to the notion of causality and so-called logical connection, it will be helpful first to examine the way in which Kharms's general stance against causality is supported by Bergsonian philosophy before addressing the specific parallels between *Le rire* and Kharms's prose.

As noted earlier, what is known as Bergson's revolution in philosophy was largely motivated by his rejection of nineteenth-century scientific determinism in favor of a "creative evolution" of life in which an organism's vital impulse for growth takes precedence over any mechanistic formula for progress. Kharms, who was instructed by Malevich to "go and stop progress," also rebelled against the concept of logical determinism as embodied in Soviet society, wherein all human activity ostensibly was geared toward the attainment of a single goal. As with Bergson, Kharms's rebellion may be seen as an attempt to preserve the individual's vital impulse for creativity and ultimately for life itself. Examples of how Kharms subverts the notion of deterministic progress in his works are numerous. In "Sonnet" (Sonet), for example, the Kharmsian narrator cannot remember which comes first: seven or eight. "An Unsuccessful Performance" (Neudachnyi spektakl') features a planned stage performance where nobody can appear because each in turn becomes sick (*rvet*) and has to run from the stage. A story entitled "Connection" (Sviaz') subverts the very idea of connection as the narrator begins with the completely illogical sequence: "1. I am writing in answer to your letter, which you are planning to write me in answer to my letter, which I wrote you." In one of his best-known prose works, "Blue Notebook No. 10" (Golubaia tetrad' No. 10), Kharms parodies the concept of narration by attempting to describe a person who does not, at least in narratorial terms, exist. After listing everything that the "red-haired man" does not possess—eyes, ears, mouth, nose, arms, legs, stomach, spine, and, indeed, hair—finally Kharms exclaims: "There was nothing! So it is not clear about whom we are speaking." Underneath "Blue Notebook No. 10" Kharms originally wrote "against Kant,"[27] a postscript that provides a broader philosophical prism through which to view the story (or anti-story) about the red-haired man. The significance of Kharms's postscript might be elucidated by recalling Bergson's main criticism of Kant, namely that Kant categorically restricts man's epistemological capability to the function of the intellect: "The human intellect is enough: such is precisely the Kantian solution" (*CE* 357). By writing "against Kant" under "Golubaia tetrad' No. 10," Kharms rejects both the limitation of literature to a strictly intellectual, logical progression of events, as well as the restriction of human knowledge to phenomenal perception, excluding the spiritual or noumenal element of reality.[28] Kharms's exclamation, "There was nothing!" thus points to the need to escape causality in literature and, by implication, life. Here is a story, declares Kharms, as well as a human being with no logical motivation behind them.[29] In the same way that Bergson takes note of "that unforeseeable nothing which is everything in a work of art," and Malevich comments on the necessity of creating forms "from nothing," so Kharms's assertion of "nothing" at the heart of his story proclaims the freedom and necessity of both art and the individual to exist independent of the oppressively logical demand that there be "something." Kharms's pointed alogicality may be read as a direct political and aesthetic challenge to the enforced Stalinist philosophy of optimistic determinism in the 1930s.

Like his subversion of traditional narration, Kharms's treatment of language—rarely a source of any true communication in his prose works—is oriented toward the breakdown of causal relationships, the sabotage of the conventional, logical connection between word and meaning. As Jaccard has observed, "a mistrust vis-à-vis words and the affirmation of their incapacity to express anything of the world but its incoherence is a fundamental element of the theatre of the absurd,"[30] and he points to one of Kharms's unpublished sketches as a prime example of the decomposition of language in the Kharmsian world:

KOKA BRIANSKY: I'm getting married today.
MOTHER: What?
KOKA BRIANSKY: I'm getting married today.
MOTHER: What?
KOKA BRIANSKY: I said I'm getting married today.
MOTHER: What did you say?
KOKA BRIANSKY: To-day—ma-rried!
MOTHER: Ma? What's *ma?*
KOKA BRIANSKY: Ma-rri-age!
MOTHER: Idge? What's this idge?
KOKA BRIANSKY: Not idge, but ma-rri-age!
MOTHER: What do you mean, not idge?
KOKA BRIANSKY: Yes, not idge, that's all!

MOTHER: What?

KOKA BRIANSKY: Yes, not idge. Do you understand! Not idge!

MOTHER: You're on about that idge again. I don't know what idge's got to do with it.[31]

As with "Blue Notebook No. 10," Kharms again echoes the Bergsonian dissatisfaction with Kantian reliance on intellect as the sole means of attaining knowledge; by emphasizing the inability of everyday language to convey meaning, Kharms highlights the individual's willful renunciation of socially imposed codes of logical conduct in life and art.[32] Although Anatolii Lunacharskii, the first Communist commissar of education, does not explicitly mention him by name, it is very possible that Kharms is one of the writers Lunacharskii has in mind when he criticizes the "Bergsonian" trend of certain writers in 1929 to strip the word of its logical meaning:

> Several artists of the recent past have said that . . . in no way can one fully express in words the inner experience of man. Even on the part of writers themselves, we see a certain aversion to the word. . . . This conception of the inadequacy of the intellect . . . (which, for example, lies at the foundation of Bergson's philosophy) leads to the opinion that art . . . has nothing in common with thought or ideology.[33]

In the same way that Bergson rejects the rigid, mechanical nature of the intellect as being incapable of apprehending the fluidity of life, so Kharms reacts negatively to the concept of automation in life, be it the nature of causality in human events where "7" automatically leads to "8," or the nature of language, where signifier automatically links to signified. It is precisely this notion of mechanism or the automatic that serves as the essence of the comic for Bergson, who writes in *Le rire:* "it is certainly a type of mechanism that makes us laugh."[34] Mechanism or the automatic also serves as the essence of the absurd for Kharms,[35] eliciting a rebellious laughter (or "anti-laughter," as Aleksandrov terms it) at a society that isolates, dehumanizes, and mechanizes the individual.[36] In this sense, Kharms most likely shared Bergson's feeling that "laughter must be . . . a type of *social gesture*" in that laughter forces the lifeless essence of the mechanical "to the surface of the social body" (20) where it can be exposed and hopefully combated. Noting that Kharms turned his life into an "astonishing spectacle," Aleksandrov goes on to remark that "in the most basic sense, this spectacle was a protest against automatic existence" (introduction to Kharms 1990, 8).

According to Bergson's conception of life as duration, repetition becomes manifest only when the life force is absent, the automatic acting in place of what should be life's fluid change.[37] Laughter ensues when repetitive mechanical movement imitates life:

> The idea is a thing which grows, buds, flowers, matures. . . . It never stops, it never repeats itself. It must continuously change, because if it ceased to

> change, it would cease to live. If only gesture could be animated in a similar fashion! If only it would accept the fundamental law of life which is never to repeat itself! But here is a certain movement of an arm or head, always the same, which seems to me to recur periodically. If I remark on it, if it succeeds in distracting me . . . I will laugh involuntarily. Why? Because now I have in front of me a mechanism which functions automatically. It is no longer life, it is the automatic installed in life and imitating life. It is comic. (32)

Kharms's use of repetition in his prose, central to his aesthetic of the absurd, may be seen to function in the Bergsonian sense of the comic as "automation installed in life and imitating life." Thus, Kharms's sketches include a woman who tries (unsuccessfully) to chop wood while repeatedly propping up her falling pince-nez, all the time imploring her husband to stop repeating the same word, "tiuk," after every chop ("Tiuk"); a conversation between two characters, each of whom repeats his sentences three or four times ("The Mathematician and Andrei Semenovich"); a character who falls asleep and wakes up five times in a row, each time dreaming a variant of the same dream ("Dream" [Son]); and six old women who fall, in turn, from the same window ("Plummeting Old Women" [Vyvalivaiushchiesia starukhi]). In each case, the mechanical or automatic has replaced life, creating a situation of artificial stasis in place of the fluidity and novelty of true existence. Bergson states: "That which is laughable is a certain *mechanistic rigidity* in the place where one would like to find the living flexibility of a person" (10).

Kharmsian characters engaged in lifelessly repetitive language and activity inevitably become isolated, mechanical, listless figures, dysfunctional within society. Bergson similarly emphasizes the unsociability of the comic figure, who "above all else expresses a particular inadaptation of the individual to society" (135). A typical example of such a mechanized, unsociable character in Kharms's prose is the carpenter Kushakov, who falls down four times in a row on the street, and when he returns all bandaged up to his apartment building, his neighbors don't recognize him and won't let him in ("The Carpenter Kushakov" [Stoliar Kushakov]); in this way, mechanism leads to depersonalization, another major aspect of the comic according to Bergson: "*We laugh whenever a person gives us the impression of being a thing.* One laughs at Sancho Panza when he is thrown down on a rug and tossed up into the air like a plain old ball. One laughs at Baron Münchhausen once he has become a cannon ball hurtling through space" (58).[38] Kharms also often depicts the transfiguration of a person into a thing; thus in his prose works, "What They're Selling These Days in Stores" (Chto teper' prodaiut v magazinakh), wherein a man is killed with a large cucumber, and "Losses" (Poteri), in which a man dreams of brushing his teeth with a candlestick-holder, "[a] man's life is equated with a cucumber or a bronze candlestick" (Aleksandrov, introduction to Kharms 1990, 5). In another sketch, the character Kalugin, who repeatedly awakes and falls asleep again, suddenly becomes unrecognizable to those whom he has always greeted at the bread store, is pronounced "unsanitary" by the Sanitary Commission and ultimately is folded up in two by his neighbors to be thrown out as trash ("Dream"). While the image of Baron Münchhausen as a cannonball might actually elicit laughter, one reads of Kalugin's transformation into trash more with a sense of horror than levity, given the obvious contemporary parallel to the fate of so many in Stalinist Russia. Although the dual themes of automation and depersonalization are central to both Bergson's conception of the comic and Kharms's aesthetic of the absurd, only the laughter inspired by the latter is marked by "tragic lucidity" precisely because of the reader's differing response to Kalugin as opposed to Baron Münchhausen. Laughter in the Bergsonian sense draws attention to the depersonalized mechanism of human activity in order to become free of it ("correct" it) and return "life" to movement. Bergson comments on the nature and function of laughter in this respect:

> Rigid mechanism . . . is like a *distraction* from life. If events could be ceaselessly attentive to their own course, then there would be no coincidences or chance encounters . . . everything would take place as planned and *always progress*. . . . The comic is . . . that aspect of human events which imitates . . . pure mechanism or simple automation: in short, movement without life. [The comic] thus expresses an individual or collective imperfection which calls for immediate correction. Laughter is that very correction. (87; my emphasis on "progress")

In order to "put a stop to progress," as Malevich had instructed, Kharms makes a "social gesture" in the Bergsonian spirit of the comic by emphasizing the automatic, lifeless nature of existence through which the individual comes to resemble a thing. However, despite their often similar treatment of the automatic (and common rejection of Kant and causality), the differences between the Kharmsian absurd and the Bergsonian comic remain perhaps of greater significance, reflecting the widely divergent social and political realities faced by each author. The Bergsonian comic of pre–World War I France was a naively enthusiastic predecessor of the terrorized, weary Kharmsian absurd of the Soviet 1930s. In place of Bergson's optimistic belief in laughter as a positive correction to automated dehumanization,[39] Kharmsian "anti-laughter" is a Gogolian "laughter through tears," or, as Alice Nakhimovsky (1982) terms it, "laughter in the void"—a tragic comprehension that in the unstoppable, uncorrectable course of "progress," the human being, like Kalugin, will be folded up in two and thrown away as trash.

Chapter Five

The Death of Intuition

> Ohé, Bergson [*sic*]! We have left your philosophy behind! No more imprévisibilité! All that remains is calculation [*uchet*]—according to Lenin.
> —Zinaida Hippius

WRITING IN 1931, Vladimir Jankélévitch (1931) observes that in Paris, "[t]he salons have become very anti-Bergsonian, and the Prophets who abound among us have proclaimed the bankruptcy of 'intuitionism'" (viii). The discussion of intuition as a viable mode of cognition had also come to an end by this time in Russia with Stalin firmly in control of cultural expression as well as all other aspects of Russian life. Until approximately 1929, however, topics in art such as intuition and the subconscious were for the most part tolerated while the outline of the new political, economic, and social landscape was being sketched.[1] Nonetheless, Bergsonian philosophy—criticized by Georgii Plekhanov almost as soon as it became popular in Russia[2]—continued to be attacked by Marxist-Leninist critics following the Bolshevik Revolution, which brought with it growing ideological demands on culture.[3] By the end of the twenties, almost all independent literary groups had been subordinated to RAPP, the Russian Association of Proletarian Writers. The last vestiges of artistic freedom as embodied in Boris Pil'niak and Evgenii Zamiatin—the two leading figures of the nonideological Union of Writers—were destroyed as the RAPP campaign against the two ended with Pil'niak's "recantation" and Zamiatin's emigration. With the advent of the Stalinist era and the First Five-Year Plan, Aleksandr Voronskii, having mentioned intuition in some of his writings, was soon made the scapegoat for those believed to be harboring "intuitivist" inclinations, and he was thus condemned in 1930 for holding "Bergsonian" views.[4]

It is not surprising that both before, but especially after, the Revolution, Marxist-Leninist thinkers would try to discredit Bergsonian philosophy. Intuition was considered an unorthodox and therefore dangerous epistemological tool because its adherents claimed that the human mind rather than the material world was the main organizing principle of reality. Thus, intuition was seen to reside outside the boundaries of the officially sanctioned philosophical method of dialectical materialism. One Soviet critic takes note of what he considers to be Bergson's treatment of matter as a "negative" phenomenon of life:

> Life [for Bergson] is composed of that which is unseen by the eye, the immediately and intuitively grasped inner essence of things. No kind of matter exists for intuition, which in its content is only an inexhaustible flow, reminiscent of a melody. . . . Thus, for Bergson, matter is in essence only the negative condition for the manifestation of life, an obstacle that life must overcome. (Davydov 1988, 404)

As noted earlier, however, Bergson straddles the idealist/materialist boundary, refusing to posit Platonic Ideas at the base of duration and insisting instead that the ceaseless flow of life, of becoming and change, must be the primary reality from which all other metaphysical discoveries follow. In fact, Bergson consistently wrote that matter was not something to be overcome, but rather that matter played an integral role in various parallelisms with the nonmaterial world—for example, psycho-physiological parallelism, metaphysics/science (*IM*), soul/body (*MM*). Because of both the materialist and dialectical aspects of Bergsonian duration,[5] it was even more imperative for Marxist-Leninist thinkers to discredit him as a false prophet of the "true" philosophical method of dialectical materialism as put forth by Marx and Engels.

As was the case with some Russian religious thinkers also intent on distancing themselves from Bergson (especially Losskii), the objective, intellectual component of Bergson's philosophy was almost entirely overlooked by Marxist-Leninists. As a result, Bergson was often lumped together with Kant and Mach as a thorough (and thoroughly misguided) idealist who constructed chimeras of meaning from subjective intuitive whimsy. Examples of the "lumping together" of Bergson with other suspect idealist thinkers believed to be hostile to Marxist thought may be found in one of Georgii Plekhanov's essays written in 1911, wherein Plekhanov (1956–58) laments the fact that in Russia, "Marx has been supplemented by Kant, Mach, and Bergson" (5:623). In addition, Lunacharskii, who in 1913 writes from Paris of Bergson as one of his teachers (1913, 345), the same year criticizes Briusov for the latter's mystical belief in the hidden, inner essence of things, inaccessible to the human mind, a belief that "in general parallels the Kantian position, revived by the fashionable Bergson."[6] Lunacharskii would later add Husserl to the "hopeless idealist" list; writing in 1930, Lunacharskii (1970) comments that while Lenin encouraged the study of certain eighteenth-century French materialist thinkers like Holbach and Diderot, he looked with contempt on the contemporary philosophy of Husserl and Bergson: "Lenin said: study Holbach and Diderot because they represent the highest point in the development of bourgeois culture, and we must learn much from them. . . .

Vladimir Il'ich and Plekhanov regarded with merciless irony all of the supposedly great men of contemporary bourgeois philosophy, all of the Husserls, Bergsons" (92).

If, as Lenin believed, appearance and reality are one and the same, then there is no "inner essence" to be apprehended within material form; reality, or the "thing-in-itself," is readily apparent to the intellect because the material world, the "thing," *is* the essence of meaning. As with Malevich, form is considered essence, although Malevich's forms are discovered by Intuitive Reason, whereas, according to Lenin, form may be reflected in the mind but in no way relies on the mind for its genesis.[7] Lenin (1960–69) writes in *Materialism and Empiriocriticism:* "There is, in principle, decidedly no difference between appearance and the thing-in-itself, nor can there be. . . . Philosophical fabrications . . . according to which the thing-in-itself exists 'beyond' appearances (Kant) . . . are complete rubbish" (18:102). Marxist-Leninists criticized Kant for claiming it was impossible to know the "thing-in-itself" (didn't Kant know that being determines consciousness, rather than vice versa?) and attacked Bergson for claiming that we *can* know the essence of things but only with the aid of intuition and not by intellect alone. As B. P. Vysheslavtsev (1971) points out, however, the Marxist-Leninist philosophy of dialectical materialism—according to which the objective reality of the constantly developing material world serves as the only true source of meaning—represents a form of "bad" metaphysics, and ultimately not a form of metaphysics at all, given that there can be no genuine search to understand the essence of things if this essence is already thought to be self-evident in the material world:

> Dialectical materialism affirms that the "thing-in-itself" *is reflected* (and even is photographed) in the consciousness, and that the absolute is matter. This . . . is *bad metaphysics,* affirming knowledge of that which is not known. . . . It is necessary to go beyond ("meta") the physical, chemical existence of atoms in order to see their connection to other forms of being and to understand their place in the fullness of objective reality. (39-40)

According to Lenin, philosophy must express *partiinost',*[8] and art, as Lunacharskii states, is class-oriented.[9] Bergsonian intuition as an aesthetic, metaphysical method was considered, in its "mysticism," to be an impediment to the purely intellectual expression of ideology and understanding of the all-important material world. The 1961 entry for Bergson in the Soviet *History of Philosophy in Six Volumes* (Istoriia filosofii v shesti tomakh) includes the following two statements, both juxtaposing Bergson's "subjective, mystical" philosophy with orthodox, objective materialism: "The basic line of Bergson's philosophy is the defense of idealism and religion, and the fight against materialist philosophy, [undertaken] by means of the discreditation of human intellect and by opposing to the latter mystical intuition" (5:600), and furthermore, in regard to art: "Bergson advocates individualism and subjectivism in art, proclaims the absolute opposition of art and reason, and tears artistic creativity away from the realm of practical activity" (604). Bergsonian intuition was thus seen by Soviet critics as a threat to the communist definition of art and reality as utilitarian and objective.

In his study of the literary critic and theorist, Aleksandr Voronskii, Frederick Choate (1987) outlines the Soviet campaign against the editor of the immensely popular literary journal *Red Virgin Soil* (*Krasnaia nov'*). The campaign was based in part on allegations of "Bergsonianism" stemming from Voronskii's occasional treatment in his works of the role of intuition in the artistic process (see especially Voronskii 1928). Whether Voronskii was in fact a follower of Bergson (Choate argues that he was not) is not as important as how Voronskii's alleged "Bergsonianism" was used against him in the name of socialist realism. Looking back at this period, Soviet critic A. I. Metchenko (1967) states that in Voronskii's articles and books, "Marxist ideas are crowded out by the ideas of Kant and Bergson," and he accuses Voronskii and those who share his beliefs of rejecting the Marxist-Leninist worldview in favor of intuition as the prime vehicle for artistic creation: "The main organ 'through which art functions' is 'intuition.' . . . For critics who took this position, the struggle for progressive ideas, for the attainment of the Marxist-Leninist worldview . . . had no direct relationship to artistic creation. . . . Intuitivism contained within itself the destruction of art, the rejection of realism" (156). Much as the idealist hero of Olesha's "The Cherry Pit" (Vishnevaia kostochka, 1929) is accused by his Marxist neighbor of holding Bergsonian views,[10] so Metchenko condemns Voronskii as an enemy of the Party for advocating "Bergsonian" idealist aesthetics.

While discussing Raisa Messer's much earlier article, "Bergson's Aesthetics and the Voronskii School" (Estetika Bergsona i shkola Voronskogo, 1930), Choate notes that Messer does not offer "any coherent explanation of Voronskii's 'Kantianism' or 'Bergsonianism,'" but instead simply tries to discredit Voronskii for "appealing for the cognition of reality" rather than uncritically accepting Stalin's policies of the First Five-Year Plan. After attempting in the first half of her article somehow to link Voronskii to Bergson's ideas on intuition, Messer devotes the entire second half to a denunciation of Bergson's philosophy. As with many Marxist and Soviet critics, a focal point in Messer's attack on Bergson is the notion of the dialectic and how Bergson corrupts it.

> The outward appearance of Bergson's "dialectics" and originality lie in his absolutization of change. But uninterrupted change, uninterrupted becoming, turns into a simple stream of becoming which lacks any kind of transition from one state to another. Such a stream of becoming turns into a series of immobile states. Therefore, Bergson's "dialectics" are absolutely incapable of pointing the way to a solution of the system's antinomies. (51)[11]

Already evident in nineteenth-century Hegelian philosophy is the conception of reality as historical consciousness. Bergson may be seen to continue in the Hegelian tradition if one considers duration as a type of dialectical process whereby thought is propelled through the creative tension between the opposing faculties of intuition and intellect. In *Creative Evolution,* Bergson describes his notion of the dialectical nature of philosophy:

> Dialectic is necessary . . . in order for intuition to break itself up into concepts and so be propagated to other men. . . . The same effort, by which ideas are connected with ideas, causes the intuition . . . to vanish. The philosopher is obliged to abandon intuition, once he has received from it the impetus, and to rely on himself to carry on the movement by pushing the concepts one after the other. But he soon feels he has lost foothold; he must come into touch with intuition again. . . . In short, dialectic is what ensures the agreement of our thought with itself. (*CE* 238)

Unlike Hegel, however, and certainly unlike Marxist-Leninist thinkers, Bergson's dialectic (so he claims) is not teleological in that there is no concept of the perfection of the Absolute Idea or a communist utopia posited as the ultimate goal of the dialectical flux. Rather, Bergson conceives of his "dialectic" as simply representing the checks and balances of the thought process by which we experience the world; the dialectic for Bergson is thus nothing more and nothing less than the process of living, with whatever outcome such a journey might bring.

Marxists like Aleksandr Bogdanov, however, rejected the notion of a dialectic that seemed to encompass the thought process alone, with no evident practical application to life. In his *The Philosophy of Living Experience* (*Filosofiia zhivogo opyta*), Bogdanov (1913) points to the metaphysics of Heraclitus (often mentioned as a source for Bergson's concept of duration), as an example of the dialectic at work: "He negates all stasis, all immobility, any immutable foundation of phenomena: 'everything flows'—such is the universal formula of his philosophy. . . . What then remains in this cosmic flow? Only one thing: the regularity of its changes . . . [or], to use the latest philosophical jargon—only the dialectic itself" (183). Despite the pure dialectical nature of Heraclitus's worldview, Bogdanov goes on to condemn it as theory without practice, yet another useless interpretation of the world instead of a practical program for changing it:

> Here is Heraclitus, who accepts that the essence of the world is movement and who finds in the universe nothing but the eternal transformations of the primordially active, divine fire. But how does his own philosophy relate to this flow of being? Marx defined the difference between the contemplative and active world view as follows: "Previous philosophers only *interpreted the world* in different ways, whereas it is now a question of changing it." Does Heraclitus's system offer anything other than an interpretation of the world? No . . .

> from it follows no kind of *program* for the active transformation of the world by man. (192)

Although in some respects Bogdanov held orthodox Marxist views, in others he came closer to idealism than materialism, which is what caused Lenin to expel him from the Party in 1909 and later to brand him an idealist and false Marxist. In *Materialism and Empiriocriticism,* Lenin criticizes Bogdanov for suggesting that there exists some "unchanging essence of things" within life's flux. According to Lenin (1960–69), such a statement betrays a fundamental misunderstanding of the dialectic and consequently of reality itself, which is ceaselessly moving, changing, and progressing:

> Bogdanov's arguments in 1899 regarding the "unchanging essence of things" . . . are also the fruits of his ignorance of the dialectic. From Engels's point of view, the only thing that remains unchanged is the reflection in human consciousness (when human consciousness exists) of the external world, which exists and develops independent of the human mind. No other "immutability," no other "essence," no "absolute substance" . . . exists. (277)

Lenin considered Bogdanov's statement regarding the "unchanging essence of things" to be a dangerous manifestation of idealism, whereby the Platonic Idea of a thing becomes more important than the thing itself, and the objective material world is therefore subordinated to the subjective determination of meaning. Although, as Loren Graham (1972) points out, "dialectical materialism incorporates features of both absoluteness and relativity, of both . . . commitment to the immutable . . . and a Heraclitean belief in flux" (24), Lenin maintained that the only immutable thing in the universe is the reflection in human consciousness of the developing external world of matter. Writing in 1914, Lenin explains that the reason Bogdanov's work was no longer being printed in workers' newspapers was because of Bogdanov's perceived attempts to inculcate the working class with "refurbished idealistic conceptions of bourgeois philosophers." Therefore, concluded Lenin, Bogdanov was not a Marxist.[12]

What may have bothered Lenin the most was Bogdanov's theory of "psycho-physiological parallelism," or the belief, despite claims of "monism," in two ways of organizing experience (such as by intuition and intellect in Bergson's metaphysics). Like Frank's monodualism of life-knowledge and thought-knowledge, Bogdanov (1908) distinguishes between "life in its immediate essence" and "life objectified for cognition," noting that in consideration of these two modes of knowledge, "let there be no room for any type of dualism. This is simply the vision of *empiriomonism*" (129). Bogdanov goes on to describe the workings of psycho-physiological parallelism in the human consciousness as the continual mutual verification between the subjective and objective realms of experience: "All the different degrees and forms of the organization of immediate experience are reflected objectively in different degrees and forms. This is the *psycho-physiological parallelism of life*, not dualistic, but strictly monistic in essence" (135). Bergson, who himself wrote a short work entitled "Le Paralogisme psycho-physiologique" (1904), similarly states in that work: "One thus oscillates from idealism to realism and from realism to idealism, but so rapidly that a sense of immobility is created, as if straddling two systems which have been united into one. This apparent reconciliation of two irreconcilable views is the very essence of the thesis of parallelism" (906). Bergson first delivered "Le Paralogisme psycho-physiologique" as a paper at the Second International Congress on Philosophy held in Geneva in September 1904. Interestingly, Bogdanov had joined Lenin in Geneva the summer prior to the congress, during which time he showed Lenin his work in progress, *Empiriomonism.* It then became clear that Bogdanov had strayed from Lenin's brand of Marxism, as Lenin wrote to Gor'kii in 1908: "in the summer and fall of 1904, Bogdanov and I finally parted ways as Bolsheviks" (Lenin 1960–69, 47:142). Whether Bogdanov actually attended the congress in Geneva that September and heard Bergson's paper is unknown; it is only possible to note that Bergson's theory of psycho-physiological parallelism may have played a role in the formation of Bogdanov's ideas on the same as expressed in his work, *Empiriomonism,* first published in 1905.

Bogdanov's condemnation of Heraclitus's worldview as theory without practice expresses the same practical impulse to change the world that is seen in Bely's theurgic impulse to create reality through the word, or in Khlebnikov's desire to unite mankind through universal language. Whereas Bely and Khlebnikov would have been able to accommodate this practical impulse through the Bergsonian philosophy of duration (with its inherent focus on the creation of new forms), Marxist-Leninist thinkers, driven by the need for a rigid ideological definition of dialectical materialism that had to exclude the intuitive in the name of pure objectivity, categorized Bergson as an idealist thinker with nothing to offer the practical, material world. In the Marxist-Leninist viewpoint, then, Bergson, like Heraclitus, was far removed from the realities of class struggle, given what they believed to be his devotion to mystical intuition over reason. Bergson was consequently labeled a bourgeois idealist thinker in the mold of Plato and Kant whose philosophy contradicted the precepts of dialectical materialism by failing to provide an ideological program for social progress.[13]

In his 1909 review of *Creative Evolution,* Plekhanov argues that Bergson's dialectic—the process of ceaseless change and becoming—is ultimately bogus because it lacks the material element of existence (*bytie*), just as Platonism rejects the material world in favor of transcendental Ideas. Although, as has been noted, Plekhanov first admits to both the materialist and dialectical tendencies in Bergson's philosophy put forth in *Creative Evolution,* he soon reverts to a sardonic critique of Bergson while attempting to discredit him on both accounts. For those who consider life to be one giant, creative élan vital, and matter to represent the blunt cessation of this dynamic impulse, Plekhanov offers congratulations and wishes for "further insight, under the direction of Bergson, into the essence of life." For those, however, who are not hoodwinked by the philosophical fashion of the day—idealism—and who assign more value to the material world, Plekhanov points out that Bergsonian thought amounts to no more than a mist of cloudy sophistry.[14]

Despite Plekhanov's denunciation of Bergsonian idealism, his concession earlier in the review to a certain "materialist element" in Bergson's philosophy, along with a general admiration for Bergson as a thinker, was enough to elicit scorn from later Soviet critics like Viacheslav Polonskii (1934):

> Plekhanov's short article on "Bergson's *Creative Evolution*" misleads the reader. . . . This article was written very "liberally" with regard to Bergson. "Bergson," writes Plekhanov, "is a real expert in his treatment of ideas"; in Plekhanov's words, [Bergson] "actually comes close to [expressing] the theory of historical materialism" . . . ; there are "materialist elements" in Bergson's views, but he "does not know how to free himself from . . . *a disposition toward idealism.*" . . . As if the crux of the matter lay in the inability to throw off a "disposition" toward idealism! (197)

Whereas the Marxist Plekhanov was able to take what Polonskii calls a "liberal" view of Bergson in 1909, admitting to some of Bergson's seemed strengths while focusing on his weaknesses, this was no longer possible in the much more ideologically oppressive Stalinist era beginning in the late twenties when a charge of "Bergsonianism" was enough to destroy a career and ultimately a life.[15]

Renato Poggioli (1968) takes note of the "tendency of the Russian critical spirit to translate artistic and cultural facts into religious or political myths" (6), one of the main reasons why, according to Poggioli, "the one current in Russian criticism which was obliged to give sustained and careful attention (however ill-disposed) to the concept of the avant-garde was the radical, sociological or Marxist, school" (7). In this sense, Marxist-Leninists may be compared to Russian religious thinkers in that both groups strove to "translate artistic facts into myth," each claiming that absolute knowledge is already in our possession, and that the artistic form, of necessity, must express what we essentially already know (for example, the icon as a representation of the divine, or the novel as a reflection of socialist realism). The reflection in human consciousness of the one, true, objective reality in its revolutionary development comes to replace the intuition of the one divine Truth.

An important difference between the two groups, however, remains: Russian religious thinkers, while admitting to one divine truth, still grappled with the so-called cursed or eternal questions regarding the nature of the world, how to live a meaningful life, and so forth, whereas for the Marxist-Leninists, no questions remained unanswered on the well-lit path to socialism. In reference to this notion of unanswered questions, Lunacharskii (1970) writes in 1930 that "nothing in them is cursed or eternal; nothing in them is cursed because we should and can answer them, although so far they (these questions) have not found answers. . . . And nothing in them is eternal because we will answer them and move on to new questions" (88). The path to a clearly foreseeable future was not so well-lit for religious thinkers, who still maintained a sense of, and even respect for, the unknown in the struggle to approach the divine. Frank's concept of the incomprehensible (*nepostizhimoe*) in life represents just such an element of the unknown or unforeseen. Writing about the Bergsonian concept of the continuous "flow of time," Frank (1990) states in his work *Nepostizhimoe:*

> Where does this uninterrupted flow come from . . . [and where] is it going? And in particular: what exactly is this incomprehensible "something" that we express in the obviously inadequate image of a "flow of time"? . . . If science and rational knowledge can define and measure movement and generally cognize becoming, then this is accomplished only by virtue of the fact that becoming is viewed as already *become, completed*. . . . The unique essence of becoming as such—the moment of dynamism within, that which is "being made," "being completed"—remains beyond the field of vision. (245)

The idea that life should be lived with the notion of the unforeseeable, a dynamism "beyond the field of vision," is precisely what Bergson has in mind when he writes about the importance of *l'imprévisibilité* and precisely what is missing in the Marxist-Leninist world view. André Joussain comments on this fundamental incompatibility between the two philosophies in his article, "Bergsonisme et marxisme":

> In effect, Bergsonian spiritualism is the negation of dialectical materialism itself; [Bergson's] deism goes against Bolshevik atheism; the freedom that he places in man and in God is in formal opposition to Marxist determinism, according to which the future, *far from being unforeseeable*, on the contrary is rigorously certain, the evolution of societies necessarily resulting in the final triumph of communism which will spread across the land; finally, the idea of history as conceived by the "progressive" Marxists was opposed to *Bergson's notion of the creation of the unforeseeable form*. (54; my emphasis)

The notion of Marxist determinism in which thought is subordinated to a single human goal, "the final triumph" of communism, is similarly pointed to by Jaccard (1985) in his discussion of why Kharms's poetics were incompatible with the ideological 1930s. According to Jaccard, the "ideological word"—static in meaning and oriented toward a "final triumph" of the "good"—destroyed the subject's ability to investigate meaning in the world by positing one foreseeable goal common to all (273). Along the same lines,

N. Georgopoulos (1979) states in his study of Kazantzakis, Bergson, and Lenin that, despite an early belief in communist goals, Kazantzakis ultimately rejects the "Russian experiment" as a failure because it didn't allow for the existence of the unforeseeable: "Reverting to Bergson's notion of the invisible vital impulse, [Kazantzakis] pointed out that moral, intellectual, [and] artistic . . . changes are the results of invisible forces—forces too fluid and anonymous to become slogans for the masses" (42). As opposed to the deterministic Marxist-Leninist certainty in what the future holds, Bergson argues against what he considers to be the Platonic presupposition of absolute truth: "Plato was the first to set up the theory that to know the real consists in finding its Idea, that is to say, in forcing it into a pre-existing frame already at our disposal—as if we implicitly possessed universal knowledge. . . . Nowhere is the inadequacy of this method so obvious as in theories of life" (*CE* 48–49). On the contrary, life, according to Bergson, is a creative evolution, and as such "transcends finality, if we understand by finality the realization of an idea conceived or conceivable in advance" (*CE* 223–24). For Bergson, the "unforeseeable" is the essence of duration, the creative process of ceaseless becoming, the "continual elaboration of the absolutely new." To foresee the future would mean to fragment this fluid process of interpenetrating moments, to deny duration by isolating the past from the present, the present from the future; in short, to foresee the future would mean to conceive of life in terms of the intellect alone, which is incapable of "sympathizing" with the creative nature of reality:

> To speak of an end is to think of a pre-existing model which has only to be realized. It is to suppose, therefore, that all is given, and that the future can be read in the present. It is to believe that life, in its movement and in its entirety, goes to work like our intellect, which is only a motionless and fragmentary view of life, and which naturally takes its stand outside of time. . . . Life, on the contrary, progresses and *endures* in time. (*CE* 51)

Furthermore:

> The intellect lets what is *new* in each moment of history escape. It does not admit the unforeseeable. It rejects all creation. That definite antecedents bring forth a definite consequent, calculable as a function of them, is what satisfies our intellect. . . . But that each instant is a fresh endowment, that the new is ever upspringing, . . . could never have been foreseen. . . . All this we can feel within ourselves and also divine, by sympathy, outside ourselves, but we cannot think it, in the strict sense of the word. (*CE* 163–64)

Bergson employs the metaphor of an artist creating a portrait to illustrate what he means by the unforeseeability of the newly created form:

> The painter is before his canvas, the colors are on the palette, the model is sitting—all this we see, and also we know the painter's style: do we foresee what

> will appear on the canvas? We possess the elements of the problem; we know in an abstract way, how it will be solved, for the portrait will surely resemble the model. . . . But the concrete solution brings with it that unforeseeable nothing which is everything in a work of art. And it is this nothing that takes time. Nought as matter, it creates itself as form.[16] The sprouting and flowering of this form are stretched out on an unshrinkable duration, which is one with their essence. So of the works of nature. Their novelty arises from an internal impetus which . . . makes succession, or *continuity of interpenetration* in time, irreducible to a mere instantaneous juxtaposition in space. This is why the idea of reading in a present state of the material universe the future of living forms, and of unfolding now their history yet to come, involves a veritable absurdity. (*CE* 340–41)

As long as the human mind lasts, according to Bergson, so will the illusion that "even now, unrollable, . . . the future is there, rolled up, already painted on the canvas." It is therefore the artist's duty to preserve the element of the unforeseeable in the artistic act so that true creativity—and consequently, true freedom—may also be preserved.[17]

Thus, duration, creativity, and freedom are all interconnected in Bergson's metaphysics. By conceiving of the present as only a precursor to the foreseeable glorious future of a communist utopia, Marxism-Leninism destroys Bergsonian *imprévisibilité* and along with it the creative impulse in Russian modernism; if all is foreseeable, already painted on the canvas, then the free artistic act becomes impossible, as well as the free act in general, which Bergson considers an outgrowth of the expression of our true, whole selves: "But if our action be one that involves the whole of our person and is truly ours, it could not have been foreseen, even though its antecedents explain it when once it has been accomplished" (*CE* 47). When Hippius laments the end of Bergsonian *imprévisibilité,* she is mourning the loss both of artistic and personal freedom in an era marked only by "calculation—according to Lenin."

Conclusion

> The fundamental idea of the artist—the genuine artist, of course—is formed in what Bergson would call an "open" society.
> —Nadezhda Mandel'shtam

WHILE TAKING NOTES on Bergson's *Creative Evolution,* V. A. Volkovich (1912) copied out almost word for word the following two sentences from the first Russian translation of Bergson's most popular work: "The *theory of knowledge* is inseparable from the *theory of life.* They must unite so that each may move the other forward" (2). Volkovich's personal notation helps to elucidate the nature of the Russian attraction to Bergson, who believed philosophy (and art as its highest form) serves not as a static system of knowledge but as an "active principle" guiding one's participation in existence. Some Russian modernists, however, including Mandel'shtam and Khlebnikov, embraced the notion of "system" (active rather than static) as they sought a type of intellectual framework through which revelation might be achieved. Thus, for example, Mandel'shtam praises Bergson's "system of phenomena" as a model for a system of language based on the Hellenistic Russian "word," which continually astonishes the poet with its organicity and dynamism.

Bergson's compatibility with Russian thought, therefore, owes much to what Zenkovskii calls the tradition of Orthodox ontologism in Russia, whereby the theory of knowledge is considered valuable only when serving as part of our total activity or "being" in the world. Thus the intertwining in Russian culture of metaphysics, aesthetics, religion and science into an organic Whole (expressed most clearly perhaps in Solov'ev's conception of "all-unity"), which crystallizes into the Russian concern with the primary link between art and life, art serving both as a way of knowing and transforming reality (a concern once again found in Solov'ev, who stresses the theurgic role of art). As one contemporary critic of the avant-garde observes: "The overcoming of the gap between art and life is often defined as the fundamental task of the avant-garde, and for the Russian avant-garde this task proved especially compelling" (Romanovskaia 1994, 12). While the link between art and life in the Russian literary consciousness certainly does not begin with modernism (one need only recall, among many other examples, Dostoevsky's belief that "beauty will save the world"), such a link took on a greater urgency in the early twentieth century as new scientific discoveries—such as those of quantum mechanics—exploded traditional notions of time, space, and movement, and Russian modernists scrambled for new artistic ways of apprehending and taking part in the rapidly changing, modern world.

Contrasting the theurgic art of Solov'ev and the Symbolists on the one hand, and Malevich on the other, Boris Grois (1992) observes that the primary goal of the former was the artistic revelation of a hidden, ideal order of both cosmos and society (*sofiinost'* and *sobornost'*), while Malevich's *Black Square* symbolized "nonbeing" or the "absolute chaos" from which all things stem (45). Although the means for the theurgic transformation of the world may differ, the end result is the same; if the Symbolists sought to awaken in the reader the capacity to perceive an ideal order of cosmos and society (and thus to be active participants in this divine order), Malevich's *Black Square* proclaimed the nonbeing of conventional forms while trumpeting a new realism based on the ideal Suprematist form. In both cases an ideal order is sought, an absolute, through which one may feel oneself an active participant in the divine, creative process of existence. (Grois goes on to state that the theurgic goal of the Russian avant-garde was consistent with Marx's dictum that "philosophy must advance from an explanation of the world to its transformation" [46], and thus that socialist realism was simply the active "reanimation" of the more contemplative ideal of the avant-garde.)

As noted earlier, the parallels between Solov'ev's and Bergson's metaphysics are numerous, especially in terms of their common view of the role of artistic intuition in "lowering the veil" from reality. Solov'ev equates the artistic act with free theurgy (*svobodnaia teurgiia*), art serving as the means by which to intuit the divine essence of reality—"the subject of great art is man's realization of the divine source in all of nature's empirical reality"—and through the intuition of reality to transform it (by establishing inner, organic connections between the realms of God, man, and nature): "The full task of art, as free theurgy, consists . . . in the re-creation of existing reality."[1] Solov'ev's view of the theurgic nature of art is echoed by both Losskii and Frank and serves as a common backdrop for the Russian modernist attempt to dissolve the boundary between art and life. Aside from offering a similar view of the interrelationship between art and life, Bergson appealed to modernists as a secular, international figure whose writings on such topics as time, space, and movement—at a historical threshold when the conventional notions of such were being radically transformed—seemed to herald a new era in artistic perception and expression.

The attempt to unify word and world helped to integrate the "diverse tendencies and trends" of Russian modernism. Because this attempt was rooted in the intuitive apprehension of "the word," or for Malevich, the form (respective manifestations of the patristic intuition of Logos and the icon), Russian modernists could find in the Bergsonian conception of artistic intuition (and in Solov'ev's earlier pronouncements on artistic theurgy) a compatible philosophical grounding for their own aesthetics/metaphysics. Through intuition and a dedication to theurgy, Russian modernists sought to become creators of the wor[l]d. In one of her notebooks, Hippius criticizes decadent literature because "this literature has no relationship to the movement of life and thought, nor is life related to it"; Bely writes in "The Magic of Words": "In the sound is reconstructed a new world, within which I feel myself to be the creator of reality" (1994b, 131–32); Mandel'shtam relishes being "master of his own house," thanks to the Hellenistic nature of the word that "humaniz[es] and warm[s] . . . the surrounding world" (Harris 1979, 127); Khlebnikov writes in "Artists of the World!": "Let one written language . . . unify the human race" (1987, 621); Malevich states in his essay, "To the New Image": "And we declare our time to be the square of our age on which we shall spread out our forms" (1978, 51); and Kharms (1988) comments in a 1933 letter on the meaning of art in his life: "I am the creator of the world, and this is the most important thing about me" (482–83). Russian modernists who considered art as the means for self-realization and participation in existence found a model not only in Solov'ev's statements on free theurgy, but also could look to the metaphysics of Bergson, who believed that through philosophy, the artistic intuition of duration, "we shall feel we are participating, creators of ourselves, in the great work of creation which is the origin of all things, and which goes on before our eyes."

Whether espousing a Symbolist, post-Symbolist, or absurdist metaphysics, Russian modernists embraced a Bergsonian type of intuition as the means by which to "bridge the Kantian gap" between scientific phenomena and spiritual noumena, or between static appearance and an object's dynamic "logical essence."[2] By stressing the sanctity of *imprévisibilité,* or the unforeseeable (*nepostizhimoe*) element in life, as well as offering a means—intellectual intuition—of penetrating to the hidden essence of things, Bergson presented just the quasi-paradoxical philosophical mix inherent to Russian thought, wherein the acceptance of that which cannot be known through intellect coexists with the intellectual striving for absolute knowledge of the neo-Platonic "thing-in-itself."[3] For Bergson and Russian modernists alike, philosophy was valuable only insofar as it represented what Bergson called the "art of living" (*CM* 124), creativity serving first as the key to the intuitive apprehension of life's divine (and therefore logical, according to Solov'ev) essence, and ultimately as the means for taking part in the divine, creative flux of reality,[4] the "great work of creation." Bergson's notions of time and consciousness as a qualitative, immeasurable flow of ceaseless change (duration), intuition as the means by which to penetrate this flow, and the knowability of the logical essence of the "thing-in-itself" were all ideas embraced by Russian modernists as well in their self-appointed role as creators of, and participators in, the essence of reality.

With the collapse of the Soviet Union, Russia again finds itself in transition, much as it was earlier in the twentieth century in the vortex of scientific, cultural, and political revolutions. Like some of their modernist predecessors Russian thinkers of the 1990s are also discussing Bergsonian thought in their attempt to create a new reality after seventy years of communist rule, although now the interest in Bergson has broader implications. Whereas Bergson's notion of creative evolution was especially appealing to modernists interested in preserving creative freedom and discovering new ways of artistic expression and growth, the same notion now is taking on a more sociological tenor as contemporary Russians grapple with the monumental task of overseeing the evolution of a more open and free post-totalitarian society. As a result, Russian interest in Bergsonian philosophy today is focused on Bergson's concept of the "open" versus "closed" society as expressed in his last major work, *Les deux sources de la morale et de la religion* (*Dva istochnika morali i religii*), originally published in 1932 and translated for the first time into Russian in 1994.[5]

According to Bergson, true, free existence is possible only in a creatively evolving, open society, characterized by the "dynamic" morality of love for humanity and God (in this, his last major work, Bergson (1932) finally identifies the "creative energy" of "divine spirituality" as the source of the dynamic élan vital (275), an acknowledgment that would have made Losskii and Frank much more comfortable with the notion of Bergsonian duration). The closed society, on the other hand, marked by a godless, "static" morality, is incapable of creative evolution given its dedication to strict discipline and the authoritarian preservation of stability.[6] In his commentary to the 1994 Russian translation of *Les deux sources de la morale et de la religion,* A. B. Gofman finds Bergson's "closed/open" distinction especially apt when considering Russia's current transition from a "closed" totalitarian society and mind-set to a more "open" democratic future:

> The questions and answers, the problems and solutions put forth by Bergson . . . are extraordinarily important today for the post-totalitarian societies that have arisen on the territory of the former Soviet Union. [These societies] were formed over the course of many years as parts of a [larger] closed society, founded on the closed morality of class struggle . . . and on the static religion incarnated in communist ideology. . . . Inherent in this regime [of the closed society] were the classic anti-democratic traits of which Bergson writes: authoritarianism, hierarchy, immobility.
>
> Today, Russia and other post-totalitarian societies are going through radical social transformations. These countries have inscribed on their flags the slogans of democracy, freedom, and human rights. In order to carry out these slogans, however, they still need to travel a long and difficult path, for, after

all, they have inherited societies and peoples with a closed, "defensive" consciousness. As long as this consciousness does not become more open, totalitarianism in its diverse manifestations will once more come to rule the land. (Bergson 1994, 370–71)

Another thinker who is enjoying renewed attention in Russia today is Mikhail Bakhtin. It is interesting to compare Bergson's concept of *l'obligation morale* (as expressed in his *Les deux sources*) with the Bakhtinian concept of responsibility (*otvetstvennost'*), especially since the issue of personal responsibility is becoming more prominent in the more open Russian society. For both Bakhtin and Bergson, the notion of responsibility or obligation serves as the unifying factor of self and humanity. Bakhtin writes in 1919: "What could possibly guarantee the inner link between the elements of a person? Only the unity of responsibility."[7] Bergson (1932) similarly states: "The sense of obligation that we imagine to be a bond between men first must bind each of us to ourselves" (8). Furthermore, the burden of responsibility for both thinkers lies in the relationship of artist to life; both Bakhtin and Bergson write of the individual's responsibility to combine word and world, a task considered by Russian modernists to be a moral imperative. Thus Bakhtin notes in the aforementioned article: "I must answer with my life for that which I have experienced and understood in art so that everything experienced and understood does not remain inactive in it" (3), and Bergson comments in *Les deux sources* on one's obligation to "translate" art into life: "It is we . . . who are truly obliged to bring together the feeling created by the artist with that which resembles it most in life" (1932, 36–37). It would seem that the deep-rooted concern in Russian thought with the link between art and life—endowed with the present-day call for greater personal responsibility demanded by a more open society—will continue to guide Russian thinkers in their attempt to create a new conception of self (*lichnost'*) as artist and member of humanity.

It is perhaps not surprising that the first Russian translation of Bergson's *Les deux sources de la morale et de la religion* has appeared on the heels of new editions of the works of Solov'ev, Losskii, Frank, Shestov, Florenskii, and other Russian religious thinkers of the early twentieth century. Apparently Solov'ev and Bergson—whose kindred philosophies found fertile ground in Russian modernism—are both still relevant sources for today's Russian thinkers who once again are focusing on how to create, and participate freely in, a new social, political, and artistic landscape with its concomitant new notions of responsibility to oneself and to others. The recent renaissance of Russian religious thought, along with the renewed interest in Bergsonian philosophy, suggests that a mixture of notions shared more or less by each—intuitivism, Neoplatonism, artistic theurgy, and love of humanity—is helping to fuel Russia's attempt in the postcommunist era to "creatively evolve" into a more open society wherein the idea of the "true artist," according to Nadezhda Mandel'shtam, may once again be conceived and expressed.

Notes

PREFACE

1. Also of interest are Curtis (1976) and two dissertations: Choate (1987) and Swoboda (1992).

2. Lehan (1992), 323. Unfortunately, Lehan does not mention Russia in his essay.

3. See, for example, Kristeva's 1966 essay, "Word, Dialogue, and Novel" (in Moi 1986) and Barthes's 1971 essay, "From Work to Text" (Barthes 1977).

4. Clayton and Rothstein (1991), 3. As noted by Clayton and Rothstein, some see intertextuality as a broadening of the notion of influence, while others consider it a new concept that should replace the latter.

5. Huyssen (1986) considers the "historical avant-garde" (examples of which being Russian Constructivism and Futurism) to have emerged from early or "high" modernism in the form of an "attack on aestheticist notions of the self-sufficiency of high culture." According to Huyssen, once Stalinism liquidated the historical avant-garde, "its remnants were later retrospectively absorbed by modernist high culture even to the extent that 'modernism' and 'avant-garde' became synonymous terms in the critical discourse" (vii–viii).

6. Gibian and Tjalsma (1976), 11. Bely (1908) reaches a similar conclusion (although writing very early in the modernist period): "By 'modernism' is understood a variety of literary schools that have nothing in common with each other. . . . Once again, modernism turns out to be fragmented into a multitude of ideological tendencies" (38–39).

INTRODUCTION

1. In a description of her life in Paris with Merezhkovskii from 1906 to 1908, Hippius (1951) notes that Bergson's "brilliant" lectures were "always overcrowded" (167).

2. Remarking upon the philosophical interests of students at Moscow University before the beginning of World War I, Pasternak (1970) recalls that "the majority were carried away by Bergson" (20).

3. See Gunter's (1986) invaluable bibliography of Bergson's works for a comprehensive listing of translations. Bergson's *Collected Works* were published in Russia between 1913 and 1914 (see Selected Bibliography).

4. Bergsonian thought is often referred to as "revolutionary." Two holders of such a view (from each end of the twentieth century) include James (1928), 273, and Rousseau (1992), 55.

5. This parallel is noted by Grogin (1988), 8–12.

6. Gourmont, in a review of French literature for *Apollon* in 1911, writes the following about Bergson's popularity: "Mr. Bergson, that new Messiah of free will who has revealed a bit of mystical ash at the bottom of the crucible of science, Bergson has given a new spiritualism to those people suffering from a loss of faith and is their true savior" (1911, 70).

7. "Le Parallélisme Psycho-Physique," in Bergson (1972), 494.

8. See Gruson (1960), 171–90. In addition, Scharfstein (1943) notes that "when Bergson began to write, the regular way of formulating a thesis was to ask how Kant had approached it and how Kant's theory might be surpassed" (30).

9. Copleston (1946–53) points out quite rightly that the term "metaphysics" is not always used by Kant in exactly the same way, given that he distinguishes between metaphysics as natural disposition and metaphysics as science. Copleston writes of this distinction in Kant's lexicon:

> The mind has a natural tendency to raise such problems as God and immortality; and though we should try to understand why this is the case, Kant neither wishes to eradicate the tendency nor believes that it is possible to do so, even if it were desirable. Metaphysics as a natural disposition is actual, and therefore it is obviously possible. But metaphysics as a science, if we mean by this a scientific knowledge of supersensible beings, has never, according to Kant, been a reality. (6:216)

Bergson, who defines metaphysics as "the science which claims to dispense with symbols" (*IM* 162), attacks Kant's *Critique of Pure Reason* for resting upon *"the postulate that our thought is incapable of anything but Platonizing,* that is, of pouring the whole of possible experience into pre-existing molds" (*IM* 197, emphasis in original). By breaking free of these molds, one can discover new modes of thought, namely intuition, by which the material, intellectual knowledge of science works together with metaphysical reflection, just as "the visible movements in the clock [depend on] the tension of the spring" (*IM* 200).

10. The distinction between *rassudok* and *razum* is roughly equivalent to that between the German *Vernunft* and *Verstand.*

11. Nekrasov comments in *O znachenii form russkogo glagola* on the ontological difference between an imperfective action that takes place in duration (outside of spatialized, mathematical time) and a perfective one governed by the laws of mathematical time: "The duration of a manifestation is

the strength, heart and life of the action itself. An action manifested in terms of mathematical time is abstract and formal, whereas an action manifested in terms of duration (energy) is full of life" (as quoted in Vinogradov 1986, 442). It is also interesting to compare Bergson's definition of duration with Tynianov's (1929) description of the "unceasing dynamism" (*nepreryvnaia dinamika*) of the literary system, the concept of which is "constantly changing, complex, evolving" (15–16).

12. Chaadaev (1991), 1:94 and 99 (Lettre Première).

13. Ibid., 1:127 (Lettre Troisième).

14. In his Fifth Philosophical Letter, Chaadaev (1991) criticizes Kant for his "deceitful teaching about the *autonomy* of human intellect, about a type of imperative law located within our intellect itself which gives it the ability, by virtue of its own impulse, to raise to the fullness of perfection that which is intelligible to it" (1:388).

15. Bakunin, "Die Reaction in Deutschland," trans. Zeldin, in Edie, Scanlan, and Zeldin (1965), 1:406. Original German in Ruge (1842).

16. Belinskii, "Ideia iskusstva," in Belinskii (1953–59), 4:585 (emphasis in original). See Terras (1974), especially 164–65, for more on Belinskii and intuition.

17. As noted by Terras (1974), see Belinskii (1953–59), 2:160; 3:353, 413–14, 493–94; 4:143, 237–38; 6:13, 22, 107.

18. Kireevskii, "O neobkhodimosti i vozmozhnosti novykh nachal dlia filosofii," in Kireevskii (1861), 2:296.

19. Khomiakov, "Neskol'ko slov Pravoslavnogo Khristianina o zapadnykh veroispovedaniiakh," in Khomiakov (1900), 2:62. Russian Symbolists would come to define art in similar terms; for example, Hippius (1970) writes in 1904: "The task of art is to give people the bliss of faith in the unseen, as if it were the seen" (252).

20. Khomiakov, "O sovremennykh iavleniiakh v oblasti filosofii," in Khomiakov (1900), 1:337.

21. Gratieux (1939), 263. Berdiaev (1912) states that Bergsonian Pragmatism was already apparent in Khomiakov's Slavophile philosophy, but "pragmatic philosophy differs from Slavophilism in its ignorance of positive religious experience and of the Logos . . . in the practical activity of life" (126).

22. Losev, "V poiskakh smysla," in Losev (1990b), 16. Zinaida Hippius (1957) also points to the "idea of creation" which links Solov'ev's "idea of ascent" with Bergson's notion of the "élan vital," both of which depend on the animation (*ozhivlenie*) of matter (4–5).

23. Caryl Emerson, AAASS Conference, Philadelphia, 1994.

24. Solov'ev (1966), 316. Solov'ev often equates "intellectual intuition" with what he calls "imagination" (*voobrazhenie*), through which the essence or "ideal image" (*ideal'nyi obraz*) of an object is apprehended.

25. Solov'ev (1994), 113. In addition, according to Solov'ev, one of the ways in which to conceive of the "divine Word" (*bozhestvennyi Logos*) is as an inner force whereby "the human soul strives to find its own true content" (1994, 178).

26. Santayana (1957) characterizes Bergson as "instinctively a mystic" (62), and Berdiaev (1908) expresses a similar view: "In France there is now a talented philosopher, Bergson, a fighter against intellectualism who puts forth a philosophy of action, and with his philosophy is throwing the doors open to mysticism and religion" (81).

27. It has been suggested that Bergson's secular concepts of intuition and the creative flow of life—duration—as put forth in his work *Creative Evolution* were merely early manifestations of a fundamentally religious outlook. One Soviet scholar, critical of the notion of "intuitivism" in general, comments that "if Bergson avoids using the term 'God' in his book, *Creative Evolution* (1907), then in his work, *Two Sources of Morality and Religion* (1932), the link between a 'creative impulse' and 'divine creation'—as well as between intuition and knowledge of the divine—becomes perfectly clear" (Chueva 1963, 121).

28. Solov'ev's conception of history as the gradual realization of the ideal of "all-unity" belonged more to the suspect Hegelian camp of teleological historical progress.

29. Douglass (1983) notes:

> Popularizations of [Bergson's] philosophy exaggerated his aversion to science, and although many who attacked him came later to see they had misunderstood his fundamental direction, the popular image prevailed: Bergson is the opponent of anything *stable* or *precise*, the proponent of the irrational *élan vital* and the inarticulable melange of the *duree reelle* [*sic*]. (235)

30. It is worth mentioning that the term "intellectual intuition" (*intellektuelle Anschauung*) was originally put forth by Kant as a faculty that man does not possess due to the impossibility of approaching the metaphenomenal world ("things-in-themselves") by means of the intellect (the cognitive function of the categories).

31. Prince Vladimir Odoevskii is often singled out as an anticipator of Bergsonian intuition in Russia because of his emphasis on instinct over intellect as the prime means of uncovering the divine truths of the universe. See, for example, Gennadii (1981): "Long before Bergson, Odoevskii taught of the cognitive value of intuition, which he called an 'instinctual force'" (208).

32. Even the idea of a Nietzschean "superman," however, is rejected by Solov'ev (1966) as redundant of man's inherent striving toward deification: "No new superhuman form of the organism has arisen through history or is

needed because the human form can perfect itself limitlessly both inside and out, *remaining all the while only itself*: it is capable of being a form of perfect all-unity, or divinity" ("Ideia sverkhcheloveka," 9:270).

33. As quoted by Rosenthal (1986), 27.

34. See, for example, Nietzsche (1967), 33, 38, 43, 45, and (1989), 230.

35. See, for example, Nietzsche (1979), 7, 20–21, 29–30, 49.

36. For more on the comparison of Bergson and Nietzsche, see Schwartz (1985), especially 36–38 and 45–48.

CHAPTER ONE

The epigraph is an excerpt from a speech given by Paul Valéry at the January 1941 meeting of the French Academy, dedicated to the memory of Bergson, who had passed away earlier that month. The Russian translation of the speech is printed in Bergson (1992), 1:49.

1. Other religious philosophers, such as Shestov (*Na vesakh Iova*) and Berdiaev (*Smysl tvorchestva*), comment on Bergson briefly in various passages, but their remarks do not represent as coherent a critique of Bergsonian philosophy as do those of Losskii and Frank.

2. Solov'ev, "Filosofskie nachala tsel'nogo znaniia," in Solov'ev (1988), 2:231.

3. Bergson, "Introduction à la métaphysique," 29; emphasis in original.

4. As stated above, Bergson's definition of duration is only suggestive of *sobornost'*, which in essence is a strictly theological concept referring specifically to the Orthodox Church as the mystical body of Christ.

5. Levitskii (1981) points out that during the time Losskii was constructing his doctrine of intuitivism in Russia, "in France Henri Bergson developed his doctrine of intuition as the basic method of cognition. . . . The significance of Losskii's theory of intuitivism can be properly understood only in the context of [such] Western epistemological investigation" (80).

6. Originally published in *Voprosy filosofii i psikhologii* in 1913, "Nedostatki gnoseologii Bergsona i vliianie ikh na ego metafiziky" was added a year later as the last chapter to Losskii's "Intuitivnaia filosofiia Bergsona." About his work on Bergson, Losskii (1968) writes: "Having received an invitation to give several public lectures in Moscow, I elucidated the essence of Bergsonian philosophy and how it differs from my own views. I printed these lectures in the pamphlet, 'The Intuitive Philosophy of Bergson' (publishing house 'Put,' Moscow 1913)" (128).

7. See Kohanski (1936) for a more complete discussion of Losskii's epistemology. Bergson also recognized the inseparability of epistemology and ontology, writing in his introduction to *Creative Evolution:* "It is necessary that these two inquiries, theory of knowledge and theory of life, should

join each other, and, by a circular process, push each other on unceasingly" (*CE* xiii).

8. In his chapter "Nedostatki gnoseologii Bergsona" from the same work, Losskii (1913) explains more fully that "*intellect is* nothing other than a *form of intuition:* it is the *ability to contemplate ideas* (in the Platonic sense), it is a vision of the timeless principles that lie at the base of the temporal world" (110–11).

9. Losskii's (1968) more detailed criticism of Bergson is as follows: "But I rejected, of course, Bergson's anti-Platonism, his epistemological dualism, his rationalism" (128).

10. In his review of Losskii's *Intuitivnaia filosofiia Bergsona,* Askol'dov (1914) comments that Losskii's criticism of Bergson is for the most part unfounded, given that Bergson's main focus is not on epistemology at all. After praising Losskii's basic exposition of Bergson's philosophy, Askol'dov goes on to state:

> We find Losskii's criticism of Bergson, put forth in the last chapter of his book, to be less successful. It is entirely unfair to reproach Bergson for mixing up epistemological investigation with that of psychology and physiology. . . . The logical and generally rational structure of knowledge is for the moment of no interest to Bergson; all his attention is directed towards the problem of perception, the theory of memory, matter and biological evolution. (51)

11. Frank reviewed Bergson's *La Perception du changement* (Vospriiatie izmenchivosti) and *Le paralogisme psychophysiologique* (Psikhofiziologicheskii paralogizm) in 1913 (see Selected Bibliography). Frank also wrote a review of Bergson's talk, "L'Intuition philosophique," which appeared in the *Revue de Métaphysique et de Morale* in 1911. Frank's review, entitled "O filosofskoi intuitsii," appeared in the journal *Russkaia mysl'* in 1912. In addition, Bergson's name comes up frequently in Frank's major writings, including *Filosofiia i zhizn'* (1910), *Predmet znaniia* (1915), and *Dusha cheloveka* (1917). Several critics, including Losskii, have noted Frank's interest in Bergsonian thought. See, for example, Losskii (1919): "On the basis of intuitivism a rapprochement is possible between such heterogeneous teachings as, for example . . . Hegelianism on the one hand, and Bergsonism on the other. S. L. Frank succeeded in bringing about such a rapprochement" (238); Radlov (1991): "These days many people are carried away by Bergson's philosophy; many of Bergson's ideas, for example, that of time, etc., have been taken up by Russian thinkers like S. L. Frank" (124); Lapshin (1922): "It is completely natural that Frank would hold in particularly high esteem the representatives of mysticism: . . . Bergson, Vl. Solov'ev, and Losskii are especially dear to his heart" (141); Florovskii, foreword to Frank (1965): "Frank is close to the famous aphorism of Bergson: *La vie déborde la raison*" (xiii); Curtis (1986): "Frank was greatly influenced by Nicolas of

Cusa and Bergson" (349); Boobbyer (1995): "[Frank] . . . attempt[ed] to grasp the moment of Bergsonian dynamism in the world" (215).

12. Chueva (1963) notes that Frank seeks to create a union between science and religion, "with priority given to the latter" (49). Similarly, it could be said of Bergson that he seeks to create a union of intellect and intuition while maintaining the priority of the latter.

13. Frank (1939), 209, 167; emphasis in original. Although *Nepostizhimoe* is a much more mature work than others of Frank here discussed, his concepts of monodualism, and, as will be seen later, those of duration and the "unforeseeable," do not represent new aspects of his philosophy, but rather elaborate upon certain concepts of a worldview already well established in earlier articles such as "Pragmatizm, kak filosofskoe uchenie" (1910) and "Krizis sovremennoi filosofii" (1916).

14. As noted earlier, Losskii criticizes Bergson for what he considers to be the latter's "epistemological dualism," a charge Losskii (1919) also levels at Frank, whom he sees as similarly espousing two different kinds of knowledge, "thought-knowledge" and "life-knowledge" (236). However, Losskii (1919) admits that, to his credit, Frank values the objectivity of logical thought more than does Bergson:

> This teaching . . . of the necessity of two types of knowledge contains a number of vague and inconsistent elements. What first comes to mind is that logical knowledge for S. L. Frank, as for Bergson, is a subjective knowledge, constructed only in the mind of the cognizing individual. However, S. L. Frank does not denigrate the value of logical knowledge to such a degree [as does Bergson]. (239)

In November 1939, P. B. Struve wrote to Frank: "You are much more logical . . . than Bergson [*sic*]" (quoted in Zenkovskii 1954, 62).

15. Frank (1913) states that "Bergson is one of those philosophical writers, *all* of whose works deserve attention and contain fresh and impressive ideas. In saying this we do not at all wish to number ourselves among that enthusiastically complimentary chorus which now proclaims Bergson to be the exclusive genius and leader of present-day thought" (49).

CHAPTER TWO

1. Bely, "Emblematika smysla," in Bely (1969), 87.

2. Ibid., 88, 95.

3. Evelyn Bristol (1983) has observed that while the French poets emphasized verbal suggestiveness, Russian Symbolists were more concerned with religious discovery, or truth (69).

4. Blok (1980–83) outlines the artist's obligation to listen to the music of the "world orchestra" and then, in the spirit of revolution, to transform life: "The task of the artist, the *duty* of the artist . . . is to listen to the music

which thunders in the 'air torn by the wind.' What is the plan? *To remake everything.* To create everything anew" ("Intelligentsiia i revoliutsiia," 4:231–32). Blok refers to Bergson only once in his collected works. In a 1908 journal entry on Merezhkovsky's essay "Intelligentsia and the People," Blok suggests that both groups struggle with the question of faith, and he then goes on to note the "Bergsonian" opposition of artistic intuition and intellect within himself (Blok 1971, 6:160).

5. See Rosenthal (1986, 1991, 1994), Clowes (1988), Sarychev (1991), Asmus (1937), Vengerov (1972), and West (1970) for discussion of Nietzschean influence on Russian Symbolists.

6. Terras (1991) notes:

> Symbolism as a whole took the romantic position of claiming intuitive cognitive power for art in general and for poetry in particular. The subject and presumed range of cognition vary greatly from author to author. Vladimir Solovyov and his followers spoke of mystical entities like the World Soul and the Eternal Feminine (*das Ewig-Weibliche*). Merezhkovsky and Hippius thought of themselves as founders of a new church. Bely and Ivanov saw their intuitions as a vehicle of spiritual regeneration and the birth of a higher humanity. (393)

In each case, the Bergsonian intuition of duration could be seen as the essence of the Symbolist pursuit.

7. Anton Kovač (1976) has pointed out that the satirical thrust of Bely's *Second Symphony* is directed against "the naive and simplistic interpretations of the works and ideas of [Bely's] favorite authors: Kant, Schopenhauer, . . . Nietzsche," but Kovač goes on to note that despite such satire, "the marked degree of cynicism in the symphony speaks also of the first germs of the author's own doubts" about these thinkers (128, 130).

8. Ada Steinberg (1982) rightly points out that Verlaine's slogan was not discovered by the Symbolists but was rather an "echo of the romantic's approach to art," revived and deepened in their poetics (18).

9. It is interesting to recall Belinskii's (1953–59, 12:390) distinction in "Ideia iskusstva" between the two contradictory worlds of "organism" and "mechanism," the former ceaselessly in motion, free, creative, "loud and sonorous" (*shumnyi i zvuchnyi*), while the latter represents a static realm of the enslaved, lifeless, "mute and silent" (*nemoi i bezglasnyi*).

10. Blok (1980–83), 6:37; emphasis in original. In a description of his creative impulses around the turn of the century, Bely remarks that music was much more important to him than was writing: "I felt more like a composer than a poet, and as a result, music long hid from me the writer's path." Once having chosen to pursue writing as a career, however, Bely further notes that he "became more of a composer of language . . . than a writer in the usual sense of the word" ("O sebe kak pisatele," in Lesnevskii and Mikhailov 1988, 19–20).

11. Although Bergson gained widespread popularity in Russia somewhat later than did Schopenhauer, his notion of the musical nature of duration as put forth in *Time and Free Will* and elsewhere may still have held value for Russian modernists like Bely. Furthermore, it is often problematic when considering the philosophical influences on Russian Symbolism to distinguish between Bergson's "musical" duration and Nietzsche's idea of the spirit of music, the Dionysian musical stream of life that sweeps everything up in its tumultuous path. It does seem to be true that Nietzsche's concept of music tends to emphasize the elemental life force, a chaotic stream flowing beneath serene Apollonian pools, whereas Bergson uses musical metaphors to describe his notion of time (duration ultimately representative of life/reality). For an interesting discussion of the connection between Bergson and the phenomenology of music, see Alexander Haardt, "Aleksej Losev and the Phenomenology of Music," in Scanlan (1994), esp. 200–203. I am grateful to James Scanlan for bringing this essay to my attention.

12. In "A. I. Chekhov," Bely praises the "music" of Chekhov's art, which results precisely from Chekhov's successful synthesis of the realistic image and the symbol, the phenomenal and noumenal (1994a, 358). It is also worth noting that a drama critic in 1914 drew a parallel between Chekhov and Bergson as kindred spirits of antideterminism: "[Chekhov's] drama stands with the philosophy of Bergson, with the whole movement of the scattered Art Theatres of Europe, as a revolt against the determinate philosophy that weakened even the drama of Ibsen, and the promise of as noble a dramatic rhythm as the world has known" ("Storm Jameson on Chekhov as Anti-Determinist," in Emeljanow 1981, 121).

13. Briusov (1916) similarly equates music with "pure movement, pure time" (73), and Mandel'shtam's *Shum vremeni* (1922–23) speaks to the same association of music and time (although, as will be seen, for Mandel'shtam the noise of time is fundamentally representative of the timeless harmony of an organic, verbal system).

14. Introduction to "The Forms of Art" in Keys and Elsworth (1986), 156.

15. Bely's *Second Symphony* (*2-ia dramaticheskaia*) was the first of four Symphonies to be published, and throughout his life Bely considered it one of his best works (Bugaeva and Petrovskii 1937, 578). His other Symphonies include the *Severnaia simfoniia* (*1-ia geroicheskaia*) (1904); *Vozvrat. III simfoniia* (1905); and *Kubok metelei* (1908).

16. Kšicova (1989), 67. I am indebted to Ondrej Tucek for his help in translating this article. Although I share Kšicová's view that there seem to be certain Bergsonian elements in Bely's *Second Symphony,* it should be noted once again that there is no evidence of a direct Bergsonian influence on Bely at this time.

17. I agree with Kšicová's general premise here, although instead of the word "sequence" (*sledu*) I would substitute "interpenetration" in order to emphasize the nonlinear, noncausal nature of Bergsonian duration.

18. Bely (1991), 100–101. All quotations from Bely's *Second Symphony* are taken from this edition and will be indicated by page number only.

19. In this early work of Bely's, Musatov is, in a sense, defeated by time, fleeing Moscow for the country without having received satisfying answers to his questions about the meaning of life and death from either Father Ioann or the rather bizarre fat orator, Petr (Peten'ka, Petrushka), who identifies himself as "the essence," the "thing in itself" (184). Later literary manifestations of Musatov—including Nikolai Apollonovich in *Peterburg* and Kotik Letaev—make progressively more headway in their respective searches for meaning, with Kotik actually achieving immortality (thus conquering time) through self-crucifixion and deification.

20. Another view of Bely's use of music is expressed by Renato Poggioli (1960), who states that "music is for Bely not an echo of the harmony of the spheres but the prophetic din of that 'last cataclysm' which will destroy creation itself" (146). (See Bethea 1989 for a detailed discussion of apocalyptic imagery in Bely's works.) These two views need not be contradictory if one considers that the "musical" harmony of the temporal and supratemporal realms (*dvoemirie*) is necessary for apocalyptic resurrection, or for what Cioran (1973) terms the apocalyptic "call to eternity" (71–91).

21. Describing her first lengthy stay in Paris with Merezhkovskii from March 1906 to July 1908, Hippius (1951) notes that "then in Paris . . . we knew very few of those who in one way or another were attached to the modernist movement: Le Roy [*sic*], Bergson" (167).

22. Bely makes this link explicit in "Magiia slov" and "Mysl i iazyk (Filosofiia iazyka A. A. Potebni)" (*Logos* 2 [1910]: 240–58). See Anschuetz (1976, 1983) for more on the influence of Nietzsche and Potebnia on Bely's theory of language. See also Anna Khan (1991) for another interesting discussion of Potebnia's influence on Bely.

23. In his study of Bely's Symbolist fiction, Vladimir Alexandrov (1985) supports the idea that Bely does in fact find a balance "between noumenal suggestiveness and phenomenal specificity" (29) in his *Second Symphony*.

24. Bely (1913), 3.

25. Bely's wife recalls that Bely struggled with Kantian philosophy his whole life: "Kant always was his main enemy. But he was an enemy worthy of the fight" (Bugaeva 1981, 272).

26. Losev, "V poiskakh smysla," in Losev (1990b), 16.

27. Briusov characterizes this first period of Hippius's career, in the 1890s, as a time "when her worldview was becoming progressively weakened by pure aestheticism" (Vengerov 1972, 178).

28. See also Hippius's poem, "Liubov'—odna" (1912), in Hippius (1972), 24.

CHAPTER THREE

1. With occasional minor modifications, translations of Mandel'shtam's prose are taken from Harris (1979).

2. In a discussion of the ethics of creativity, Berdiaev (1931) notes that "the task of the ethics of creativeness is to make the perspective of life independent of the fatal march of time. . . . The creative act is an escape from time, it is performed in the realm of freedom, not of necessity" (157; quoted in Schmemann 1977, 269).

3. Clark (1995) identifies the avant-garde conception of revolution with that of secular revelation, or "the acquisition of a 'new vision' (*novoye zreniye*)" (30). Although the "new vision" of Mandel'shtam, Khlebnikov, and Malevich lacked the ostensible allegiance to the divine so palpable in the vision of Lossky or Bely, post-Symbolist revelation—like that of the religious philosophers and Symbolists—was nonetheless characterized by the clearer seeing of an ideal order, a Whole, perceived through intuition, at the base of the ceaseless flow of reality.

4. Rusinko, who originally observes Bergson's and Mandel'shtam's common use of the axiom "A = A" in her "Acmeism, Post-Symbolism, and Henri Bergson" (1982), notes that the "unadorned fact of existence" expressed in the "law of identity" put forth by Bergson in the axiom A = A became a "sacred commandment of Acmeism" (508), reflecting Bergson's early influence on Mandel'shtam. In addition, Freidin (1978) poses the question: "What did Mandel'shtam oppose to the symbolists' view of the world as a reality concealing a higher reality (Ivanov's *a realibus ad realiora*)?" and answers that Mandel'shtam turned to Schelling's "famous law of identity between the subject and the object, nature and consciousness, the finite and the infinite" in order to ground his aesthetic and philosophical views. Freidin goes on to state that Schelling "prepared Mandel'shtam for exposure to the current philosophical fashions—the 'intuitivist' philosophy of Henri Bergson" (430).

5. Voloshin, who was a student of Bergson's in 1907, writes in his autobiography that the reason he spent so many years of his life in Paris was in order "to study . . . logic from Gothic cathedrals . . . and the structure of thought from Bergson" (1925, 5).

6. For more on Mandel'shtam's creative misinterpretation of this passage, see Harris (1982), 116.

7. Futurists attacked Symbolism in much the same way as did Acmeists. For example, the Futurist artist Victor Khovin, like Mandel'shtam, blamed the Symbolists for turning the world into a lifeless shell, a static, meaningless realm of "gutted images": "Please understand that a living feeling for the

world has been lost, a living sense of its life, its movement, its dynamism; indeed, the dead reign of dead things has begun' ("Vetrogony, sumasbrody, letateli!" 8). Both Futurists and Acmeists rejected the Symbolist focus on other-worldly significance and called for a return to the law of identity, A = A, whereby the image is "interesting in itself" and the word is "self-sufficient." One is reminded of Bergson's statement in similar defiance of philosophical systems (that is, those of Kant, Schelling, Schopenhauer, and others) that obscure, rather than help to uncover, the "thing-in-itself": "Let us have done with great systems embracing all the possible, and sometimes even the impossible! Let us be content with the real, mind and matter" (*CM* 77).

8. Mandel'shtam, "January 1, 1924," in Mandel'shtam (1993).

9. Mandel'shtam, *Shum vremeni,* in Mandel'shtam (1993), 384.

10. Ibid.

11. "I myself know . . . that it isn't the underground that's better, but something different, something for which I thirst but can in no way find!" (Dostoevsky 1979, 314).

12. Mandel'shtam, "On the Naturalists," in Harris (1979), 333–34.

13. The scientist K. A. Timiriazev—best known perhaps as the greatest popularizer and defender of Darwin in Russia—claimed, in the name of Darwin, that nature is ruled by "blind, mechanistic" forces and denounced the Lamarckian "nonscientific" belief in an "inner principle" at work in evolution. Since Bergson's popular conception of "creative evolution" had much in common with Lamarck's theory of the same, Timiriazev considered Bergson a similar enemy of science. Thus in 1920 Timiriazev denounced "the present-day fighters against human intellect and its loftiest manifestation, science, beating a retreat back to the realm of intuition or instinct (all those Bergsons and their numerous worshipers among us)" ("Solntse, zhizn' i khlorofill." *Izbrannye sochineniia,* t. I, 84–85). Bergsonian notions on evolution and biology became especially popular in Russian scientific circles around 1914, when a publication on current developments in biological theory, *New Ideas in Biology,* featured a survey of Bergson's thoughts in these areas (Vucinich, *Darwin in Russian Thought,* 254).

14. Nadezhda Mandel'shtam notes in her memoirs (1972) that her husband considered Armenia to be the "outpost of Christianity, of the Hellenic and Judaic world" (551). In his poem "Armenia," Mandel'shtam (1993, 3:37) writes of his introspective activities during his time there: "Ia bestolkovuiu zhizn', kak mulla svoi koran, zamusolil" (I pored over my incoherent life, like a mullah his Koran).

15. Marinetti himself denied any Bergsonian influence on his Futurist aesthetics, seemingly also to stress his own originality. After mentioning the importance of "a new intuitive apprehension of the world" during his visit to Russia in 1914, a rather defensive Marinetti was questioned by the Futurist artist Nikolai Kulbin about Bergson (related by Livshits):

> "Bergson . . . ," sputters Kulbin.
> "Bergson has nothing to do with it! Clearly you have not read my *Addendum to the Technical Manifesto of Futurist Literature?*" retorts an offended and surprised Marinetti. . . . "Why is it," he continues, his agitated voice becoming gradually louder, "that the figure of Bergson always crops up the moment the word 'intuition' is uttered? One would think that before he came around, only pure rationalism existed in the world." (Livshits 1978, 153)

16. Russian Formalists like Viktor Shklovskii pursued a similar goal of "fresh" perception through *ostranenie* (defamiliarization or estrangement). James Curtis (1986) has observed that "the Formalists drew heavily on the work of Bergson. Shklovskii's famous concept of (*ostranennie*) [*sic*], for example, clearly derives from some principles of perception which Bergson sets forth in *Laughter*" (353). In addition, Curtis (1976) writes: "One could hardly ask for a better summary of Bergson's concept of art than Shklovskii's statement, 'The goal of art is to give the feeling of a thing as seeing, not as recognition.' . . . Estrangement as a device embodies Bergson's concept of the effect of art" (114–15). As Peter Steiner (1984) points out, however, Shklovskii modified his notion of *ostranenie* as early as 1919 when he adopted Aleksandr Veselovskii's theory of literary change, whereby "it was the evolution of life that revitalized petrified artistic forms" and not artistic forms that revitalize petrified life (as with artistic estrangement). For more on Shklovskii, Bergson, and *ostranenie,* see Any (1990), 416.

17. Khlebnikov, "Truba marsian," in Khlebnikov (1928–33), 5:153.

18. Khlebnikov, "Razgovor dvukh osob," in Khlebnikov (1928–33), 5:183.

19. Malevich (1978) calls Kruchenykh, rather than Khlebnikov, "the alpha of zaum'," because he thought of Khlebnikov more as an "astronomer" charting man's course through the universe than as a poet: "The alpha of Futurism is Marinetti, the alpha of zaum'-poetry is Kruchenykh. . . . To me this is Khlebnikov's main task, he is the draughtsman of the human orbit, rather than a poet, generally speaking, or a Futurist, or zaum'-poet in particular" ("About Zangezi," 94).

20. In several of his essays, Khlebnikov (1928–33) demonstrates how a system of roots might be organized around different letters of the alphabet. For example, in "Razlozhenie slova," he focuses on the letter "kh": "Nouns with a forceful, destructive bent: . . . mischief-maker (*okhal'nik*), boor (*kham*), plunderer (*khishchnik*). . . . Words indicating a weak nature, something in need of protection: decrepit (*khilyi*), fragile (*khrupkii*), withered (*khiryi*)" (5:200–201).

21. Khlebnikov (1928–33) asks in "Nasha osnova" (1919): "Who would travel from Moscow to Kiev via New York? And what line of modern bookish language is free of such excursions? This is because there is no science of word formation" (5:228). Khlebnikov had already been concerned with the link between science and poetry seven years earlier, stating in his essay

"Uchitel' i uchenik" (1912): "Only through the growth of science will it be possible to discover the whole wisdom of language, which is wise because it once was a part of nature itself" (5:172). Like Mandel'shtam, Khlebnikov is interested in a "biology" of language through which an organic unity of words, phenomena, and moments of time may be discovered. As in Bergsonian philosophy, each poet seeks a combination of science and metaphysics through intuition; by intuitively penetrating conventional "outer" forms to reach the "inner" forms of poetry and language, pure meaning and organic connections between words are uncovered, thus providing a systemic model for human existence in the universe.

22. Khlebnikov (1987), 480. In "Magiia slov," Bely (1994a) makes a comparable statement about the illuminating power of language to transform reality: "The creation of living speech always represents man's battle with the hostile elements surrounding him; the word victoriously lights up the darkness which surrounds me" (229).

23. In a letter written to his family in 1915, Khlebnikov (1928–33) states: "Thus will I go down in the history books—as the one who discovered the laws of time" (5:304). One example of Khlebnikov's mathematical search for the Laws of Time may be found in his essay, "Uchitel' i uchenik":

> I wish only to say that if one considers the Orthodox States—Bulgaria, Serbia and Russia—and looks at how many years they existed before their first loss of freedom, then all together it turns out to be equal to the number of years that Byzantium was in existence. Byzantium 395–1453 = 1058; Russia 862–1237 = 375; Bulgaria 679–1018 = 339; Serbia 1050–1389. 375 + 339 + 339 = 1053. This resembles a law for the preservation of strength. (5:176)

24. Khlebnikov, "Nasha osnova," in Khlebnikov (1928–33), 5:235.

25. Khlebnikov, "Khudozhniki mira!" in Khlebnikov (1928–33), 5:220.

26. In his article on contemporary Futurism, Khovin (1916) emphasizes the link between an intuitive, emotional appreciation of the word as unit of sound (that is, the word as any verbal utterance) and the apprehension of the inner, spiritual essence of life:

> Why should one try to express one's heartfelt emotion through thought, through logic? The blacked boots of the intellect have no business with spiritual nuances, which can be grasped only through intuition.
>
> For such intuitive comprehension, however, it is essential to grasp the emotional foundation of words, to sense them, not in their written form, but as sounds. Then the word bridles experience, saddles it, will cease to be a shadow. (8)

Poliakov similarly notes: "Transrational words were created outside the system of the Russian language as a means of nontraditional communication. They demanded an emotional and intuitive apprehension of their meaning" (introduction to Khlebnikov 1987, 23). A possible source for Khlebnikov in this context could have been Potebnia's theory of the inner versus the outer form of the word as expressed in his 1862 work, *Mysl' i iazyk*.

27. Khlebnikov, "O stikhakh," in Khlebnikov (1928–33), 5:225.

28. Khlebnikov, "Nasha osnova," in Khlebnikov (1928–33), 5:229.

29. One is reminded here of Hippius's distinction between "everyday routine" and "event" in her 1904 essay, "Byt i sobytie" (Hippius 1970). In terms of the distinction between the "pure" and "unpure" word, see Nilsson (1980, esp. 475, 480) for more on what he calls the "spoiled"-"original" opposition in avant-garde literature.

30. Malevich (1968), "From Cubism and Futurism to Suprematism," 27. Unless otherwise indicated, all page references to Malevich's essays correspond to the latter source.

31. Ibid., 38.

32. Douglas (1976), 59. Douglas's point here recalls that of the first-century iconophiles, who held that the icon is a revelation of divine truth rather than a representation. While examining the Bergsonian subtext to Cubism, Mark Antliff (1988) poses the parallel question of "how the painted *medium* induces a state of *immediacy* or intuition in the beholder" when "Bergson regarded all forms of representation as distorted refractions of a profound, ineffable self" (344). In answer, Antliff quotes a passage from Bergson's *Introduction to Metaphysics* in which Bergson seems to suggest that the splintered Cubist image may allow the consciousness to "seize on" a certain intuition. "No image will replace the intuition of duration, but many different images, taken from quite different orders of things, will be able, through the convergence of their action, to direct the consciousness to the precise point where there is a certain intuition to seize on" (Antliff 1988, 345; *CM* 195). Although Bergson does not comment specifically on Suprematist art in his writings, he does suggest in *Creative Evolution* that "irreducibility" (of, for example, a square) originally lends itself to philosophical, intuitive apprehension rather than to the intellectual grasp of science: "Anything that is irreducible and irreversible in the successive moments of a history eludes science. To get a notion of this irreducibility and irreversibility, we must break with scientific habits that are adapted to the fundamental requirements of thought. . . . But that is just the function of philosophy" (*CE* 29–30).

33. Malevich (1968), "From Cubism and Futurism to Suprematism," 29, 36.

34. Malevich (1968), "Suprematism. 34 Drawings," 123.

35. Malevich (1968), "To the New Image," 51.

36. Malevich (1968), "On the Museum," 68; my emphasis.

37. Malevich (1919), "O muzee," 2.

38. Malevich (1968), "God is Not Cast Down," 190.

39. Malevich (1968), "From Cubism and Futurism to Suprematism," 29.

40. Malevich (1978), "Suprematism," 146.

41. Malevich (1968), "On New Systems in Art," 100.

42. Malevich (1968), "From Cubism and Futurism to Suprematism," 31, 33.

43. Douglas (1976), 55.

44. Matiushin (1976), 174. Matiushin worked on this lengthy article between the years 1912 and 1926 (*Ezhegodnik rukopisnogo otdela Pushkinskogo doma na 1974 god* 1976, 8) and perhaps had Bergson in mind when he was formulating his thoughts on Russian Futurism. In a notebook entry entitled "Bergson," undated though most likely written in or around 1915, Matiushin devotes two pages of random thoughts to the French philosopher (Manuscript Division, Gosudarstvennyi Muzei Maiakovskogo, fond 11, opis 1, edinoe khranilishche 14). Matiushin focuses his remarks on the primacy of the qualitative ("emotion and feeling," *emotsiia i oshchushchenie*) over the quantitative ("muscular exertion," *muskul'noe usilie*). This is a distinction similar to Bergson's in *Creative Evolution* wherein he compares the relationship between "quality" and "quantity" to that of "soul" and "body," the former of each pair characterized by inner change and becoming (apprehended through intuition), while the latter is marked by static, external spatiality (apprehended by intellect) (*CE* 350). Given the fact that Matiushin's notebook entry on Bergson corresponds in time to the writing of "Opyt khudozhnika novoi mery," the possibility is raised that Matiushin's statements regarding the ability of Russian Futurist art to reveal the qualitative "inner world" of phenomena—inaccessible to the "everyday eye"—might have been inspired to some degree by Bergsonian philosophy, according to which art is defined in precisely the same way. I am grateful to Professor Katherine Lahti of Trinity College for bringing Matiushin's notebook to my attention.

45. "Content and Form" (1910), quoted in Bowlt (1976), 19. In noting Kandinsky's transitional status between Symbolism and the avant-garde, Günther (1992) comments that "Kandinsky's aesthetics are built on the boundary of two stylistic systems. The conceptions of Symbolism serve as the ideological source of Kandinsky's aesthetics, however, the tendency toward avant-gardism is unquestionably evident in certain key ways, such as in the emancipation of art from imitative tasks" (62).

46. Malevich (1978), "Suprematism," 145.

47. As Blauberg notes in his introduction to the first (and so far only) volume of Bergson's collected works republished in Moscow in 1992: "For Bergson, freedom, duration and creation are synonymous" (introduction to Bergson 1913–14, 1:21).

CHAPTER FOUR

1. As one early twentieth-century thinker observes: "All self-respecting '-ists' [Cubists, Futurists, etc.—H. F.] are presently busy interpreting the

fourth dimension. . . . They have decided that art must . . . sing of the fourth dimension" (Makovskii 1913, 56).

2. Tufanov, "O zhizni i poezii"; reprinted in Tufanov (1991), 124.

3. The last letter of OBERIU was added just for fun, perhaps to accord with the children's rhyme "potomu, chto konchaetsia na 'u'" (because it ends in "u"), or else simply to contradict the conventional logic of acronyms (Aleksandrov, introduction to Kharms 1990, 9).

4. Meilakh's introduction to Vvedenskii (1993), 1:21; quoted by Gibian (1987), 13. Besides Kharms, the other principal members of the OBERIU were Aleksandr Vvedenskii, Nikolai Zabolotskii, and Konstantin Vaginov, while those associated with the group though not official members included Iakov Druskin, Igor Bakhterev, and Nikolai Oleinikov. In regard to Malevich's inscription, "Go and put a stop to progress," one is reminded of how Mandel'shtam turns to Bergsonian thought in his 1922 essay, "On the Nature of the Word," as an antidote to "the bad infinity of evolutionary theory, not to mention its vulgarized corollary—the theory of progress."

5. *Afishi Doma pechati*, no. 2 (1928): 11–12.

6. Like Bely, who believed that "Symbolism becomes a living method," or Mandel'shtam, for whom Acmeism served not only as an aesthetic system but also as a metaphysical force, a guide to the organic participation in existence, Kharms similarly sought to live according to his art, free from the "logical" expectations of conformity to ideological "progress." Druskin recalls that "Kharms said at the end of the thirties that the most important thing to him had always been life, not art: to make his life like art. This is not aestheticism; for Kharms, 'the creation of life like art' was not an aesthetic category but, as they now say, an existential one." Druskin also relates Aleksandr Vvedenskii's (1993) now well-known characterization of his close friend Kharms: "Kharms does not create art; he is art" ("Chinari," 108; quoted in Cornwell 1991b, 6).

7. Zabolotskii, "Poeziia oberiutov," in Kushner (1994), 538.

8. Noted by Kobrinskii, introduction to Kharms (1991), 10. According to the eyewitness account of Lidia Ginzburg, the Oberiuty answered a student's query regarding the meaning of this sign by asking in return: "Do you really think we are pies?" ("A razve my—pirogi?"). This reply is a good example of the type of absurd logic often employed by Kharms in his prose.

9. Nil'vich (1930), emphasis in original; reprinted in Vvedenskii (1993), 2:153.

10. Although the proletarian writers' association (RAPP) exerted more and more control over literature in Russia once Stalin assumed power, the Party would not declare socialist realism the official policy for writers until 1934, two years after RAPP itself had been disbanded.

11. "I consider Khlebnikov, Vvedenskii, and Marshak to be my teachers" (introduction to Kushner 1994, 22).

12. In a discussion of Kharms's work, Druskin (1989) observes: "That which is called nonsense or alogicality is to be found in his stories and verses. However, his stories are not nonsensical and alogical—the life he describes in them is" (112).

13. Kharms, "O kruge," in Kharms (1993), 63.

14. See especially Chances (1982, 1985), Vishevsky (1986), and Cassedy (1984). Mention should also be made of the pronounced Gogolian nature of Kharms's prose as repetition, dehumanization, and the unreliability of language are emphasized in the works of both authors.

15. See Cornwell (1991a), Jaccard (1985, 1991a, 1991b), and Anemone in Cornwell (1991a). In attempting to define French Surrealism, Isaev observes that the Oberiuty may be considered a similar aesthetic phenomenon:

> The creative work of the oberiuty (D. Kharms, A. Vvedenskii, Ia. Druskin, L. Lipavskii) represents a concrete literary effort that may help us to understand surrealism, although surrealism, of course, is much broader, both as a movement and as a cultural phenomenon. Practically coinciding in time period, they also coincide in the most essential way: in the production of ontological sense-less images. (Isaev and Gal'tsova 1994, 8–9)

The view of French Surrealism as a "cultural phenomenon" may also be applied to the art of the Oberiuty, suggesting the sociological motivation of the absurd in their works.

16. Jaccard (1991b) remarks that "the absurd outlook on the world . . . isolates each part of the world and negates the link between them" (53). Like Kharms, Vvedenskii distrusted the world of conventional logic and causal linkages, believing instead that only through the breakdown of such a "logical" system of connections may the essential meaning of life be apprehended. Vvedenskii writes in 1933: "I am convinced of the falsity of all previous connections but cannot say which should take their place. . . . I have a fundamental sense of the world's incoherence . . . and since this contradicts reason, then it means that reason does not comprehend the world" (Vvedenskii 1993, 2:157).

17. Kharms, "O vremeni, o prostranstve, o sushchestvovanii," in Jaccard (1985), 304.

18. *Afishi Doma pechati,* no. 2 (1928): 11.

19. Ibid.

20. Tufanov (1924), 11. Jaccard suggests that the primary reason Kharms and Tufanov became acquainted could have been their shared admiration for Khlebnikov (Jaccard and Ustinov 1991, 160).

21. Tufanov, "Avtobiografiia Predsedatelia Zemnogo Shara Zaumi Aleksandra Tufanova," quoted in Tufanov (1991), 173 (earlier in the autobiography Tufanov remarks that by 1917, "I had already freed myself . . . from Kant and Schopenhauer, and was moving toward Bergson"). Following Bergson as

"closest" to Tufanov in 1925 is the original "president of the earth," Velimir Khlebnikov, along with the Futurist artist, Mikhail Matiushin.

22. One is reminded of Matiushin's distinction between the qualitative and quantitative in his notebook entry devoted to Bergson around 1915; in fact, Jaccard states that Matiushin, Tufanov, and the Oberiuty were all influenced by Bergsonian philosophy: "[Tufanov's works] are an integral part of one particular current of creative thought in the 1920s, a current linked with the name Matiushin and, later, with the oberiuty poets, and influenced by the philosophical, scientific and literary theories of Uspenskii, Einstein, Bergson" (Tufanov 1991, 22–23). Meilakh similarly notes that Tufanov's [Bergsonian] emphasis on the qualitative, nonspatial apprehension of time owed much to Matiushin's analogous concept of "penetrating vision" (*zorkoe videnie*), which resulted in the "widened apprehension of the world" (Vvedenskii 1993, 1:18). In addition, Tufanov's (1991) "Declaration" that "in *zaum'*, there is no room for the intellect with its spatial perception of time" (44)—echoing Bergson's belief in the inability of the intellect to grasp the essence of "real time"—held, according to Meilakh, "particular meaning in terms of the sources for Vvedenskii's interpretation of the problem of time, the central problem of his poetry" (Vvedenskii 1993, 1:18); thus Vvedenskii's statement, with which Kharms certainly would have agreed: "Our human logic and our language do not conform to time in any type of understanding. Our logic and our language glide over the surface of time" (1993, 2:79).

23. Tufanov (1924), 7. In an earlier article, Tufanov explicitly identifies the artistic impulse with the dynamic Bergsonian élan: "We worship life's dynamism . . . , the Bergsonian élan vital, the need for creation" ("O zhizni i poezii" [1918], reprinted in Tufanov 1991, 125). Aleksei Tolstoy (1924) similarly states: "The process of artistic creation is carried out not by means of logical thinking but through an ecstatic élan" (9).

24. Tufanov (1924), 26. Three years before Tufanov published *K zaumi*, Losev (1990a) similarly connects the notion of "musical being" to the Bergsonian concept of nonspatial, "real time":

> Observing the mechanical movement in space of a watch's hands, the natural scientist does not suspect that he, in fact, is measuring space instead of time. *Bergson* has brilliantly exposed this general delusion on the part of science. . . .
>
> Musical being . . . does not exist in spatially measurable time but demands real time, which is independent of space and which is not measured by any type of ruler. ("Muzyka kak predmet logiki," 237)

25. Aleksandrov (1990), 69. Tufanov's emphasis on the "fluidity" (*tekuchest'*) of time and poetry (which he seems to have appropriated from the Bergsonian notion of consciousness/duration/life as a ceaseless, creative flow) may have been one of the concepts that Kharms "adopted" from his elder teacher. Writing in 1930, Kharms (1993) states: "One person thinks log-

ically; many people think *fluidly.* Even though I am only one person, I think *fluidly*" ("Odinnadtsat' utverzhdenii Daniila Ivanovicha Kharmsa," 56).

26. Books from the Library of New Books:

> . . . H. Bergson, vol. V:
> 1) Introduction to Metaphysics
> 2) Psychological Parallelism and Positive Metaphysics
> 3) Laughter
>
> vol. IV:
> —Questions of Philosophy and Psychology
> —Time and Free Will
> —Duration and Simultaneity
>
> H. Bergson:
> Matter and Memory. Essay on the Relation of Body to Spirit
> Time and Free Will, vol. II. Creative Evolution.
>
> Bergson. Laughter in Life and on the Stage.
>
> (Kharms 1991, 68–69)

27. Noted by Aleksandrov in his commentary to Kharms (Kharms 1988, 528). Like Bely and Kharms, Tsvetaeva (1990) also makes Kant a symbol of attack, stating in a 1923 poem about the nature of the poet: "On tot . . . kto Kanta nagolovu b'et" (335).

28. In opposition to the reliance on strictly phenomenal knowledge, Kharms (1988) states in a 1930 essay: "I only realized that I was seeing the world when I stopped seeing it" ("Myr," 314).

29. Dostoevsky's Underground Man, who obstinately insists on the human right to be illogical and thus argues that twice two need not equal four, fights a similar battle against the idea of Chernyshevskii's Crystal Palace, where everything is organized in the utmost "logical" fashion in the supposed best interest of humankind.

30. Gerasimova (1988) points to this same inadequacy of language to endow experience with meaning as the primary source of the comic in OBERIU art: "For the Oberiuty, the comic, to a certain extent, results from the realization of the verbal form's inadequacy in the expression of nonverbal experience" (55). See Shukman (1988) for a discussion of the Kharmsian absurd in terms of Roman Jakobson's six-point communications schema and the language theory of the Bakhtinian circle in the 1920s.

31. Manuscript Section of the State Public Library (Saint Petersburg), f. 1232, MS 345 (1933). Translated and quoted by Jaccard (1991b), 56. The sketch continues in the same vein for several more lines.

32. Writing in 1930 of an undefined "category E," Kharms (1993) comments of the diametrically opposed tendencies of formal logic and art: "3). Logical science ('formal logic,' 'the laws of thought') depends on the postulates of category E; thus it is not creative. 4) Art cannot depend on the postulates of category E; thus it is a creative discipline" ("Cisfinitum [*sic*]," 60).

33. Lunacharskii, "Klassovaia bor'ba v iskusstve" (1929), in Lunacharskii (1965), 8:30.

34. Bergson (1925), 17. Unless otherwise indicated, all following quotations of Bergson in this section will be noted by page number only, corresponding to *Le rire.*

35. Jaccard (1985) observes that mechanism is "the principal trait of Kharmsian poetics as seen in his prose works, as well as the principal source of the *comic* in them" (295). Although, as Jaccard points out by quoting Tynianov, "[t]he essence of parody lies in the mechanization of a particular device" (Tynianov 1921, 23; Jaccard 1985, 296), Kharms's artistic use of mechanization may still have been reinforced by Bergson's emphasis on the automatic as the essence of the comic.

36. In an article examining the nature of laughter and including a discussion of Bergson's theory of the comic, Bogdanov (1923) comments on the fine line separating the comic from its core of anger: "The most fertile soil for laughter is hostility, struggle. The kinship of laughter and rage is clear to everyone" (177). While such an element of rage is absent from the Bergsonian conception of laughter, it would seem to be very much a part of Kharmsian "anti-laughter."

37. A parallel may be drawn here to Freud's theory of defense mechanisms, including repetition of patterns of behavior that an individual might cling to in fear of/defense against creative life and action. While Freud was known to Il'ia Zdanevich and other Russian transrational artists (Jaccard 1991a, 462), there is no evidence to suggest that Kharms was influenced by Freud. One critic, however, has found parallels in Kharms's *Starukha* to Freudian ideas on death, the "uncanny," and the "aesthetic/anti-aesthetic dimension of pain and anguish" (Rosanna Giaquinta, "The Fantastic in Kharms' *Starukha,*" in Cornwell 1991a, 133–48).

38. In his discussion of the meaning of modern art, Ortega y Gasset (1948) similarly focuses on dehumanization as a defining characteristic, writing in 1925 that the modern artist is "brazenly set on deforming reality, shattering its human aspect, dehumanizing it" (21). It should be noted, however, that while Kharms's artistic use of dehumanization is meant largely as an indictment of the treatment of the individual in Soviet society, Ortega y Gasset points to the modern artist's "triumph over human matter" as the essence of "aesthetic pleasure," the enjoyment of art contingent on an audience's non-habitual perception of the world.

39. Bakhtin (1986a) would disagree in that he considered Bergson's theory of the comic to be devoid of any positive connotation: "Bergson's whole theory deals only with the negative role of laughter. Laughter is a means of correction. . . . The basic idea is true: life laughs at death (dead mechanism). But the organic *matter* of life within laughter is positive" (223). It is, however, precisely the positive, organic fluidity of life that Bergsonian laugh-

ter seeks to recapture by drawing attention to "lifeless mechanism." As opposed to Bergson, Kharms is the pessimist for whom laughter represents not a victory over death but a tragic acknowledgment that death will in fact have the last laugh. For more on Bakhtin and Bergson, see Morson and Emerson (1990), esp. 177–79.

CHAPTER FIVE

1. Hayward and Labedz (1963) observe that "the relatively mild, in retrospect almost idyllic, period" of intellectual freedom in Russia following the Revolution abruptly came to an end in 1929 with the end of the New Economic Policy and with

> Stalin's decision to make the Party, now under his undisputed personal control, into an instrument for the revolutionary transformation of society and an apparatus for the minute regulation of all aspects of life. Hence, just as the peasants were to be collectivized, so writers and intellectuals in general were to be "bolshevized." (ix)

Brown focuses on the year 1930 as a "year of acquiescence," marked by the suicide of Maiakovskii and "Pilnyak's transmogrification of *Mahogany* into a Five-year Plan novel" ("The Year of Acquiescence," in Hayward and Labedz 1963, 44).

2. Plekhanov's review of Bergson's *Creative Evolution* (which was first published in Russia in 1907) appeared in the journal *Sovremennyi mir* in 1909.

3. In his commentary to Lunacharskii's collected works, P. M. Samarin states that Lunacharskii viewed the modernist movement as an artistic manifestation of decaying bourgeois society: "'Modernism' for Lunacharskii was the broad, general definition of the art of bourgeois decline" (Lunacharskii 1965, 5:628).

4. See Messer (1930). In his study of Voronskii, Choate (1987) remarks that "the charge of Bergsonianism is only one of the many sordid footnotes in the history of Stalinist thought" (309).

5. In his review of *Creative Evolution,* Plekhanov (1909) notes what "could be called" the "*materialistic* element in Bergson's views," as well as Bergson's "ability to think dialectically" (119, 121).

6. Lunacharskii, "Molodaia frantsuzskaia poeziia," in Lunacharskii (1965), 5:283.

7. Nonetheless, Lissitzkii (1976) notes the parallel between Malevich and Lenin in a 1920 essay (lacking any capital letters): "into this chaos came suprematism extolling the square as the very source of all creative expression. and then came communism and extolled work as the true source of man's heartbeat" (154).

8. For Lenin, philosophy had to reflect and support the Party-directed class struggle against the bourgeoisie; thus Lenin states in 1922: "[W]ithout a solid philosophical basis . . . no type of materialism can maintain the struggle against the onslaught of bourgeois ideas and the re-establishment of the bourgeois worldview" ("O znachenii voinstvuiushchego materializma," *PSS*, t. XLV, 29).

9. Lunacharskii, "Klassovaia bor'ba v iskusstve," in Lunacharskii (1965), 8:29.

10. Noted by Harkins (1996), 352. To the idealist hero's claim that the practical and imaginary worlds can be combined, the Marxist neighbor replies: "I don't understand anything. It's some kind of Bergsonianism" (Olesha 1956, 265). For a brief discussion of Bergsonian duration in Olesha's *Zavist'*, see Tucker (1996), 25–28, 129–30. Nilsson (1973) has also commented on the possible Bergsonian influence on both Olesha and Voronskii (269–71). In terms of Olesha, Nilsson notes that the belief in the poet as "a man who breaks the spell of automatization, a spell which permanently threatens our perception of the world . . . was usually based on the philosophy of Henri Bergson, so popular at that time." As for Voronskii, Nilsson states that despite the fact that Voronskii never admitted to any Bergsonian influence on his work, "we can hardly presume that he was ignorant at least of the general European discussion which circled round certain of Bergson's concepts in those days."

11. While Messer charges Bergsonian duration with being unable to "resolve antinomies," Levitskii (1981) takes the opposite position and calls dialectical materialism "the greatest perversion of the true dialectic, the best practitioners of which are Plato, Hegel and Bergson" because, in order to preserve a state of constant (class) struggle, dialectical materialism never succeeds in overcoming contradictions (193).

12. Lenin, "Ob A. Bogdanove," in Lenin (1960–69), 24:338–39.

13. In the *Istoriia filosofii v shesti tomakh* (1961), Bergson gets top billing for the section entitled: "Bourgeois Philosophy at the End of the Nineteenth and the Beginning of the Twentieth Century" which begins: "Bourgeois philosophers . . . began directly or indirectly to speak out against dialectical and historical materialism. . . . Over the course of several decades, from the end of the nineteenth-century up to the 1920s, the intuitivism of Henri Bergson (1859–1941) was the main trend of idealistic philosophy" (5:599).

14. Plekhanov (1909), 122. While Plekhanov denounces Bergson for his idealism, we recall that Losskii (1913) criticizes Bergson for not being Platonic enough, for denying "the idea in the Platonic sense of the word" (113)—another example of how different aspects of Bergson's philosophy were emphasized by different groups in order to bolster a particular philosophical position.

15. Voronskii's career as a prominent critic was effectively ended after Messer's 1930 article in which he was accused of holding Bergsonian views. While allowed to work as an editor at the State Publishing House for the next five years, Voronskii was arrested in 1935. Although there are no published details of Voronskii's death, he is thought to have died in prison or in a labor camp (Brown, 1963a, 197).

16. One is reminded here of Malevich's conception of the Suprematist construction of forms "from nothing."

17. Writing in 1912, Vladimir Markov (pseudonym of Waldemars Matvejs) (1976) makes a similar connection between the unforeseeable, or "chance" (*sluchainost'*), and the free creative act: "The source of the beauty of chance can be found not only in blind, extrinsic, purely external factors, but also in the inmost recesses of man's very soul, in the unconscious movements of the artist's hand and thought. It is on this faculty of man's spirit, bestowed from above, that the principle of *free creation* is built" (30). In addition, Berdiaev (1931) qualifies the creative act as "unforeseeable," proceeding "from nothing": "Creativity is the greatest mystery of life, the mystery of a new phenomenon that has never been before, that . . . flows out of nothing, that is born of nothing" (136).

CONCLUSION

1. Solov'ev, "Kritika otvlechennykh nachal," in Solov'ev (1988), 1:744.

2. This phenomenological conflict between appearance and essence served as the focal point of philosopher Gustav Shpet's 1914 *Iavlenie i smysl.* Shpet dedicated his book to Husserl, whom he met and studied under in 1912–13 while at Göttingen University, and to a large degree *Iavlenie i smysl* represents an exegesis of Husserl's *Logical Investigations* and *Ideas I.* Some of the central issues of phenomenology as put forth by Husserl as well as by his main popularizer in Russia, Shpet, are quite similar to those addressed by Bergson, the most fundamental of which being the emphasis on intuitive (yet objective) knowledge of "things-in-themselves" as opposed to the "negative intellectualism" of Kant. In this sense Husserl claims of his school of phenomenologists: "We are the true Bergsonians" (quoted in Waldenfels 1983, 21), and Shpet (1914) asks: "But is not Bergson right that life and movement slip away from us precisely at this moment? Is he not right that the gaze of our intellect has the hypnotic, deadly power of the eyes of a poisonous snake which roots its victim to the spot and deprives it of the ability to move or struggle?" (5).

3. This quasi-paradoxical element in Russian thought perhaps stems from the Orthodox concept of deification, according to which the individual constantly strives toward the realization of the divine although it is already present in and around one.

4. Although Kharms's oeuvre would seem to deny the search for connection with the divine (or for any type of connection), he nonetheless ends his last major prose work, *The Old Woman,* with a prayer, much as Bely concludes his *Second Symphony* with a nun kindling small lights over several of the convent graves.

5. In an interesting footnote to the current Russian interest in this work as a model for a more free society, one Soviet critic in 1935 also focused on *Les deux sources* in an attempt to discredit Bergson by linking him to fascism. Ignoring Bergson's support for the "open society" as the type of society that man should, and must, grow into, L. German (1935) distorts Bergson's earlier statement that nature originally intended for man to live in a "closed" society (based on defense against enemies and preservation of social stability) into an endorsement of the closed society's nationalism and xenophobia over the open society's internationalism and love of humanity. German concludes: "After the appearance (in 1931) of Bergson's new work, *Two Sources of Morality and Religion*—wherein he sets forth the fundamentals of his social worldview—there no longer can be any doubt that his political credo [*sic*] is entirely in line with the fascist reactionary program of 'national salvation'" (125). This idea is reiterated by Novikov (1964), who links Bergson not only to German fascists but to Mussolini as well, claiming that Bergson's work *Two Sources of Morality and Religion* represents a "justification of militarism" and a "hate for democracy" (213).

6. According to Blauberg, the actual prototype for the "closed society" was the totalitarian regime (he does not specify which one) that was emerging on the world scene when Bergson was formulating his ideas on the problem of societal progress and change (introduction to Bergson 1992, 1:37–38).

7. Bakhtin, "Iskusstvo i otvetstvennost'," in Bakhtin (1986b), 3.

Selected Bibliography

WORKS BY BERGSON PUBLISHED IN RUSSIA (IN CHRONOLOGICAL ORDER)

1900. *Smekh v zhizni i na stsene.* Translated by A. E. Ianovskii. Saint Petersburg: XX vek. ["Le rire." *Revue de Paris* 7, nos. 23 and 24 (1899): 512–14, 759–90; no. 1 (1900): 146–79.]

1909. *Tvorcheskaia evoliutsiia.* Translated by M. Bulgakov. Moscow: Sotrudnichestvo. [*L'Evolution créatice.* Paris: Félix Alcan, 1907.]

1911. *Vremia i svoboda voli.* Translated by S. I. Gessen. Moscow: Russkaia mysl'. [*Essai sur les données immédiates de la conscience.* Paris: Félix Alcan, 1889.]

1912. *Vremia i svoboda voli: S prilozheniem traktata togo zhe avtora Vvedenie v metafiziku.* Translated by S. I. Gessen and M. Grunval'd. Saint Petersburg: Russkaia mysl'. ["Introduction à la métaphysique." *Revue de Métaphysique et de Morale* (29 January 1903): 1–36.]

1913a. *Vospriiatie izmenchivosti.* Translated by V. A. Flerevaia. Saint Petersburg. [*La Perception du changement: Conférences faites à l'université d'Oxford les 26 et 27 mai 1911.* Oxford: Clarendon Press, 1911.]

1913b. *Vospominanie nastoiashchego.* Translated by V. A. Flerevaia. Saint Petersburg. ["Le Souvenir du présent et la fausse reconnaissance." *Revue Philosophique de la France et de l'Etranger* 66, no. 4 (December 1908): 561–93.]

1913c. *Intellektual'noe usilie. Zametka o psikhologicheskom proiskhozhdenii nashei very v zakon prichinnosti.* Translated by V. A. Flerevaia. Saint Petersburg. ["L'Effort intellectuel." *Revue Philosophique de la France et de l'Etranger* 5 (January 1902): 1–27. "Note sur les origines psychologiques de notre croyance à la lois de causalité." *Bibliothèque du congrès international de philosophie,* vol. 1, *Philosophie générale et métaphysique.* Paris: Armand Colin, 1900.]

1913d. *Psikho-fiziologicheskii paralogizm. Snovidenie.* Translated by V. A. Flerevaia. Saint Petersburg. ["Le Paralogisme psycho-physiologique." *Revue de Métaphysique et de Morale* 12 (November 1904): 895–908. "Le Rève." *Bulletin de l'Institut Général Psychologique* 1, no. 3 (May 1901): 97–122.]

1913–14. *Sobranie sochinenii Bergsona.* Vols. 1–5. Edited by M. I. Semenov. Saint Petersburg. Vol. 1 (1913): *Tvorcheskaia evoliutsiia.* Translated by M. Bulgakov. Vol. 2 (1914): *Neposredstvennye dannye soznaniia. Vremia i svoboda voli* (*Essai sur les données immédiates de la conscience*). Translated by B. S. Bychkovskii. Vol. 3 (1914): *Materiia i pamiat'* (*Matière et mémoire: Essai sur la relation du corps avec l'esprit.* [Paris: Félix Alcan, 1896]). Translated by B. Bazarov. Vol. 4 (1914): *Voprosy filosofii i psikhologii* (*Vospriiatie izmenchivosti, Psikhofiziologicheskii paralogizm, Snovidenie, Vospominanie nastoiashchego, Intellektual'noe usilie*). Translated by V. A. Flerevaia. Vol. 5 (1914): *Vvedenie v metafiziku. Smekh* (*i drugie proizvedeniia*). Translated by V. A. Flerevaia and I. Gol'denberg.

1923. *Dlitel'nost' i odnovremennost'* (*po povodu teorii Einshteina*). Saint Petersburg. [*Durée et simultanéité: A propos de la théorie d'Einstein.* Paris: Félix Alcan, 1922.]

SOURCES IN RUSSIAN

Aleksandrov, A. A. 1980. "Materialy D. I. Kharmsa v rukopisnom otdele Pushkinskogo Doma." In *Ezhegodnik rukopisnogo otdela Pushkinskogo Doma na 1978 god.* Leningrad: Nauka.

Askol'dov, S. A. 1914. "N. Losskii. *Intuitivnaia filosofiia Bergsona.*" *Russkaia mysl'* 2, no. 35:50–51.

———. 1922. "Tvorchestvo Andreia Belogo." *Literaturnaia mysl'* 1:73–90.

Asmus, V. F. 1926. "Advokat filosofskoi intuitsii." *Pod znamenem marksizma,* no. 3:53–84.

———. 1929. "Estetika Bergsona." *Na literaturnom postu,* no. 2:4–18.

———. 1937. "Filosofiia i estetika russkogo simvolizma." *Literaturnoe nasledstvo* (Moscow) 27–28:1–53.

———. 1963. *Problema intuitsii v filosofii i matematike.* Moscow: Izd. sotsial'no-ekonomicheskoi literatury.

———. 1984. *Istoriko-filosofskie etiudy.* Moscow: Mysl'.

Babynin, B. N. 1911. "Filosofiia Bergsona." *Voprosy filosofii i psikhologii,* no. 3:251–90; no. 4:472–518.

Bakhtin, M. M. 1986a. "Iz zametok o komicheskom." *Den' poezii 1986.* Moscow: Sovetskii pisatel'.

———. 1986b. *Literaturno-kriticheskie stat'i.* Moscow: Khudozhestvennaia literatura.

Belinskii, V. G. 1953–59. *Polnoe sobranie sochinenii.* 13 vols. Moscow: Izd. Akademii nauk SSSR.

Bely, Andrei. 1904. "KritITSizm i simvolizm." *Vesy,* no. 2:1–13.

———. 1908. "Simvolizm i sovremennoe russkoe iskusstvo." *Vesy* 5, no. 10:38–48.

———. 1912. "Krugovoe dvizhenie." *Trudy i dni,* nos. 4–5:51–73.

———. 1913. "Letter to E. Metner." *Rossiiskaia gosudarstvennaia biblioteka,* f. 167, ed. khranilishche 7, 3–4.

———. 1964. *Kotik Letaev.* Munich: Eidos.

———. 1965. *O smysle poznaniia.* Chicago: Russian Language Specialties. (Originally published Saint Petersburg: Epokha, 1922.)

———. 1969. *Simvolizm.* Munich: Wilhelm Fink.

———. 1982. *Pochemu ia stal simvolistom.* Ann Arbor, Mich.: Ardis.

———. 1988. "O sebe kak pisatele." In *Andrei Bely. Problemy tvorchestva,* edited by S. S. Lesnevskii and A. A. Mikhailov, 19–24. Moscow: Sovetskii pisatel'.

———. 1990. *Serebrianyi golub: Povesti, roman.* Moscow: Sovremennik.

———. 1991. *Simfonii.* Leningrad: Khudozhestvennaia literatura.

———. 1994a. *Kritika. Estetika. Teoriia simvolizma.* Vol. 1. Moscow: Iskusstvo.

———. 1994b. *Simvolizm kak miroponimanie.* Moscow: Respublika.

Berdiaev, N. A. 1908. "Katolicheskii modernizm i krizis sovremennogo soznaniia." *Russkaia mysl'* 29, no. 9:80–94.

———. 1912. *Aleksei Stepanovich Khomiakov.* Moscow: Put'.

———. 1931. *O naznachenii cheloveka.* Paris: YMCA Press.

———. 1994. *Filosofiia tvorchestva, kul'tury i iskusstva v dvukh tomakh.* Moscow: Iskusstvo.

Bergson, Anri. 1992. *Sobranie sochinenii.* Vol. 1. Moscow: Moskovskii klub.

———. 1994. *Dva istochnika morali i religii.* Translated and with commentary by A. B. Gofman. Moscow: Kanon.

Blauberg, I. I. "Otkuda my prishli? Kto my? Kuda my idem?" *Voprosy filosofii* 1 (1990): 155–68.

Blok, A. A. 1971. *Sobranie sochinenii v shesti tomakh.* Moscow: Pravda.

———. 1980–83. *Sobranie sochinenii v shesti tomakh.* Leningrad: Khudozhestvennaia literatura.

Bogdanov, A. A. 1908. *Empiriomonizm.* Izd. 3-e. Moscow: Izd. S. Dorovatovskogo i A. Charyshnikova.

———. 1913. *Filosofiia zhivogo opyta.* Saint Petersburg: Izd. M. I. Semenova.

———. 1923. "Taina smekha." *Molodaia gvardiia,* no. 2:175–80.

Briusov, V. Ia. 1916. "O muzyke." *Trudy i dni:* 70–86.

———. 1973–75. *Sobranie sochinenii.* Moscow: Khudozhestvennaia literatura.

Bugaeva, K. N. 1981. *Vospominaniia o Belom.* Berkeley, Calif.: Berkeley Slavic Specialties.

Bugaeva, K. N., and A. Petrovskii. 1937. "Literaturnoe nasledstvo Andreia Belogo." *Literaturnoe nasledstvo* 27–28.

Bulgakov, S. N. 1903. *Ot marksizma k idealizmu. Sbornik statei* (1896–1903). Saint Petersburg: Obshchestvennaia pol'za.

———. 1993. *Sochineniia v dvukh tomakh.* Moscow: Nauka.

Chaadaev, P. Ia. 1989. *Sochineniia.* Moscow: Izd. Pravda.

———. 1991. *Polnoe sobranie sochinenii i izbrannye pis'ma.* 2 vols. Moscow: Nauka.

Chizhevskii, Dmitrii. 1939. *Gegel' v Rossii.* Paris: Dom knigi i Sovremennye zapiski.

Chueva, I. P. 1963. *Kritika idei intuitivizma v Rossii.* Leningrad: Izd. Akademii nauk SSSR.

Davydov, Iu. N. 1959. "Leninskaia kritika otnosheniia Bogdanova k filosofskoi traditsii." *Voprosy filosofii,* no. 6:111–22.

———, ed. 1988. *Kritika nemarksistskikh kontseptsii dialektiki XX veka.* Moscow: Izd. Moskovskogo universiteta.

Dostoevsky, F. M. 1979. *Povesti i rasskazy v dvukh tomakh.* Moscow: Khudozhestvennaia literatura.

Druskin, Ia. S. 1989. "Chinari." *Avrora* 6:103–23.

Ellis. 1909. "Itogi simvolizma." *Vesy,* no. 7:55–74.

El'zon, M. D., and N. A. Groznova, eds. 1994. *Nikolai Gumilev. Issledovaniia i materialy. Bibliografiia.* Saint Petersburg: Nauka.

Emel'ianov, B. V., and K. N. Liubutin, eds. 1991. *A. I. Vvedenskii, A. F. Losev, E. L. Radlov, G. G. Shpet: Ocherki istorii russkoi filosofii.* Sverdlovsk: Izd. Ural'skogo universiteta.

Ezhegodnik rukopisnogo otdela Pushkinskogo doma na 1974 god. 1976. Leningrad: Nauka.

Ezhegodnik rukopisnogo otdela Pushkinskogo doma na 1978 god. 1980. Leningrad: Nauka.

Fleishman, L. S. 1975. "Marginalii k istorii russkogo avangarda." Introductory essay to *Stikhotvoreniia,* by N. M. Oleinikov. Bremen: K Presse.

Frank, S. L. 1910. "Pragmatizm, kak filosofskoe uchenie." *Russkaia mysl'* 5, no. 31:90–120.

———. 1912. "O filosofskoi intuitsii." *Russkaia mysl',* no. 3:31–35.

———. 1913. "Kriticheskoe obozrenie (Anri Bergson. *Vospriiatie izmenchivosti, Psikho-fiziologicheskii paralogizm*)." *Russkaia mysl',* no. 2: 49–51.

———. 1915. *Predmet znaniia.* Petrograd: R. G. Shreder.

———. 1916. "Krizis sovremennoi filosofii." *Russkaia mysl'* 9, no. 3:33–40.

———. 1917. *Dusha cheloveka.* Moscow: Izd. G. A. Lemana i S. M. Sakharova.

———. 1939. *Nepostizhimoe.* Paris: Dom knigi i Sovremennye zapiski.

———. 1990. *Sochineniia.* Moscow: Pravda.

Gennadii, I. 1981. "Liubomudry i slavianofily." *Novyi zhurnal,* no. 142:206–20.

Gerasimova, A. 1988. "OBERIU (Problema smeshnogo)." *Voprosy literatury,* no. 4:48–79.

German, L. 1935. "Anri Bergson kak filosof fashistskoi reaktsii." *Front nauki i tekhniki,* no. 1:116–28.

Gershenzon, M. O. 1919. *Videnie poeta.* Moscow: Tip. Lit. M.G.S.N. Kh.

Gippius, Z. N. 1921. "Dnevnik Zinaidy Nikolaevny Gippius." *Russkaia mysl'*, no. 42:49–99.
———. 1929. *Siniaia kniga: Peterburgskii dnevnik. 1914–1919.* Belgrade: Radenkovich.
———. 1951. *Dmitrii Merezhkovskii.* Paris: YMCA Press.
———. 1970. *Literaturnyi dnevnik, 1899–1907.* Munich: Wilhelm Fink.
———. 1972. *Stikhotvoreniia i poemy.* Vol. 2, *1918–1945.* Munich: Wilhelm Fink.
———. 1973. *Novye liudi. Pobediteli.* Munich: Wilhelm Fink.
———. 1990. *Peterburgskie dnevniki, 1914–1919.* 2d ed. New York: Teleks.
Gourmont, Jean de. 1911. "Iziashchnaia slovesnost' Frantsii." *Apollon* 7: 70–75.
Grois, Boris. 1992. "Rozhdenie sotsialisticheskogo realizma iz dukha russkogo avangarda." *Voprosy literatury* 1:42–61.
Grossman, G. 1914. "Bakunin i Bergson." *Zavety,* no. 5:47–62.
Gumilev, N. S. 1911. "Pis'ma o russkoi poezii." *Apollon,* no. 5:76–78.
Günther, Hans. 1992. "Kniga *O dukhovnom v iskusstve* V. Kandinskogo i avangardnoe myshlenie." *Russian Literature* 32:53–64.
Gurevich, A. V. 1913. *Filosofskie issledovaniia i ocherki.* Edited and with an introduction by S. L. Frank. Moscow.
Iakovenko, B. V. 1912. "Chetvertyi mezhdunarodnyi kongress po filosofii." *Zhurnal ministerstva narodnogo prosveshcheniia,* no. 1:1–34.
———. 1922. *Ocherki russkoi filosofii.* Berlin.
Iakovlev, A. A., ed. 1991. *Vekhi. Sbornik statei, 1909–1910.* Moscow: Molodaia gvardiia.
Isaev, S. A., and E. D. Gal'tsova, eds. 1994. *Antologiia frantsuzskogo siurrealizma.* Moscow: GITIS.
Istoriia filosofii v shesti tomakh. 1961. Moscow: Akademiia nauk SSSR.
Iushkevich, P. S. 1914. "Bergson i ego filosofiia intuitsii." *Russkoe bogatstvo* 11, no. 2:33–59; no. 3:47–67.
Ivanov, G. V. 1952. *Peterburgskie zimy.* New York: Izd. imeni Chekhova.
Ivanov, Vasilii. 1958. "O literaturnykh gruppirovkakh i techeniiakh 20-x godov." *Znamia,* no. 5:190–208; no. 6:179–98.
Ivanov, V. I. 1916. *Borozdy i mezhi. Opyty esteticheskie i kriticheskie.* Moscow: Musaget.
Ivanov, V. V., ed. 1994. *Russkii avangard v krugu evropeiskoi kul'tury.* Moscow: Radiks.
Jaccard, Jean-Philippe, and Andrei Ustinov. 1991. "Zaumnik Daniil Kharms: Nachalo puti." *Wiener Slawistischer Almanach* 27:159–228.
Kaukhchishvili, Nina, ed. 1991. *Andrei Bely: Master slova—iskusstva—mysli.* Paris: Atheneum.
Khan, Anna. 1991. "A Potebnia i A. Bely." In *Andrei Bely: Master slova—iskusstva—mysli,* edited by Nina Kaukhchishvili, 135–50. Paris: Atheneum.

Khardzhiev, Nikolai. 1975. "Novoe o Velimire Khlebnikove." *Russian Literature* 9:5–25.

———. 1976. *K istorii russkogo avangarda.* Stockholm: Hylaea Prints.

Kharms, Daniil. 1988. *Polet v nebesa. Stikhi. Proza. Dramy. Pis'ma.* Edited and with an introduction and notes by A. A. Aleksandrov. Leningrad: Sovetskii pisatel'.

———. 1990. *Proza.* Edited by V. Grubin. Compiled and with an introduction by A. A. Aleksandrov. Leningrad: Lira.

———. 1991. *Gorlo bredit britvoiu: sluchai, rasskazy, dnevnikovye zapisi.* Riga: Glagol.

———. 1993. *Menia nazyvaiut kaputsinom. Nekotorye proizvedeniia Daniila Kharmsa.* Tver': Karavento sovmestno s firmoi Pikment.

Khlebnikov, V. V. 1928–33. *Sobranie proizvedenii Velimira Khlebnikova.* Vols. 1–5. Leningrad: Izd. Pisatelei v Leningrade.

———. 1987. *Tvoreniia.* Edited and with an introduction by M. Ia. Poliakov. Moscow: Sovetskii pisatel'.

Kholopov, I. 1912. "K voprosu o prirode intuitsii." *Voprosy filosofii i psikhologii,* no. 5:667–703.

Khomiakov, A. S. 1900. *Polnoe sobranie sochinenii Alekseia Stepanovicha Khomiakova.* Moscow: Univ. tip.

Khoroshko, V. 1915. "Filosofiia Bergsona s tochki zreniia medika." *Russkaia mysl',* no. 2:93–118.

Khoruzhii, S. S. 1994. *Posle pereryva. Puti russkoi filosofii.* Saint Petersburg: Aleteiia.

Khovin, Viktor. 1916. "Vetrogony, sumasbrody, letateli!" *Ocharovannyi strannik,* no. 10:8–13.

Kireevskii, I. V. 1861. *Polnoe sobranie sochinenii Ivana Vasil'evicha Kireevskogo.* Moscow.

Kreid, Vadim, ed. 1993. *Vospominaniia o serebrianom veke.* With introduction and notes by Vadim Kreid. Moscow: Respublika.

Kroner, R. 1910. "Filosofiia tvorcheskoi evoliutsii (A. Bergson)." *Logos* 1:85–117.

Kushchinskaia, L. 1966. "Literaturnaia diskussiia 1922–1925 godov." *Voprosy literatury,* no. 4:35–55.

Kushner, A. S., ed. 1994. *Poety gruppy "Oberiu."* Saint Petersburg: Sovetskii pisatel'.

Kuz'mina, T. A. 1979. *Problema sub"ekta v sovremennoi burzhuaznoi filosofii.* Moscow: Nauka.

Lapshin, I. I. 1922. "Misticheskii ratsionalizm prof. S. L. Franka." *Mysl',* no. 3:140–53.

Lazarev, A. 1917. "Filosofiia Bergsona." *Mysl' i slovo* 1:177–214.

Lenin, V. I. 1960–69. *Polnoe sobranie sochinenii.* 5th ed. Moscow: Izd. Politicheskoi literatury.

Lesnevskii, S. S., and A. A. Mikhailov, eds. 1988. *Andrei Bely. Problemy tvorchestva.* Moscow: Sovetskii pisatel'.

Levitskii, S. A. 1981. *Ocherki po istorii russkoi filosofskoi i obshchestvennoi mysli.* Frankfurt: Possev-Verlag.

Livshits, B. K. 1978. *Polutoraglazyi strelets.* New York: Izd. imeni Chekhova.

Losev, A. F. 1990a. *Iz rannikh proizvedenii.* Moscow: Pravda.

———. 1990b. *Strast' k dialektike.* Moscow: Sovetskii pisatel'.

———. 1990c. *Vladimir Solov'ev i ego vremia.* Moscow: Progress.

Losskii, N. O. 1908. *Obosnovanie intuitivizma.* 2d ed. Saint Petersburg.

———. 1913. "Nedostatki gnoseologii Bergsona i vliianie ikh na ego metafiziku." *Voprosy filosofii i psikhologii* 24, no. 118:224–35.

———. 1914. *Intuitivnaia filosofiia Bergsona.* 2d ed. Moscow: Russkaia Pechatnia. (3d ed., Saint Petersburg: Uchitel', 1922. 1st ed., Moscow: Put', 1913.)

———. 1917. *Mir kak organicheskoe tseloe.* Moscow: Izd. G. A. Lemana i S. I. Sakharova.

———. 1919. *Osnovnye voprosy gnoseologii.* Saint Petersburg: Nauka i shkola.

———. 1968. *Vospominaniia: Zhizn' i filosofskii put'.* Munich: Wilhelm Fink.

———. 1994a. *Bog i mirovoe zlo.* Moscow: Respublika.

———. 1994b. *Istoriia russkoi filosofii.* Moscow: Progress.

Lovtskii, G. 1923. "Vremia Einshteina i dlitel'nost' Bergsona." *Sovremennye zapiski* 14:417–23.

Lunacharskii, A. B. 1913. "Pis'mo iz Parizha." *IMLI,* f. 16, op. 3, no. 28, 345.

———. 1965. *Sobranie sochinenii v vos'mi tomakh.* Moscow: Khudozhestvennaia literatura.

———. 1970. "Aktual'nye voprosy khudozhestvennoi literatury." *Literaturnoe nasledstvo,* 82:73–100. Moscow.

Makovskii, S. 1913. "Novoe iskusstvo i 'chetvertoe izmerenie' (po povodu Sbornika 'Soiuza molodezhi')." *Apollon* 7:53–60.

Malevich, K. S. 1919. "O muzee." *Iskusstvo kommuny* 12:2.

Malmstad, John. 1988. "Andrei Bely i antroposofiia. Material k biografii (intimnyi). Perepiska s M. K. Morozovoi." *Minuvshee* 6:337–448.

Mandel'shtam, N. Ia. 1972. *Vtoraia kniga.* Paris: YMCA Press.

Mandel'shtam, O. E. 1993. *Sobranie sochinenii v chetyrekh tomakh.* 1993. Moscow: Art-biznes-tsentr.

Matiushin, M. V. 1976. "Opyt khudozhnika novoi mery." In *K istorii russkogo avangarda,* edited by Nikolai Khardzhiev, 159–87. Stockholm: Hylaea Prints.

Messer, Raisa. 1930. "Estetika Bergsona i shkola Voronskogo." *Literatura i iskusstvo,* no. 1:43–53.

Metchenko, A. I. 1967. "Formirovanie teorii sotsialisticheskogo realizma." In *Sovetskoe literaturovedenie za piat'desiat let.* Moscow: Izd. Moskovskogo universiteta.

Miloradovich, K. M. 1913. "Dva ucheniia o vremeni: Kanta i Bergsona." *Zhurnal ministerstva narodnogo prosveshcheniia,* no. 18:323–39.

Mochul'skii, K. V. 1955. *Andrei Bely.* Paris: YMCA Press.

Mokievskii, P. 1909. "Filosofiia Anri Bergsona." *Russkoe bogatstvo* 6:152–68.

Nil'vich, L. 1930. "Reaktsionnoe zhonglerstvo (ob odnoi vylazke literaturnykh khuliganov)." *Smena,* no. 81 (9 April).

Novikov, A. V. 1964. "Kritika teorii dramy i komicheskogo A. Bergsona." In *Voprosy marksistko-leninskoi estetiki.* Moscow: Izd. Moskovskogo universiteta.

———. 1976. *Ot pozitivizma k intuitivizmu. Kriticheskie ocherki burzhuaznoi estetiki.* Moscow: Iskusstvo.

Ocheretianskii, Aleksandr, and Gerald Janecek, eds. 1993. *Zabytyi avangard.* New York and Saint Petersburg.

Olesha, Iu. K. 1956. *Izbrannye sochineniia.* Moscow: Khudozhestvennaia literatura.

Pasternak, B. L. 1970. *Okhrannaia gramota.* Rome: Aquario.

Pisateli ob iskusstve i o sebe. 1924. Moscow: Krug.

Plekhanov, G. V. 1909. "Anri Bergson." *Sovremennyi mir* 3, no. 2:118–22.

———. 1956–58. *Izbrannye filosofskie sochineniia.* Moscow: Izd. Politicheskoi literatury.

Polonskii, V. P. 1934. *Soznanie i tvorchestvo.* Leningrad: Izd. Pisatelei v Leningrade.

Potebnia, A. A. 1913. *Mysl' i iazyk.* 3d ed. Khar'kov: Mirnyi trud.

Radlov, E. L. 1991. "Ocherki istorii russkoi filosofii." In *A. I. Vvedenskii, A. F. Losev, E. L. Radlov, G. G. Shpet: Ocherki istorii russkoi filosofii,* edited by B. V. Emel'ianov and K. N. Liubutin, 96–216. Sverdlovsk: Izd. Ural'skogo universiteta.

Romanovskaia, T. B. 1994. "Avangard i nauka." In *Russkii avangard v krugu evropeiskoi kul'tury,* edited by V. V. Ivanov, 10–26. Moscow: Radiks.

Rozenfel'd, I. 1913–14. "Intuitivizm i futurizm." *Maski* 6:17–26.

Ruge, A. 1911. "Chetvertyi mezhdunarodnyi kongress po filosofii v Bolone 6–11 apr. 1911 g." *Voprosy filosofii i psikhologii* 3:394–431.

Sarychev, V. A. 1991. *Estetika russkogo modernizma.* Voronezh: Izd. Voronezhskogo universiteta.

Sazhin, V. N., ed. 1994. *David Burliuk. Fragmenty iz vospominanii futurista. Pis'ma. Stikhotvoreniia.* With an introduction by N. A. Zubkova. Saint Petersburg: Pushkinskii fond.

Semenova, S. G. 1988. "Sem'ia idei." *Znamia,* no. 3:185–201.

Shcheglov, A. V. 1967. "Filosofskie diskussii v SSSR v 20-x i nachale 30-x godov." *Filosofskie nauki,* no. 5:110–18.

Shestov, L. I. 1993. *Sochineniia v dvukh tomakh.* Moscow: Nauka.

Shpet, G. G. 1914. *Iavlenie i smysl.* Moscow: Germes.

Sokolov, I. 1920. *Renessans XX veka. Manifest.* Moscow.

Sologub, F. K. 1915. "Iskusstvo nashikh dnei." *Russkaia mysl'*, no. 12:35–62.

Solov'ev, V. S. 1966. *Sobranie sochinenii V. S. Solov'eva.* Brussels: Foyer Oriental Chrétien.

———. 1988. *Sochineniia v dvukh tomakh.* Moscow: Mysl'.

———. 1994. *Chteniia o bogochelovechestve.* Saint Petersburg: Khudozhestvennaia literatura.

Spektorskii, E. V. 1976. "Znachenie filosofii N. O. Losskogo." *Zapiski russkoi akademicheskoi gruppy v S. Sh. A.* 10:127–32.

"Spor o pragmatizme." 1910. *Russkaia mysl'* 5, no. 31:121–56.

Starchenko, N. N. 1982. *Filosofiia intuitivizma v Rossii i sovremennost'.* Moscow.

Svas'ian, K. A. 1978. *Esteticheskaia sushchnost' intuitivnoi filosofii A. Bergsona.* Erevan: Izd. AN Armiansko i SSR.

Timiriazev, K. A. 1948. *Izbrannye sochineniia v chetyrekh tomakh.* Moscow: Sel'khozgiz.

Tolstoi, A. N. 1924. "Literaturnye zametki. Zadachi literatury." In *Pisateli ob iskusstve i o sebe,* 3–16. Moscow: Krug.

Tolstoi, Lev. 1960–65. *Sobranie sochinenii v dvadtsati tomakh.* Moscow: Khudozhestvennaia literatura.

Trotskii, L. D. 1923. *Literatura i revoliutsiia.* Moscow: Krasnaia nov'.

Tsvetaeva, Marina. 1990. *Stikhotvoreniia i poemy.* Leningrad: Sovetskii pisatel'.

Tufanov, A. V. 1924. *K zaumi. Stikhi i issledovaniia soglasnykh fonem.* Petrograd: A. Tufanov.

———. 1991. *Ushkuiniki.* Modern Russian Literature and Culture 27. Compiled by Jean-Phillipe Jaccard and Tat'iana Nikol'skaia. Edited by Lazar Fleishman, Joan Delaney Grossman, Robert Hughes, Simon Karlinsky, John Malmstad, and Olga Raevsky-Hughes. Berkeley, Calif.: Berkeley Slavic Specialties.

Tynianov, Iu. N. 1921. *Dostoevskii i Gogol'* (*k teorii parodii*). Saint Petersburg: OPOIAZ.

———. 1929. "Literaturnyi fakt." In *Arkhaisty i novatory.* Leningrad: Priboi.

Uspenskii, P. D. 1992. *Tertium Organum. Kliuch k zagadkam mira.* Saint Petersburg: Andreev i synov'ia.

Vengerov, S. A. 1972. *Russkaia literatura XX veka.* Munich: Wilhelm Fink.

Vinogradov, V. V. 1986. *Russkii iazyk.* Moscow: Vysshaia shkola.

Volkovich, V. A. 1912. "Anri Bergson, 'Tvorcheskaia evoliutsiia.' Zametka, 1912, marta 9." *RGB,* f. 55, ed. khr. 14, 2.

Voloshin, M. A. 1991. *Avtobiograficheskaia proza. Dnevnik.* Moscow: Kniga.

———. 1925. "Avtobiografiia." *RGB,* f. 461, ed. khr. 6, 5.

Voronskii, A. K. 1928. *Iskusstvo videt' mir: sbornik statei.* Moscow: Krug.

"Vtoroi mezhdunarodnyi filosofskii kongress." 1904. *Vesy* 1, no. 10:59–62.

Vvedenskii, A. I. 1993. *Polnoe sobranie sochinenii v dvukh tomakh.* Edited with introduction and notes by Mikhail Meilakh. Moscow: Gileia.

Vysheslavtsev, B. P. 1971. *Filosofskaia nishcheta marksizma.* Frankfurt: Posev-Verlag.

Zenkovskii, V. V., ed. 1954. *Sbornik pamiati Semena Liudvigovicha Franka.* Munich.

SOURCES NOT IN RUSSIAN

Alexandrov, Vladimir E. 1985. *Andrei Bely. The Major Symbolist Fiction.* Cambridge: Harvard University Press.

———, ed. 1995. *The Garland Companion to Vladimir Nabokov.* New York: Garland.

Amrine, Frederick. 1992. "'The Triumph of Life': Nietzsche's Verbicide." In *The Crisis in Modernism: Bergson and the Vitalist Controversy,* edited by Frederick Burwick and Paul Douglas, 131–49. Cambridge: Cambridge University Press.

Anschuetz, Carol. 1976. "Recollection as Metaphor in *Kotik Letaev.*" *Russian Literature* 4, no. 4:345–55.

———. 1983. "Bely's *Petersburg* and the End of the Russian Novel." In *The Russian Novel from Pushkin to Pasternak,* edited by John Garrard, 125–53. New Haven: Yale University Press.

Antliff, Mark. 1988. "Bergson and Cubism: A Reassessment." *Art Journal* 47 (Winter): 341–49.

———. 1993. *Inventing Bergson: Cultural Politics and the Parisian Avant-Garde.* Princeton: Princeton University Press.

Any, Carol. 1990. "Boris Eikhenbaum in OPOIAZ: Testing the Limits of the Work-Centered Poetics." *Slavic Review* 49, no. 3:409–26.

Bal'mont, K. D. 1904. "Les carnets de Bal'mont." Bibliothèque Nationale. *Slave* 98, 2–3.

Barta, Peter I., ed. 1991. *The European Foundations of Russian Modernism.* New York: Edwin Mellen Press.

Barthes, Roland. 1977. *Image, Music, Text.* Translated by Stephen Heath. New York: Hill & Wang.

Barthelemy-Madaule, Madeleine. 1966. *Bergson adversaire de Kant.* Paris: Presses universitaires de France.

Beguin, Albert, and Pierre Thevenaz, eds. 1943. *Henri Bergson. Essais et témoignages inédites.* Neuchatel: Editions de la Baconnière.

Bely, Andrei. 1978. *Petersburg.* Translated, annotated, and with an introduction by Robert A. Maguire and John E. Malmstad. Bloomington: Indiana University Press.

Benda, Julien. 1912. *Le Bergsonisme; ou, Une philosophie de la mobilité.* Paris: Mercure de France.

Bergson, Henri. 1904. "Le Paralogisme psycho-physiologique." *Revue de métaphysique et de morale* 12 (November): 859–908.

———. 1925. *Le rire*. Paris: Félix Alcan.

———. 1932. *Les deux sources de la morale et de la religion*. Paris: Félix Alcan.

———. 1972. *Mélanges*. Paris: Presses Universitaires de France.

Berlin, Isaiah. 1978. *Russian Thinkers*. New York: Penguin Books.

Berman, Art. 1994. *Preface to Modernism*. Champaign: University of Illinois Press.

Berthelot, René. 1913. *Un Romantisme utilitaire*. Vol. 2, *Le Pragmatisme chez Bergson*. Paris: Félix Alcan.

Bethea, David. 1989. *The Shape of Apocalypse in Modern Russian Fiction*. Princeton: Princeton University Press.

Billington, James H. 1970. *The Icon and the Axe: An Interpretive History of Russian Culture*. New York: Vintage Books.

Bloom, Harold. 1973. *The Anxiety of Influence*. New York: Oxford University Press.

Boobbyer, Philip. 1995. *S. L. Frank: The Life and Work of a Russian Philosopher, 1877–1950*. Athens: Ohio University Press.

Bowlt, John, ed. and trans. 1976. *Russian Art of the Avant-Garde: Theory and Criticism, 1902–1934*. New York: Viking.

Bristol, Evelyn. 1983. "From Romanticism to Symbolism in France and Russia." In *American Contributions to the Ninth International Congress of Slavists*, edited by Paul Debreczeny, 69–79. Kiev.

Broms, Henri, and Rebecca Kaufman, eds. 1988. *Semiotics of Culture. Proceedings of the 25th Symposium of the Tartu-Moscow School of Semiotics, Imatra, Finland, 27th–29th July, 1987*. Helsinki: Arator.

Brown, Clarence. 1973. *Mandel'shtam*. London: Cambridge University Press.

Brown, Edward J. 1963a. *Russian Literature Since the Revolution*. London: Cromwell-Collier.

———. 1963b. "The Year of Acquiescence." In *Literature and Revolution in Soviet Russia, 1917–1962*, edited by Max Hayward and Leopold Labedz, 44–61. London: Oxford University Press.

———, ed. 1973. *Major Soviet Writers: Essays in Criticism*. London: Oxford University Press.

Burwick, Frederick, and Paul Douglas, eds. 1992. *The Crisis in Modernism: Bergson and the Vitalist Controversy*. Cambridge: Cambridge University Press.

Carden, Patricia. 1976. "Ornamentalism and Modernism." In *Russian Modernism: Culture and the Avant-Garde, 1900–1930*, edited by George Gibian and H. W. Tjalsma, 49–64. Ithaca: Cornell University Press.

Cariou, Marie. 1976. *Bergson et le fait mystique*. Paris: Aubier Montaigne.

Cassedy, Steven. 1984. "Daniil Kharms's Parody of Dostoevskii: Anti-Tragedy as Political Comment." *Canadian-American Slavic Studies* 18, no. 3:268–84.

———, ed. and trans. 1985. *Selected Essays of Andrey Bely.* Berkeley and Los Angeles: University of California Press.

———. 1987. "Bely the Thinker." In *Andrey Bely: Spirit of Symbolism,* edited by John E. Malmstad, 313–35. Ithaca: Cornell University Press.

Cavanagh, Clare. 1995. *Osip Mandelstam and the Modernist Creation of Tradition.* Princeton: Princeton University Press.

Challaye, Félicien. 1954. "Bergson vu par les Soviets." *Preuves* 4, no. 44: 62–63.

Chances, Ellen. 1982. "Čexov and Xarms: Story/Antistory." *Russian Language Journal* 36, nos. 123–24:181–92.

———. 1985. "Daniil Charms' 'Old Woman' Climbs her Family Tree: 'Starucha' and the Russian Literary Past." *Russian Literature* 17, no. 4: 353–66.

Choate, Frederick S. 1987. "Aleksandr Konstantinovich Voronskii's Literary Criticism." Ph.D. diss., Stanford University.

Chomiak, Martha, and Bernice Rosenthal, eds. 1982. *A Revolution of the Spirit: Crisis in Value in Russia, 1890–1918.* Translated by Marian Schwartz. Newtonville, Mass.: Oriental Research Partners.

Cioran, Samuel D. 1973. *The Apocalyptic Symbolism of Andrej Belyj.* The Hague: Mouton.

Clark, Katerina. 1995. *Petersburg, Crucible of Cultural Revolution.* Cambridge: Harvard University Press.

Clayton, Jay, and Eric Rothstein, eds. 1991. *Influence and Intertextuality in Literary History.* Madison: University of Wisconsin Press.

Clowes, Edith. 1988. *The Revolution of Moral Consciousness: Nietzsche in Russian Literature, 1890–1914.* DeKalb: Northern Illinois University Press.

Coignet, Clarisse. 1904. "Kant et Bergson." *Revue Chrétienne* 1, no. 7:27–41.

———. 1911. *De Kant à Bergson: Reconciliation de la religion et de la science dans un spiritualisme nouveau.* Paris: Félix Alcan.

Colletti, Lucio. 1979. "From Bergson to Lukacs." *Marxism and Hegel.* London: Verso.

Cooke, Raymond. 1987. *Velimir Khlebnikov: A Critical Study.* Cambridge: Cambridge University Press.

Copleston, Frederick C. 1946–53. *A History of Philosophy.* 9 vols. Westminster, Md.: Newman.

———. 1986. *Philosophy in Russia.* Notre Dame: University of Notre Dame Press.

Cornu, Auguste. 1968. "Bergsonianism and Existentialism." In *Philosophic Thought in France and the United States,* edited by Marvin Farber. Albany: State University of New York Press, 151–68.

Cornwell, Neil, ed. 1991a. *Daniil Kharms and the Poetics of the Absurd: Essays and Materials.* London: MacMillan.

———. 1991b. "Daniil Kharms, Black Miniaturist." In *Daniil Kharms and the Poetics of the Absurd: Essays and Materials,* edited by Neil Cornwell, 3–21. London: MacMillan.

Croce, Benedetto. 1915. *What is Living and What is Dead of the Philosophy of Hegel.* 3d ed. Translated by Douglas Ainslie. London: Macmillan.

Curtis, James M. 1976. "Bergson and Russian Formalism." *Comparative Literature* 28:109–21.

———. 1986. "Michael Bakhtin, Nietzsche, and Russian Pre-Revolutionary Thought." In *Nietzsche in Russia,* edited by Bernice Rosenthal, 331–54. Princeton: Princeton University Press.

Delaney, C. F. 1972. "Bergson on Science and Philosophy." *Process Studies* 2, no. 1:29–43.

Deleuze, Gilles. 1988. *Bergsonism.* Translated by Hugh Tomlinson and Barbara Habberjam. New York: Zone Books.

Delhomme, Jeanne. 1976. "Le Sens interne." *Etudes Bergsoniennes* 11: 35–65.

Donchin, Georgette. 1958. *The Influence of French Symbolism on Russian Poetry.* The Hague: Mouton.

Douglas, Charlotte. 1973–74. "Colors Without Objects. Russian Color Theories, 1908–1932." *The Structurist,* nos. 13/14:30–41.

———. 1975a. "Suprematism: The Sensible Domain." *Russian Review* 34, no. 3:266–81.

———. 1975b. "Views From the New World. A. Kruchenykh and K. Malevich: Theory and Painting." *Russian Literature Triquarterly,* no. 12: 353–70.

———. 1976. *Swans of Other Worlds: Kazimir Malevich and the Origins of Abstraction in Russia.* Ann Arbor: UMI Research Press.

Douglass, Paul. 1983. "The Gold Coin: Bergsonian Intuition and Modernist Aesthetics." *Thought* 58, no. 229:234–50.

Dyrssen, Carl. 1922. *Bergson und die deutsche Romantik.* Marburg: N. G. Elwert.

Edie, James M., James P. Scanlan, and Mary-Barbara Zeldin, eds., with the collaboration of George L. Kline. 1965. *Russian Philosophy.* 3 vols. Chicago: Quadrangle Books.

Emeljanow, Victor, ed. 1981. *Chekhov: The Critical Heritage.* London: Routledge & Kegan Paul.

Erlich, Victor. 1994. *Modernism and Revolution: Russian Literature in Transition.* Cambridge: Harvard University Press.

Foster, John Burt. 1993. *Nabokov's Art of Memory and European Modernism.* Princeton: Princeton University Press.

Frank, Semen. 1965. *Reality and Man. An Essay in the Metaphysics of Human Nature.* Translated by Natalie Duddington, with a foreword by Georges Florovsky. New York: Taplinger.

Freidin, Gregory. 1978. "The Whisper of History and the Noise of Time in the Writings of Osip Mandel'shtam." *Russian Review* 37, no. 4:421–37.

Garrard, John, ed. 1983. *The Russian Novel from Pushkin to Pasternak.* New Haven: Yale University Press.

Gasparov, Boris. 1990. "Notes on the 'Metaphysics' of Russian Aspect." In *Verbal Aspect in Discourse,* edited by Nils B. Thelin, 191–212. Amsterdam: John Benjamins.

Georgopoulos, N. 1979. "Kazantzakis, Bergson, Lenin and the 'Russian Experiment.'" *Journal of the Hellenic Diaspora* 5, no. 4:33–44.

Gibian, George, ed. and trans. 1987. *The Man in the Black Coat: Russia's Literature of the Absurd.* Evanston: Northwestern University Press.

Gibian, George, and H. W. Tjalsma, eds. 1976. *Russian Modernism: Culture and the Avant-Garde, 1900–1930.* Ithaca: Cornell University Press.

Gillies, M. A. 1986. "The Influence of Henri Bergson on Early Modern British Literature." Ph.D. diss., Oxford University.

Graham, Loren. 1972. *Science and Philosophy in the Soviet Union.* New York: Knopf.

Gratieux, Albert. 1939. *A. S. Khomiakov et le Mouvement Slavophile.* Paris: Editions du Cerf.

Grogin, R. C. 1988. *The Bergsonian Controversy in France, 1900–1914.* Calgary: University of Calgary Press.

Gruson, Françoise Fabre Luce de. 1960. "Bergson, lecteur de Kant." *Etudes Bergsoniennes* 5:171–90.

Guillén, Claudio. 1959. "The Aesthetics of Influence Studies in Comparative Literature." In *Proceedings of the Second Congress of the International Comparative Literature Association,* edited by Werner P. Friederich, 1:175–92. Chapel Hill: University of North Carolina Press.

Gunter, P. A. Y. 1986. *Henri Bergson: A Bibliography.* Rev. 2d ed. Bowling Green: Philosophy Documentation Center, Bowling Green State University.

Haardt, Alexander. 1993. *Husserl in Russland.* Munich.

———. 1994. "Aleksej Losev and the Phenomenology of Music." In *Russian Thought After Communism: The Recovery of a Philosophical Tradition,* edited by James P. Scanlan, 197–205. Armonk, N.Y.: M. E. Sharpe.

Harkins, William E. 1966. "The Philosophical Stories of Jurij Oleša." In *Orbis Scriptus. Dmitrij Tschiżewskij 70. Geburtstag.* Munich: Wilhelm Fink, 349–54.

Harris, Jane Gary, ed. and trans. 1979. *Osip Mandelstam: Critical Prose and Letters.* Ann Arbor, Mich.: Ardis.

———. 1982. "Mandelstamian Zlost', Bergson, and a New Acmeist Esthetics?" *Ulbandus Review* 2, no. 2:112–30.

———. 1988. *Osip Mandel'shtam.* Boston: G. K. Hall.

Hausheer, Herman. 1933. "Thought Affinities of Bergson and Schelling." *Personalist* 14, no. 2:93–106.

Hayward, Max, and Leopold Labedz, eds. 1963. *Literature and Revolution in Soviet Russia, 1917–1962.* London: Oxford University Press.

Henderson, Linda Dalrymple. 1978. "The Merging of Time and Space: The 'Fourth Dimension' in Russia from Ouspensky to Malevich." *Soviet Union/Union Sovietique* 5, pt. 2:171–203.

Hippius, Zinaida. 1975. *Between Paris and St. Petersburg: Selected Diaries of Zinaida Gippius.* Translated and edited by Temira Pachmuss. Urbana: University of Illinois Press.

Huyssen, Andreas. 1986. *After the Great Divide: Modernism, Mass Culture, Postmodernism.* Bloomington: Indiana University Press.

Jaccard, Jean-Philippe. 1985. "De la réalité du texte: L'Absurde chez D. Harms." *Cahiers du Monde russe et soviétique* 26, nos. 3–4:269–312.

———. 1991a. *Daniil Harms et la fin de l'avant-garde russe.* Bern: Peter Lang.

———. 1991b. "Daniil Kharms in the Context of Russian and European Literature of the Absurd." In *Daniil Kharms and the Poetics of the Absurd: Essays and Materials,* edited by Neil Cornwell, 49–70. London: MacMillan.

James, William. 1928. *A Pluralistic Universe.* 6th ed. New York: Longmans, Green.

Janecek, Gerald. 1974. "Anthroposophy in *Kotik Letaev.*" *Orbis Litterarum* 29:245–67.

———. 1976. "The Spiral as Image and Structural Principle in Andrej Belyj's *Kotik Letaev.*" *Russian Literature* 4, no. 4:357–64.

Jankélévitch, Vladimir. 1931. *Bergson.* Paris: Félix Alcan.

———. 1948. *Pragmatism.* New York: Longmans, Green.

Jensen, Kenneth. 1978. *Beyond Marx and Mach: A. Bogdanov's Philosophy of Living Experience.* Dordrecht, Holland: Reidel.

Jordan, Bruno. 1912. "Kant and Bergson." *Monist* 22, no. 3:404–14.

Joussain, André. 1956. "Bergsonisme et marxisme." *Ecrits de Paris,* no. 137: 50–55.

Kandinsky, Wassily. 1977. *Concerning the Spiritual in Art.* Translated by M. T. H. Sadler. New York: Dover.

Kaukhchishvili, Nina, ed. 1991. *Andrei Bely: Master slova—iskusstva—mysli.* Paris: Atheneum.

Keys, Roger. 1987. "Bely's Symphonies." In *Andrey Bely: Spirit of Symbolism,* edited by John E. Malmstad, 19–59. Ithaca: Cornell University Press.

———. 1996. *The Reluctant Modernist: Andrei Bely and the Development of Russian Fiction, 1902–1914.* Oxford: Clarendon Press.

Keys, Roger, and John Elsworth. 1986. *The Dramatic Symphony and The Forms of Art.* Edinburgh: Polygon Books.

Khlebnikov, Velimir. 1985. *The King of Time: Velimir Khlebnikov.* Edited by Charlotte Douglas. Translated by Paul Shmidt. Cambridge: Harvard University Press.

Kohanski, Alexander S. 1936. *Losskii's Theory of Knowledge.* Nashville, Tenn.: Mennonite Press.

Kovač, Anton. 1976. *Andrej Belyj: The "Symphonies" (1899–1908).* Frankfurt: Peter Lang.

Kšicová, Danuše. 1988. "K. D. Balmont—Básník impresionismu a secese." *Ceskoslovenská Rusistika* 33, no. 3:108–15.

———. 1989. "Poetika ruské secesní poezie." *Slavia, časopis pro slovanskou filologii* 58, nos. 1–2:65–70.

Kujundžić, Dragan. 1997. *The Returns of History. Russian Nietzcheans After Modernity.* Albany: State University of New York Press.

Lacey, A. R. 1989. *Bergson.* London: Routledge.

Laird, John. 1917. *Problems of the Self: An Essay Based on the Shaw Lectures Given in the University of Edinburgh, March 1914.* London: MacMillan.

Landes, Margaret W. 1924. "A Suggested Interpretation of Bergson's Doctrine of Intuition." *Philosophical Review* 33, no. 5:450–62.

Lehan, Richard. 1992. "Bergson and the Discourse of the Moderns." In *The Crisis in Modernism: Bergson and the Vitalist Controversy,* edited by Frederick Burwick and Paul Douglas, 306–29. Cambridge: Cambridge University Press.

Lissitzkii, El. 1976. "Suprematism in World Reconstruction, 1920." In *Russian Art of the Avant-Garde: Theory and Criticism, 1902–1934,* edited and translated by John E. Bowlt, 151–58. New York: Viking.

Lovejoy, A. O. 1914. *Bergson and Romantic Evolutionism.* Berkeley and Los Angeles: University of California Press.

Lutzow, Thomas H. 1977. "The Structure of the Free Act in Bergson." *Process Studies* 7, no. 2:73–89.

Maguire, Robert A. 1968. *Red Virgin Soil: Soviet Literature in the 1920s.* Ithaca: Cornell University Press.

Maguire, Robert A., and John E. Malmstad. 1987. "Petersburg." In *Andrey Bely: Spirit of Symbolism,* edited by John E. Malmstad, 96–144. Ithaca: Cornell University Press.

Malevich, K. S. 1968. *Essays on Art.* Edited by Troels Andersen. Translated by Xenia Glowacki-Prus. 4 vols. Copenhagen: Borgen.

———. 1978. *The Artist, Infinity, Suprematism: Unpublished Writings, 1913–33.* Edited by Troels Andersen. Translated by Xenia Hoffman. Copenhagen: Borgen.

Malmstad, John E., ed. 1987. *Andrey Bely: Spirit of Symbolism.* Ithaca: Cornell University Press.

Markov, Vladimir. 1968. *Russian Futurism: A History.* Berkeley and Los Angeles: University of California Press.

Markov, Vladimir (Waldemars Matvejs). 1976. "The Principles of the New Art." In *Russian Art of the Avant-Garde: Theory and Criticism, 1902–1934,* edited and translated by John E. Bowlt, 23–38. New York: Viking.

Matich, Olga. 1972. *Paradox in the Religious Poetry of Zinaida Gippius.* Munich: Wilhelm Fink.

Mochul'skii, K. V. 1977. *Andrei Bely: His Life and Works.* Ann Arbor: Ardis.

Moi, Toril, ed. 1986. *The Kristeva Reader.* Oxford: Basil Blackwood.

Morson, Gary Saul, and Caryl Emerson. 1990. *Mikhail Bakhtin: Creation of a Prosaics.* Stanford: Stanford University Press.

Mozejko, Edward. 1986. "Two Versions of Classicism: O. Mandel'shtam and T. S. Eliot." *Russian Language Journal* 40, nos. 136–37:111–21.

Nakhimovsky, Alice Stone. 1982. *Laughter in the Void. An Introduction to the Writings of Daniil Kharms and Alexander Vvedensky.* Vienna: Wiener Slawistischer Almanach.

Nethercott, Frances. 1991. "Elements of Henri Bergson's *Creative Evolution* in the Critical Prose of Osip Mandel'shtam." *Russian Literature* 30–34: 455–66.

———. 1995. *Une rencontre philosophique: Bergson en Russie (1907–1917).* Paris: L'Harmattan.

Nietzsche, Friedrich. 1967. *The Birth of Tragedy and the Case of Wagner.* Translated by Walter Kaufmann. New York: Vintage Books.

———. 1979. *The Use and Abuse of History.* Translated by Adrian Collins. Indianapolis: Bobbs-Merrill.

———. 1989. *Beyond Good and Evil.* Translated by Walter Kaufmann. New York: Vintage Books.

Nilsson, Nils Åke. 1973. "Through the Wrong End of the Binoculars: An Introduction to Jurij Oleša." In *Major Soviet Writers: Essays in Criticism,* edited by Edward J. Brown, 254–79. London: Oxford University Press.

———. 1980. "Futurism, Primitivism and the Russian Avant-Garde." *Russian Literature* 8:469–82.

Ortega y Gasset, José. 1948. *The Dehumanization of Art and Notes on the Novel.* Translated by Helene Weyl. Princeton: Princeton University Press.

Pachmuss, Temira. 1971. *Zinaida Hippius: An Intellectual Profile.* Carbondale: Southern Illinois University Press.

Papanicolaou, Andrew C., and Pete A. Y. Gunter, eds. 1987. *Bergson and Modern Thought: Towards a Unified Science.* Chur, Switzerland: Harwood Academic Publishers.

Paperno, Irina, and Joan Delaney Grossman, eds. 1994. *Creating Life: The Aesthetic Utopia of Russian Modernism.* Stanford: Stanford University Press.

Perlina, Nina. 1991. "Daniil Kharms's Poetic System: Text, Context, Intertext." Translated by Ann Shukman. In *Daniil Kharms and the Poetics of the Absurd: Essays and Materials,* edited by Neil Cornwell, 175–91. London: MacMillan.

Pike, Christopher, ed. 1979. *The Futurists, the Formalists, and the Marxist Critique.* Translated by Christopher Pike and Joe Andrew. London: Ink Links.

Pilkington, Anthony E. 1976. *Bergson and His Influence: A Reassessment.* Cambridge: Cambridge University Press.

Poggioli, Renato. 1960. *The Poets of Russia, 1890–1930.* Cambridge: Harvard University Press.

———. 1968. *The Theory of the Avant-Garde.* Translated by Gerald Fitzgerald. New York: Harper & Row.

Politzer, Georges. 1967. *La fin d'une parade philosophique: Le Bergsonisme.* Paris: J. J. Pauvert.

Robinet, André, ed. 1972. *Mélanges.* With an introduction by Henri Gouhier. Paris: Presses Universitaires de France.

Rosenthal, Bernice Glatzer, ed. 1975. *D. S. Merezhkovsky and the Silver Age: The Development of a Revolutionary Mentality.* The Hague: Martinus Nijhoff.

———, ed. 1986. *Nietzsche in Russia.* Princeton: Princeton University Press.

———. 1991. "A New Word for a New Myth: Nietzsche and Russian Futurism." In *The European Foundations of Russian Modernism,* edited by Peter Barta, 219–50. New York: Edwin Mellen Press.

———, ed. 1994. *Nietzsche and Soviet Culture.* Cambridge: Cambridge University Press.

Rousseau, George. 1992. "The Perpetual Crises of Modernism and the Traditions of Enlightenment Vitalism: With a Note on Mikhail Bakhtin." In *The Crisis in Modernism: Bergson and the Vitalist Controversy,* edited by Frederick Burwick and Paul Douglas, 15–75. Cambridge: Cambridge University Press.

Rudova, Larissa. 1994. *Pasternak's Short Fiction and the Cultural Vanguard.* New York: Peter Lang.

Ruge, Arnold, ed. 1842. *Jahrbücher für Wissenschaft und Kunst,* Leipzig, 5, nos. 247–51:985–1002.

Rusinko, Elaine. 1979. "Gumilev in London: An Unknown Interview." *Russian Literature Triquarterly,* no. 16:73–85.

———. 1982. "Acmeism, Post-Symbolism and Henri Bergson." *Slavic Review* 41, no. 3:494–510.

Russell, Bertrand. 1945. *A History of Western Philosophy.* New York: Simon and Schuster.

Santayana, George. 1936. *Works.* Vol. 6. New York: Scribner.

———. 1957. *Winds of Doctrine.* New York: Harper & Brothers.

Scanlan, James P., ed. 1994. *Russian Thought After Communism: The Recovery of a Philosophical Tradition.* Armonk, N.Y.: M. E. Sharpe.

Scharfstein, Ben-Ami. 1943. *Roots of Bergson's Philosophy.* New York: Columbia University Press.

Schmemann, Alexander, ed. 1977. *Ultimate Questions: An Anthology of Modern Russian Religious Thought.* Crestwood, N.Y.: St. Vladimir's Seminary Press.

Schopenhauer, A. 1969. *The World as Will and Representation.* Translated by E. F. J. Payne. 2 vols. New York: Dover.

Schwartz, Sanford. 1985. *The Matrix of Modernism: Pound, Eliot, and Early Twentieth-Century Thought.* Princeton: Princeton University Press.

Setschkareff, Wsewolod. 1939. *Schellings Einfluss in der russischen Literatur der 20er und 30er Jahre des XIX Jahrhunderts.* Grafenhainichen: C. Schulze.

Shukman, Ann. 1988. "Towards a Poetics of the Absurd: The Prose Writings of Daniil Kharms." In *Semiotics of Culture: Proceedings of the 25th Symposium of the Tartu-Moscow School of Semiotics, Imatra, Finland, 27th–29th July, 1987,* edited by Henri Broms and Rebecca Kaufman, 81–95. Helsinki: Arator.

Stallman, R. W. 1955. "The Scholar's Net: Literary Sources." *College English* 17:20–27.

Steinberg, Ada. 1982. *Word and Music in the Novels of Andrey Bely.* Cambridge: Cambridge University Press.

Steiner, Peter. 1984. *Russian Formalism: A Metapoetics.* Ithaca: Cornell University Press.

Steiner, Rudolf. 1946. *Theosophy.* Translated by Henry B. Monges. New York: Anthroposophic Press.

———. 1991. *Earthly Knowledge and Heavenly Wisdom.* Translated by Sabine H. Seiler. Hudson, N.Y.: Anthroposophic Press.

Stelleman, Jenny. 1991. "The Transitional Position of *Elizaveta Bam* Between Avant-Garde and Neo-Avant-Garde." In *Avant Garde: Interdisciplinary and International Review,* edited by Jan van der Eng and Willem Weststeign, 5/6:207–29. Amsterdam: Rodopi.

Swoboda, Philip J. 1992. "The Philosophical Thought of S. L. Frank, 1902–1915: A Study of the Metaphysical Impulse in Early Twentieth-Century Russia." Ph.D. diss., Columbia University.

Szathmary, Arthur. 1937. *The Aesthetic Theory of Bergson.* Cambridge: Harvard University Press.

Terras, Victor. 1974. *Belinskij and Russian Literary Criticism.* Madison: University of Wisconsin Press.

———. 1991. *A History of Russian Literature.* New Haven: Yale University Press.

Toker, Leona. 1990. "Philosophers as Poets: Reading Nabokov with Schopenhauer and Bergson." *Russian Literature Triquarterly* 24:185–96.

———. 1995. "Nabokov and Bergson." In *The Garland Companion to Vladimir Nabokov,* edited by Vladimir E. Alexandrov, 367–73. New York: Garland.

Trillo Clough, Rosa. 1961. *Futurism: The Story of a Modern Art Movement.* New York: Philosophical Library.

Tucker, Janet G. 1996. *Revolution Betrayed: Jurij Oleša's "Envy."* Columbus, Ohio: Slavica Publishers.

Vietroff, J. 1912. "L'Influence de la philosophie de M. Bergson. VI." *Mouvement Socialiste* 31, no. 237:62–64.

Visan, Tancrède de. 1911. *L'Attitude du lyrisme contemporain.* Paris: Mercure de France.

Vishevsky, Anatoly. 1986. "Tradition in the Topsy-Turvey World of Parody: Analysis of Two OBERIU Plays." *Slavic and East European Journal* 30: 355–66.

Vucinich, Alexander. 1988. *Darwin in Russian Thought.* Berkeley and Los Angeles: University of California Press.

Waldenfels, Bernhard. 1983. *Phänomenologie in Frankreich.* Frankfurt: Suhrkamp.

Walicki, Andrzej. 1979. *A History of Russian Thought.* Translated by Hilda Andrews-Rusiecka. Stanford: Stanford University Press.

Webb, Clifford Wellington. 1957. "Space and Time in the Philosophies of Kant and Bergson." Ph.D. diss., University of Toronto.

West, James. 1970. *Russian Symbolism. A Study of Vyacheslav Ivanov and the Russian Symbolist Aesthetic.* London: Methuen.

———. 1991. "Kant, Kant, Kant: The Neo-Kantian Creative Consciousness in Bely's *Peterburg.*" In *The European Foundations of Russian Modernism,* edited by Peter I. Barta, 87–135. New York: Edwin Mellen Press.

Zenkovskii, V. V. 1953. *A History of Russian Philosophy.* 2 vols. Translated by George L. Kline. New York: Columbia University Press.

Zernov, Nicolas. 1963. *The Russian Religious Renaissance of the Twentieth Century.* New York: Harper & Row.

Index